P9-DNA-032

Creative Conflict®

Creative Transformation

by Christopher Hills

Edited by Deborah Rozman, Ph.D.

The term Creative Conflict® refers to a specific process that has been outlined in this book. Creative Conflict® is an official service mark registered with the U.S. Department of Patents and Trademarks.

the secret of heart to heart communion learning to love with total openness

UNIVERSITY
OF THE TREES PRESS

Copyright© 1980, by Christopher Hills

The author freely grants anyone the right to quote up to 350 words of text from this book (excluding material quoted from other sources) without applying for specific permission, as long as proper credit is given.

Printed in the United States
by Banta

Front Cover: Design & Photography: John Hills

Library of Congress Cataloging in Publication Data

Hills, Christopher B
    Creative conflict.

    1. Conflict (Psychology)   2. Social conflict.
3. Psychotherapy.   I. Title.
BF503.H54   158'.2   80-5562

ISBN 0-916438-36-8

UNIVERSITY OF THE TREES PRESS
*—A Registered Trust and Common Ownership business
jointly owned and operated by its employees.*
P.O. Box 644, Boulder Creek, Calif. 95006

TABLE OF CONTENTS

ACKNOWLEDGEMENTS

Names are not important but hearts are. May I thank all those who have participated and put all their hearts into Creative Conflict, both in its development over the years as a way of self-discovery and now in its production as a book by the staff of the University of the Trees Press. Particular gratitude should go to the editor who not only sorted the contents from mounds of taped and written materials but actually tried out and used Creative Conflict over a number of years, teaching it to educators and becoming herself the living proof of its efficacy. There can be no greater thankfulness in a teacher than when his students prove the teachings in everyday life. To be blessed with willing helpers in addition is beyond gratitude.

—Christopher Hills

Editor's Note:

To have an original insight into how the cosmos designs and motivates the inner workings of man and to what glorious end, can only be the work of a master of consciousness who so tunes his mind and heart, his own intelligence to the cosmic intelligence that he shares in the cosmic perception. Everything you will read in the pages to follow has been tapped by Christoher Hills from the universal consciousness and channeled through the minds and hearts of those who have partaken in Creative Conflict and shared in the ongoing discovery of its wondrous unfolding process, like finding a jewel hiding within the bosom of nature, and proving over and over the validity of Creative Confict in their lives.

Up until now the only tangible evidence to show for Christopher's thirty years research and teachings in Creative Conflict has been the transformation and evolution in those whom these teachings have touched. During that entire period, Christopher has devoted his time and energy, his resources and life force to serving the evolution of people. From literally thousands of long hours of patiently trying to show students how they are using their consciousness to create their reality, to sharing in the struggles and breakthroughs of those he is closest to, his every action is that of untiring, selfless love. Such a life is an example of one who has seen his way through the duality of nature from which all conflict, creative or otherwise, arises. Creative Conflict is only part of a much wider insight into the nature of consciousness which Christopher calls "Nuclear Evolution", and his book of that title as well as his book "Rise of the Phoenix" contain the full force of his original vision.

—Deborah Rozman

CREATIVE COMMUNICATION

Anyone living today does not need to be a great prophet to see that the world could come to an end rapidly through escalating human conflict. Believe it or not there are some countries who are deliberately fostering class conflict, giving money to terrorists to disrupt our social fabric and create political dissension and thereby destroy our society through human conflict. The Biblical story of the confusion of tongues is nothing but the story of man's inability to talk the real language of life. That language is beyond words, beyond the ordinary communications we make every day. Unless the world learns that language soon, the human conflicts which exist at every level between man and wife, child and parent, individual and the group, will escalate, rear up their ugly heads, and destroy our capacity to love in the heart. Those who do not wake up to this new evolutionary message and who ignore the meta-language in which our reality is written, will be left in the debris of a social order that is even now rapidly disintegrating.

The root cause is our own imaginations and the ghosts and fears that lurk there. We can only discover those dark forces and learn to grapple with them through learning when and how to trust ourselves and others. We can only do this with some new way of breaking through the blocks to creativity and sharing with others.

CREATIVE COMMUNICATION

The word communication comes from the root word

communicare, to make common, to share in common with. If we
cannot share our beings, or make our feelings common with others
and with our environment, we will have conflicts within and
without. In essence, the problem with communication *is* the basic
world problem. All human problems arise from misunderstanding
which in turn emerges out of poor communication.

Everyone has conflicts and challenges to deal with in daily life.
They are the friction which spurs growth and learning. To know
how to grab hold of your conflicts and use them for growth, rather
than have them use you, is a rare talent. Most people allow
conflicts to buffet them around. The conflicts teach them lessons in
spite of themselves because they do not harness the energy of
conflict. Traditionally we have been taught to face conflict by
a) fighting back, b) staying cool and calm while trying to reason
the difficulty out, c) turning the other cheek, or d) being the "nice
guy". But how much do we really gain from our conflicts? Few
people realize how much dynamic energy gets bound up in a
conflict. That energy can be taken hold of and released into higher
creative potential when we know how. Regardless of which methods
people have used to deal with conflicts we can all probably agree
that most people still do not understand themselves or others very
well.

At the University of the Trees we have evolved some very
successful communication skills that deal with the energies of
conflict. We call the practice and use of these skills "Creative
Conflict". In nature, creation evolves through continuous conflict
resolution. There is much violence, from the forceful collisions of
microscopic atoms to giant exploding stars. On earth, positive and
negative forces conflict, repel and unite in dynamic action on every
level of existence, from the atomic and cellular levels to the mental
and spiritual levels. Darwin saw conflict in nature as competition
for survival of the species. But conflict is more than survival.
Conflict is built into nature to evolve the creation, to push it along
the path of evolution. Conflict is so very important because it is the
major propelling evolutionary force, although it is not the evolutionary goal.

When together we can discover the creative keys to mastering conflict, we will be on the threshold of a new society. It is not something we can put off to the future, waiting for some government to hand it to us. We must build with every tool we have available now, because the choice is cold and clear—mastery or suffering, even destruction. Science knows that when energies build up they must eventually be released. The negative energies in the world must be understood and transmuted or they must wreak their havoc after creating too much pressure. Love is necessary, but personal devotion alone will not change the world. Neither will moralistic codes forced upon people by social, political or religious authorities change the world. Self-responsibility in each of us to take hold of the destructive energy of conflict is the only way, and everyone must do the work. No one is exempt from resolving conflict. There will always be conflict; therefore we must use its energy creatively.

THE EGO AS THE ROOT OF CONFLICT

Most people think of the ego as something they value, their individual separate uniqueness, and they cannot distinguish it from their real being. The idea of "getting rid of" or "working on" the ego seems foreign to them. They ask, "Is there any advantage in transcending the ego? How can it be beneficial to constantly look at my motives, my inner thoughts, the subtle undercurrents of my self-centeredness generated by my ego? What is the advantage of being egoless? Can I really gain anything by giving up looking out for Number One? Look around. How many people really want to give up their egos? I'll be stupid if I do. I want to *develop* the strength of my ego, not reduce it."

But what is ego really? It is the sense of "I" sitting inside our own idea of who we are. It is the shell which contains that consciousness which is in everything. The seed or nut of consciousness must express through growing into some form or body. In getting a body this seed of our being wants to be somebody unique and special, separate from other bodies and from the environment. "That's me," it says, until the ego, the "self-sense", realizes that by giving up its narrow idea of separateness, it gains a much greater sense of individuality and fulfillment and a much expanded consciousness. By giving up our separateness, we must give up our selfishness, that part of us that brings our conflicts, pains and suffering—that part that harms others, knowingly or unknowingly. Rather than being a weak, unattractive and spineless state, egolessness is *knowing who you really are*. It is becoming one with everyone and feeling that the whole environment belongs to you. Supreme selflessness builds tremendous strength, joy and courage. But it terrifies every bit of egotism left inside us.

Creative Conflict challenges every person to confront his or her ego position that separates being from being, because it is ego-revealing. It tackles the very causes that separate human consciousness from total oneness. The essentially spiritual structure of the technique we call Creative Conflict has nothing to do with religion or any belief system, but is just the pure relationship between energies. You can refer to my earlier book *Nuclear Evolution* for more explanation of the nature of these personal energies, and the link between ego, light and consciousnes   Given these facts of nature, it seems a bit absurd that so few people are really willing to work on their ego—that self-centered identity which binds and limits their real potential and personal energy. Most people would rather cling to the ego as a self identity or escape into some heavenly euphoria or into sense pleasures. But in working directly with the confrontation of our ego we release the energies that block our fulfillment. We release them permanently into a greater potential, transport our consciousness into greater light and expanded understanding.

The first step in dissolving the separating self-sense of ego is to get out of our little self and inside the inner worlds of others. All the new beginning personal growth methods available are good (such as Gestalt, psychosynthesis, EST, co-counseling, PET, etc.) for they enable us to begin to take this step. But we must then go much farther to develop our own evolution and to deepen relationships by learning to watch and confront the ego's subtle unconscious motivations and reactions. There are many, many group process methods available today. Most fall under some branch of humanistic psychology or therapy. Some are short-term intensives.

They do enhance awareness of self and others' inner worlds to varying degrees, but few have the basic purpose of penetrating the ego, which is the crux of human destiny on earth. One of the proofs of this statement is that if you put the skilled facilitators of the majority of these groups together, most often underneath the veneer of a degree of cooperation, you will find competitive, even self-righteous egos vying for recognition, esteem and one-upmanship or egos unable to really receive the full being of the other. And this is because they do not yet know how to work on the basics—their own egos. As leaders they do not yet see their *own* underlying motivations. I am not saying that all group leaders are like this, but too many are!

Creative Conflict methods can be used successfully with children, teenagers, parents, classrooms, lovers, businesses, growth groups, labor-management relations and spiritual groups. With some practice you will be able to develop and apply the process on your own in all your relationships. *The most fundamental principle which Creative Conflict is based upon is the spiritual principle that all is one, and therefore all life is a mirror of ourself.* Each situation, each person, each inner reaction, is a mirror in which you can see yourself, your own nature. Through learning to look at the mirror everywhere, you can see where it needs polishing. In a Creative Conflict group, together we can polish the mirror to see reality and reflect the glory of our own true potential unveiled. In the Creative Conflict group we learn to see how we are creating our reality and we gain the power to put in a new program. The Creative Conflict process is a modern tool for enlightenment, for breaking through the veil of ignorance, the light barrier.

I originally developed the techniques of Creative Conflict at Centre House in London, perfected them in my travels around the USA during the 1960's and finally gave them form and expression at the permanent ongoing community we call the University of the Trees. This book is a summation of this practical work done by those who were willing to expose themselves to this transforming process. Their love and their growth is a living testament to the power of Creative Conflict to transform human lives.

Two long time practitioners of the Creative Conflict process.

PART I

1

CREATIVE CONFLICT—
THE MISSING LINK

One day I was walking along a mountain path in Scotland with a friend. He was a loveable person, very talented, and came from an illustrious family of English historians. I loved him very much and was glad to be on holiday together, climbing among the Scottish highlands and crags. I wanted to get to know him much more deeply and share a very sensitive part of my being that I could not expose in public. I thought being open and direct was the best policy, so one day I broached the question of his self-image because I knew he had some secret messianic feelings about his destiny as a spiritual person. For openers I asked him directly what was his relationship to God. He became very defensive and wanted to know what mine was first. I told him that I did not feel separate from God; I felt God with me all the time. He bristled a bit and I felt the surge of some inner conflict in him as he replied, "Do you think you are God then?" I tried to explain that I had lost the feeling that I was a separate ego and so there was no way I could tell any difference between my consciousness and God, because what *is* God if not Consciousness? I didn't think that there was any less of God in my friend's consciousness than in mine, but I could see that he was missing the subtlety of my point.

We walked along in silence for awhile as I could feel him struggling with some internal conflict within himself. I pointed out that to make any difference between God and man was up to each person who projected such thoughts into their own minds. A bit further along the path I again pointed out that the ego structure of each person would determine whether they separated God from themselves and others or not. I felt in him a distinct reaction to my words though I sincerely believed them and they were the honest result of my meditations and many years of spiritual search, including two years as a wandering holy man in India where this idea is a common concept.

The silence of the mountain trail was heavy as I felt a mounting anger in my friend. "So you are claiming to be God, are you?" he said with some degree of harsh feeling. I said that God had created consciousness in humans and in everything else and that we experienced a separation only if we identified with our particular physical form; so anyone who had truly conquered the self-sense would feel that such a separation was artificial because he or she would be identifying with consciousness itself and not with the form that it took. "That to me," he answered vehemently, "sounds like a claim that you are God!" I responded that I could only speak as I experienced God and life and that I could not deny that I felt the presence of God.

My friend became even more hostile and accused me of being arrogant. I protested that being one with God was not the same thing as claiming to be God. But he would hear none of it, and he kept silent the whole way home to our hotel. He was sullen for days and I knew I had lost a dear friend, one who was insisting on twisting my words to suit his own ideas of what was spiritual and what constitutes a holy life or a wholistic approach to the possession of God Consciousness. From that moment on our relationship withered and I heard from friends later that he thought I was stuck up or superior. I could not understand it at first because I had not spoken in any superior way but merely stated the facts of my personal experience. But that experience was deliberately taken and twisted into something else by him because something about God was twisted into an ego knot of separation in himself, and this ego knot became projected onto others. In fact what had happened was typical of most human relationships—he had made a superior judgement about me and my state of consciousness. With a closed mind on the subject of God and religion, he could not hear my words as they were spoken; he could not feel my love of God or enter my inner world to probe my real meaning at the depths. There was nothing I could do, nothing I could say that would change his mind-set that I was arrogantly claiming to be God. And so I lost a good friend whom I loved deeply and with whom I wanted so much to share deeply the very essence and core of my being.

I had devoted my life to discovering that state of consciousness at the expense of everything else. But when I was real and spoke about it I lost a friend. It seemed a paradox until I realized that when I spoke of nonseparateness in the depth of being, all those who felt separated from God were repelled. This experience concerned me deeply because if we humans cannot share our deepest thoughts about life and God together with friends we care about without them rejecting, judging, and becoming hostile, then how can we ever reduce the hostility of those who consider themselves our enemies and competitors?

I pondered on this experience for a couple of years and eventually started a center for Creative Conflict where people could talk about their perceptions in depth as an exercise in deep communication. Eventually I founded a community in England, based on this type of in-depth sharing, which lasted for twelve years. It closed its doors six years after I left to start a similar community based on Creative Conflict in California. The London center closed because the community lost the lease on the building through a lawyer's error. But during that whole time my old friend, who had turned against me on that mountain trail, never once came to see what I was doing or even wrote me to open up any dialogue or communication.

This experience of rejection of one's love and one's deep being is the world problem in a nutshell. If you say what you really mean you lose friends. If you speak the truth in your heart it will be used against you. If you put honesty and integrity beyond friendship you will be risking those dear to you whom you love. Yet if you do not speak your heart or share your ultimate truths you will live a half lie, a shallow existence with only half of you alive and expressing itself. This leads to divorce, not only between married people but also between friends, lovers, parents and children. So life is lived in separate worlds, separate ego bubbles which never fully come together in any depth. The method I evolved for breaking through the barriers of self-image or self-esteem and the twisted concepts in the imagination of humans I call Creative Conflict. It was born on a Scottish mountain trail and that trail still winds through the inner ego-structure of every being on the planet. For until humans stop separating themselves in their inner worlds from God and from their fellow beings, there will never be understanding and peace in their outer worlds.

The system I evolved works directly on the ego structure to reveal the separations we have from others, from the greater Self. Many are already working on this sense of separation through centering, yoga, meditation and many other kinds of personal growth methods. *Yoga* means union—the union of the personal self with the greater Self in all. But most often we have no way of checking out our personal growth except through our own evaluation. Meditation is usually done alone and no one judges the quality of your meditations but you. Through Creative Conflict, however, you gain a mirror into your inner soul. You see just how much you are really manifesting of what you think you have realized or who you think you are. Meditation by itself is not enough for dissolving ego separation even though it can have profound effects on consciousness. Creative Conflict becomes actually a social yoga, an active meditation with others, rather than a passive meditation which one does alone.

Like a spiritual discipline equal to meditation, equal to monastic disciplines in building spiritual strength, Creative Conflict is designed for the modern person living in the everyday world. Many people feel that meditation is enough to save the world. But meditation is only a tool, only as good as its user, and if you look at the world today you can see that society has not improved much even with meditation. Greed and hostility are just as rampant now as in Christ's or Krishna's time. India has had meditation for thousands of years but the country is an economic and political mess.

As the President of a worldwide yoga conference in 1970 with

800 yogis present in New Delhi, India, I saw displays of ego and received requests by yogis for special treatment that did not fit with the philosophies they were preaching. So much did I see this that I finally asked a friend and former President of the American Association of Humanistic Psychology, Dr. Sidney Jourard, to announce to the yogis present that their egos were acting like a bunch of porcupines, which he did in full public session. Meditative yogis, many of them famous, from rival ashrams who normally would not speak to one another according to long Indian tradition, had made a great step forward in even agreeing to come to such a joint convention, but they brushed past each other with egos bristling. One internationally famous yogi who was supposed to be part of a panel of ten philosophers in a discussion took over the entire proceedings for two hours and made it a one-man show. I had to scold him like a schoolboy in front of everyone present. I realized at that time that there is nothing as subtly competitive as spiritual politics. I saw holy men competing for the lowest seat in the room, each wanting to sit lower than the other as a mark of humility. The gap between their spiritual aspirations and words and their actual manifestation in real life is a statement of the situation not only in India but among many meditators. *The uniqueness of Creative Conflict is that it provides a special link between the spiritual and the material so that the inner benefits of meditation are brought into the physical and social worlds and not lost in the spiritual ethers.* It heals the split between our inner subjective life and our outer social-material life as human beings. *In most people these are two separate realities.*

Basically, practicing Creative Conflict is learning how humans can live centered in truth, learning how to be very integral and communicating that integrity to whomever you meet. Most groups just touch on the main thing that Creative Conflict goes deeply into—the ego. It is not the major purpose of most groups, even of most *spiritual* groups, to work on the ego. The group process often enhances a certain level of communication or personal awareness or is used as group therapy; mind patterns may be exposed in groups but the basic core of man's ego separation from other egos is not penetrated. Ego is the identity with ourself as a separate being, a physical identity which comes from living in a separate body apart from others. When we are tuned to spirit we do not feel the physical identification and we can feel other spirits as blending with our consciousnesses. There is nothing wrong with having an ego; we all have one. In fact it can be our strength and our goad to work on ourself. But when in daily living the ego makes us blind to each other's inner worlds, when you can't see where I am coming from or when I can't see where you are coming from because we are set in our own self-centered mental positions, then it creates a spiritual and social communication breakdown and we have all the consequences of that, even up to hostility and war.

An example of this ego separation is putting other people down —"I'm better than you." Such judgements create a reaction and breed the whole gamut of conflict. All destructive conflict arises from ego separation and if there were no ego separation there would be no negative conflicts that threaten us. We must be careful lest our negativity destroy not only our personal fulfillment but the human race. This does not mean that there should be no human differences but that they should not be out of tune with the harmony of the whole. Inner conflict occurs when different parts of ourself are split or are not able to see each other; they become blind to each other and thus out of resonance. But these are just words until you know inside yourself what your ego is. And that may not happen right away. People often come to a realization after a few months or a few weeks of working with Creative Conflict that they do not know when they are in their ego or not. They say, "I don't know when I am putting out something that comes from a separated ego space or when it is coming from a pure space." You will soon be able to observe that most of the time people are coming from an ego space, a self-righteous state which does not know what it does not know, so it is safe to begin by assuming that you probably are speaking from ego. If you have that recognition, then you begin to look deeper. You begin to probe your own mind—workings and you begin to have humility. You listen more. You open more. And you realize, "I really need to take in at a deeper level what's happening in my surroundings," so you merge closer with the environment. Then the expansion of awareness that you experience in peak moments or in your personal meditations can happen all the time. But you have to first have the recognition of what separates you from that total experience of unity while you are walking around and busy at your work.

Why work on this ego? Because we have such a hard time living with each other. Nature works through complex creative conflict processes, and the whole method of Creative Conflict is based on carefully observing Nature and its ways. Many religious disciplines teach that pain is something we should run away from or avoid or try to transcend because no one wants suffering. With Creative Conflict you learn to see pain as a teacher. Of course you don't seek pain or wallow in it when it is there. You learn to see pain as a subtle message for yourself. When you get physical pain it is a warning. Your body is saying that something is not right. It is crying, "Pay attention to me." The same thing is true for emotional pain. It is saying to you, "There is something you need to look at; life is trying to teach you something." So how can we help each other recognize what life is trying to show us? This is Creative Conflict—trying to help each other see what life is trying to teach us through exposing our inner conflicts and pains.

The joy of being in deep communication together is very bonding to our spirits. The joys really take care of themselves, as long as you are nurturing and have a loving group. What happens in many spiritual groups is that they cling to the good feelings and avoid pain and suffering because they want to preserve that loving space. They tiptoe around each other's egos. Something then is missing and not fulfilling in the relationships. Great teachers like Christ advise going towards our sufferings and feelings of persecution. "Blessed are ye when men shall persecute you and say all manner of evil against you falsely"* is Christ's way of saying face up to painful situations and use them creatively. Creative Conflict methods deal lovingly with the sensitive areas, but do not avoid meeting truth head on, even if it means we have to disturb the peace temporarily to get to the root of the problem or the pain. Creative Conflict enables you to gain a great amount of strength by knowing how to look at pains. You can then see clearly nature's

---

* Matthew 5:11

message to you. You read the book of life. Creative Conflict is very much needed to clean out the psychic climate in any group. Many people cling to their self-pity and wallow in their pain. But Creative Conflict is only for those who are sick of wallowing, who desire transcendence and want self-mastery.

The reality in the classroom, the reality in a family, is not the outward circumstances, but it is what is happening at the inner psychic energy level. That inner body dictates the reality. When you teach Creative Conflict to teachers in a public school class-room or to adults who have no spiritual experience at all, who are for the first time being exposed to these ideas and methods, the very first and most important thing is to make them aware of this inner body or the psychic body which constitutes the atmosphere of the home or classroom. The question you must ask yourself is, what is the real psychic climate in your home life or in your classroom, or even in your workplace like? Is it confused vibra-tions all mixed up with each other? Is it pretty smooth-flowing energy? What is going on inside you to create that psychic climate or to modify it? Are there tensions that you have at home and in your personal life which you shove under the carpet and out of your mind when you go to work? Your vibration is still being broadcast to children or to people you work with at an unconscious level to condition the psychic climate.

This psychic climate is very important in businesses and in any group process, and very few groups ever look at the real cause of it. But the psychic climate *is* the reality. It is more real than what is being said verbally because it conditions everything a person says and what the group is able to manifest. Creative Conflict works on this inner level of the subjective spiritual and psychic climate. The methods attune each member to the deeper vibration going on in people, and this attuning to the dynamic of the inner body of the group develops the individual soul and its intuition.

Creative Conflict takes practice. It is not something you learn in one series of lessons or by reading a book. It only becomes totally real when it becomes part of your daily life and you can apply it in your interactions with all people. When you can tune instantly to the inner worlds of all people with whom you come in contact and at the same time stay centered, then you are manifesting the results of the methods and you will find yourself quite in harmony or in tune with the deeper beings of people. You will have empathy and will know their hearts and struggles. You apply the Creative Conflict methods to yourself as an individual as well as in groups. You don't absolutely need a group to do Creative Conflict in your life situation, but it is better if you can work with one. If you get agreement from a group to use the same communication tools, to say, "Hey, I want to work on my ego with you," then your growth is much enhanced. The group may be just one other person, or your family, some people at your job, or a group gathered together for the expressed purpose of exploring awareness, communication skills and evolving together. Society itself is made up of such groups.

If you are in a relationship where you want to work on the ego and your partner or child or associate says, "No, that's not for me," you cannot force anyone else to grow with you, but you yourself can become a living example. Use the principles and steps of Creative Conflict and it will soon have a magical effect on other people. For one thing, they will feel your integrity. There is an incredible integrity emanating from a person who has realized Creative Conflict in himself, and it makes other people want the same thing for themselves. At first direct truth can be very uncomfortable and embarrassing. But when people see or feel this integrity, they know that it is what they are missing in their own lives. And when that recognition comes, then they are more willing to go through the pain of facing themselves as they really are in order to get to the other side. Some people just are not prepared to face themselves. And these people we can only let be. Life will teach them.

Once integrity can be established within individuals, within families, within businesses, within schools and within groups of people at the social levels, then it can transform our politics and be applied even between nations. When nations sit down to talk they rarely discuss causes or probe each other's basic motivations. They rarely go beyond the politics of confrontation. And this is a reflection of the relationships between individuals in this world. In

the Arab-Israeli dispute, when you get beyond politics the motivations are deeply engrained. Israel feels it has a historical, religious
right to the West Bank and to remain in Jerusalem. It is a deeply
emotional issue. And the Arabs firmly believe that the Palestinians
have inalienable humanitarian rights to be as self-governing as
Israel and that the Arabs also have historical, religious rights to
Jerusalem. They both feel their own religion is the right one. There
is so much emotional volatility in these deeply-held, entrenched
beliefs that the only way true and lasting peace could come
between them is if they could look together at their assumptions and
challenge the truth of their emotional fervor in relation to the good
of the greater whole—total world peace. It is probably still a
millenium away before governments will make working on the ego
to reach peace a common practice. At the moment they cannot
make the deepest truth their basic purpose or motivation, since
they think only in terms of compromise. Creative Conflict goes
beyond a mere compromise between separate interests and separated egos. It is a way of skillfully getting to the greatest truth—
that deepest place where the two parties become one in spirit and
thus are no longer separated in reality.

*This symbol represents the endless interaction of opposing forces
which come together only in the center of being.*

2

WHAT EXACTLY IS
CREATIVE CONFLICT?

Creative Conflict is a way of relating to people deeply, openly from the heart. It reveals to those who practice it honestly a definite purpose in life—that there is a truth of being, a state of oneness where the ego, the feeling of separateness, disappears or is merged into a higher, more wholistic total state of consciousness. How do we make that cosmic state of being a reality in our interactions between people? Rather than separating education from spirituality, politics from spirituality or business from spirituality, Creative Conflict is actually the dynamic process of bringing them together, right from the core of being. It means we have to be willing to look at some things that we as individuals or as society have not really been prepared to look at before. And that is what you eventually learn to look for in the Creative Conflict group—*the one thing that each person does not want to look at or deal with—the gap in our consciousness.*

A father of two young children preached love and generosity to friends and clients and indeed was always ready to warmly offer his services to those in need. His demeanor was ever generous, calm and poised with friends or at work. But in the home he ignored his wife and was ice cold with his children, ordering them about, barking commands and unleashing any frustration he had with them with the belt. His young son would quiver even when his father came near, fearful of a brusque encounter. The boy became increasingly disobedient in spite of the constant beltings. The two-faced character of this man not only created severe family problems but kept him in constant inner torment, without his knowing why. He could not see the outward gap between his work life and his home life, between his self-image and his actual manifestation, let alone understand where the gap was coming from. The Creative Conflict group mirrored to him this gap between his spiritual self-image and his relationships with his children and initially he became very defensive and rejected the people's perceptions. But the frequency of the same feedback coming from so many varied and different people finally put him in touch with the painful realization that he was not as perfect as he thought and that his attitude was destroying his young son.

The intuition becomes trained to clue into that one thing—that Achilles' heel that keeps tripping us up in very subtle ways—for that is the very thing that, when probed, can give the greatest penetration and release of soul. But are people willing to do it? To reach this perception we have to be able to look clearly and ask where is inner conflict coming from in people and in ourselves? We have to be willing to risk letting go of things we think we need or ideas and images that are precious to us. To get really clear at that depth is what is needed to clean out the Augean stables of our collective psychic atmosphere.

So the first step and purpose in Creative Conflict is to train ourselves to get inside each other's inner worlds. This is what you practice in the first training period. We need to be able to experience what another person experiences from inside him or her. To some degree we can achieve this training through psychology or by doing meditation, and meditation is part of the Creative Conflict process. You cannot have pure perception without meditation, without being able to be one-pointed in your attention and expanding your awareness to include more of the other's being.

Real listening can only happen if we are in a state of meditation, where the body is calm and the emotions and mind are peaceful, not churning. If the ego is jumping around we cannot listen to the being of the other. So the first step in Creative Conflict is to learn to put the ego aside temporarily to hear the other person in depth. And it may take awhile just to get to the point where you can listen, where you can know when your ego is in the way or when it is aside and you have become receptive. It is wise to begin Creative Conflict with meditation to help get centered and put the ego aside. But if two people are really emotionally upset or hot under the collar, they are not going to be able to stop their churning ego reactions to meditate silently unless they already have some experience with meditation. For them it is important to take a moment to try to settle down and get into a peaceful state, then to share some of their feelings to get them off their chests and to ease the emotional tensions.

Once you begin to meditate you can begin to let go of the ego reactions more easily. You can release at will the restless energies of mind and emotions and this will make you more receptive, more able to listen to life's message throughout the day and from many sources. The way you can watch your receptivity or your ability to listen is to ask yourself, "Am I playing thoughts in my mind, tapes of what I want to say, while another person is talking?" "Am I thinking, 'What's for dinner?', or 'I'm bored', or 'my back hurts'?" If you are not fully concentrated on the being of the other then you are not listening. Or if you are analyzing what is happening or free associating in your mind, thinking, "that leads to that, and if that is so then I see that", etc., you are not listening. Listening is becoming one with each person so that you are hearing more than just their words, you are experiencing the frequencies of sound like listening to music as you are feeling what they are feeling: you are inside them and you feel them inside your own being. Then you can begin to read their unconscious and *know* beyond the word level where they are really coming from. If the other person really is boring, then you can choose not to listen, but most people drift off and do not make a conscious choice. They are not integral. If you are bored you need to take responsibility for changing your situation. If you choose to stay and be bored, then take responsibility for choosing your experience. If you want to be receptive then you will discipline those tapes in your mind to really listen. You will become like a photographic plate where subtle impressions from the other person are registered in your being, along with their words. Then your will and your heart are consciously involved and you radiate the aura of a person of integrity.

When you get practiced in the Creative Conflict process you can immediately scan the psychic field of a group and know the quality of the group energy. You can tell how focussed the consciousness is or who is drifting and thinking about being somewhere else or dreaming about someone else. Once you have learned how to get inside another's inner world, putting your own ego, concepts and identity aside for the moment, then you can begin gaining insight into the basic motivations underlying your own as well as the other's ego positions. This takes the communication to a deeper level of being that is very important in making conflict creative. At this deeper level we ask, "What are my motivations for saying what I am saying, doing what I am doing, and how do I look at my motivations?" We are stepping into the depths of our soul with these questions.

What, deep down, do you really want? Do you have a secret self-image that you like to feed? When you probe motivations you get to yet another and deeper layer—the different self-images that each person has. Every ego position radiates with more and more clarity the deeper you go in Creative Conflict. And the stronger the radiation, the better the group can mirror back what each person needs to work on. This is the tremendous love that the group can give you—to become a soul mirror for your ego position so that you may see yourself clearly. When you are willing and trusting, the group force can help you penetrate beyond ego, beyond self-image to your real being in a way you may have never before experienced. The group and you are not separate at that level, but are one and the same, like looking in a clear mirror and seeing your reflection so purely that you know it is a cosmic being.

Peer pressure is used creatively in Creative Conflict as the pressure of the mirror of life. And the group mirror becomes very accurate with practice. In a group that sticks to the methods, the mirror of the group becomes highly polished and this brings a feeling of peer pressure to purify oneself. The motivation to grow may not always be the purest desire for self-realization; it may sometimes be a motive of not wanting to be rejected or not wanting to be mirrored as one who doesn't want to change, which would cause the ego not to think very highly of itself. But your real nature, your real willingness to change is what eventually does get tested. Whenever the entrenched ideas of self, the self-image, are challenged, the ego churns and we are confronted inside ourself with how much we do indeed want to change or not. We eventually reach a crunch point where we are left in freedom to choose whether or not to take a step forward in evolution, just as nature or God allows us free choice to follow cosmic laws in tune with the whole or to go our own way and let life's pains be our mirror and our teacher if we can see it. Creative Conflict substitutes the loving mirror of others for the more ruthless pains of life. We use the group, the peers in the group, not as a substitute for thinking for ourselves, but as all those eyes homing in on truth to *stimulate* thinking for ourselves. This creates a tremendous challenge to the ego to look at truth and still feel love and unity in the heart at the same time. It is a lot easier to do that looking at our depths when we have a supportive environment where we can build trust and have a common purpose with others. It is too ego-threatening to be penetrated by oneself alone. So there is a need to feel the heart of the group. And for Creative Conflict to get to any depth there has to be a commitment in the heart. The commitment is to be one in the heart, although at times different in the head. We can have all the differences and disagreements we want in the head provided there is acknowledgement in the heart that we care and nurture and give each other freedom. Then conflict is creative.

In a family, in school, in business, in a group, you can make time just for the purpose of coming together to work on the ego. This is Creative Conflict in daily life. At the same time that you build trust and caring you are able to risk more in the ego. If you can acknowledge that the mirror of the group is saying something to you and you are willing to hear, you will learn easily from life. Life itself is your teacher every moment if you are in that receptive state. Most people are so blind that they go trampling through life ignoring or trying to ignore all its messages, avoiding all the mirrors that are trying to reflect one hint after the other. We get pain when we turn this way, we get pain that way, and we still go on saying, "I'm okay Jack." Then we are surprised when we come down with cancer or get a heart attack or we get divorced or something crashes down on us, which is really another mirror, still trying to get a message to us. The key to conflict is to learn how to look deeply in the mirror of our consciousness to see that *the whole of life is geared for the purpose of your evolution.* Everything that is happening, every little thing, even in your dreams, is part of yourself. Everything is a projection of consciousness in the service of evolution, your evolution. And in this sense you are a singularity, always the center of the universe. This doesn't mean your evolution is separate from my evolution or anyone's evolution, but that everything is a mirror for everything else. It's happening the same universally in all, while our personalities are all uniquely different. This is the way life grows all of its creation. How can we read the book of nature, the book of life and its message for ourselves and for each other? That is what Creative Conflict teaches.

3

WHAT DOES IT MEAN TO REALLY WORK ON THE EGO?

No one likes to have their ego revealed to them. The more insecure or blocked up you are, the more it feels like criticism or rejection when someone tries to point out your ego to you. This is as true for young children as it is for older people. This is because the ego's function is to always try to get approval, recognition and support for itself. You can watch children who are being told that they hurt someone, and their egos will just wriggle in the corner, caught. They may try to change the subject, anything to avoid facing themselves. Even if the confronting is being done in a loving, non-accusing way, the sensitive ego feels *it* is no good and *it* is being rejected. So the first thing you need to do in Creative Conflict is to help the child or adult realize that the ego is not his real being. Children and most adults are busy building their ego and they do not want to look at it or tear down what they are building. You might say to a child, "I don't like you leaving your dirty lunch box lying around the living room." And the child might respond by ignoring you and saying, "Hey what's on TV tonight?" hoping you will drop the subject and leave him alone, let his ego stay just as it is.

The ego-building process is one of the most misunderstood and biggest causes of conflict between parents and children, especially in the teen years. It is important to remember that there is nothing wrong with a strong ego, as long as you are willing to look at it and include others in it at the same time. And you can only look at it if you are identified with your real being, with the whole, and not thinking that your separate ego is your real self. If you can help children build a happy, positive self-image that includes others and help them to look truthfully at themselves at the same time, they learn to work with life and stay in tune. If they do not look, they are already building patterns that will come crushing in on them later through painful situations that will leave deep emotional and psychological scars.

Even though it is not easy working on your ego, because you are so identified with it, it is mandatory for real happiness. The ego is like feeling the splinter is part of your finger and not wanting to cut the sliver out. But working on the ego brings you tremendous feelings of relief as you realize you are not the sliver, and you are loved for your deeper self. Working on the ego is to change identifications, which is what evolving from matter to spirit, to pure consciousness, is all about. So we have to acknowledge that the ego is tricky and that it is going to be tricky in ourselves, and then we can come prepared to deal with it, and not let it set us back or defeat us. When we can learn to point it out in each other with humor, we can learn to make working on ourself a lighter process. We can laugh at ourselves and love ourselves.

A very common pattern in the practice of Creative Conflict is when someone is trying to show you a deep ego pattern in yourself which you are not in touch with and you fog out. You enter into a mental fog and can't quite register what they are saying, even though they are being perfectly clear. Everyone else can see what they are pointing out in you, but your blindspot is before you. To you it is not clear at all because your ego patterns are blocking your perception. The "fog" is an unconscious mechanism of the ego to defend itself, not to have to work on or change that part of itself. Why is the ego so desperate to maintain itself? Because you have given so much energy to building up the ego as your sense of identity, you have given so much energy to your negativity that it is like a habit that seems to have energy of its own and keeps you enslaved in spite of your desire to give up the habit. It takes on a life of its own and to change to something else is, from ego's point of view, to die. So it usually defends itself fiercely as if caught in a life-or-death struggle for existence until the heart can be touched.

Then the picture seems to change. The kaleidoscope turns and we have a different perspective; ego's hold is released even if for a moment. If you have a loving, supportive group who can intensify and focus life's mirror for you, like a lens focusing light, and can take you deeper into yourself, then you are given more energy, more power to change yourself. If you, at that moment, open and receive the focussed light and use it to look deep within to illumine your ego for you, then the fog lifts. If you have difficulty opening, the methods and techniques of Creative Conflict help you to open. First you go to the method of active listening and mirroring until you can do it accurately with your full being which can put you in touch with the light and get you out of the fog, out of your identification with ego and into the other person's heart. By getting out of yourself, you open up, and the light can enter in.

Positive support is not the same as false flattery. False flattery only massages the ego. It builds up a false self-image. Positive self-image building is a very creative process but it has to be distinguished from false self-image building. Telling someone they are really great when they have done nothing to really earn that praise can build a false sense of pride that will be shattered later by life's reality. But giving praise for something done really well creates a true mirror of their positive manifestation. You can still positively support someone's efforts and real being without giving false ego food that will only inflate their idea of who they are and give them pain later on when life mirrors back the falsity of what you have said.

Some people crave attention and ego praise so much that they are unable to hear truth about themselves unless you reinforce their egos at the same time by giving them positive feedback about their good qualities. With children this is sometimes vital because they are still forming their self-image and don't have a crystallized feeling about who they are. But the danger with adults is that positive feedback at the wrong time can block ego penetration if it is used to avoid reality and reinforce a false self-image. One woman resisted Creative Conflict because she felt no one saw or appreciated her good qualities. Everyone loved her good qualities dearly and reflected that to her at other times, but during the group session we were trying to help her see the ten percent of her being that was blind to itself, the gap, and it felt unclean to have to pander to her ego. The very thing that was keeping her from seeing the lack in her manifestation she didn't want to hear because she was afraid she would lose herself and be devastated. The fact was she didn't *want* the truth if it meant re-evaluating her idea of herself, and so she felt others did not love her. Since the group mirror could not convince her, life had to do it more painfully as her relationship with her boyfriend slowly disintegrated. In time she did learn to see that there was love even in the speaking of unpleasant truth.

We still should love each other openly and positively but we need to learn to love truthfully. Truth is different at different levels of perception, but if you adhere to the deepest truth you know, then life will assist your growing. Then your love becomes pure. There is nothing gooier than false love, false appreciation, when it is said out of sentimentality or said just because it is the thing to say. It doesn't feel clean. Sometimes parents lay ego food on so thick that children sense the falsity in it and won't receive it. They turn away from kind remarks or hugs. Of course the opposite happens even more often where parents feel so bad about themselves that they are constantly putting down their children and knocking their egos unwittingly, thus giving them a negative self-image. But the remedy is not to substitute one falsity for another. You don't really grow by icing over a negative self-image with positive feedback unless the feedback is true. Seeing truth is what makes us grow, and Creative Conflict is polishing the mirror of life to see "what is" clearly. It can be tough to face it.

WHERE WE ARE HEADED

In past years families stayed together because there was a strong economic motivation and strong insecurity about following any inner guidance. People cannot communicate any better today than they could then, but today the economic motivation to stay together as a family, or even to stay in a job that doesn't meet our ideals, is no longer so much of a priority. Women are increasingly economically independent and so do not fear starvation or social rejection if they divorce. People feel more secure in pursuing personal fulfillment and shedding old roles. Children are no longer needed by parents for an economic asset in supporting the family. They have more freedom to do what they want to do and thus more freedom to rebel. And in business, if we have many skills, we can choose our jobs. Much of our present-day unrest is because we have more choices, yet we have not improved our ability to communicate or get inside each other's worlds. This ferment in society is leading inevitably to some sort of transformation. It is up to each of us to take responsibility for making it a positive evolutionary change towards fulfilling our potential instead of dire instability or a complete breakdown of society.

Many groups come together with wonderful ideals, but fall apart because the binding force is not as strong as the ego differences between them. The Findhorn Community is an example where the leader found it very difficult to surrender the power which controls others. The group at Findhorn, at the time of this writing, is in the middle of a power struggle and has not yet learned the process that would enable them to go through their decision-making crisis to a synthesis in which all members participate. This requires knowing how to take the differences and disagreements to the level of basic motivations, and really ask, "Are our basic purposes and underlying motivations the same?" And if we find that our underlying vision or motive is different, then there is either going to be a split eventually or someone is going to have to change. It cannot be any other way. If you use Creative Conflict you understand these different motivations at work and their effect on the group consciousness. You can feel good about splitting apart if your basic purposes, your wills, are different. Or you can decide that in spite of your differences there is a bond that you want to keep. That bond has to be stronger than the differences if the group is to continue to grow to be evolutionary, and by "group" I include couples as well as larger groups. In a Creative Conflict group where people meet precisely for the purpose of evolving together, you have to constantly challenge each other's willingness to overcome separateness and ego in order to keep the heart bond strong and deep.

In every relationship you eventually come to the question of will. Do I have the willingness to overcome my separateness, my ego? In a Creative Conflict group you learn to experience this willingness only by identifying with your greater potential and wanting that more than you want your ego. Only by identifying with oneness, with the greater harmony and potential that comes from a feeling of oneness, can we have the strength to conquer ego. The choice is constantly put to us in many tests throughout life. "Do I want to sacrifice my ego for this, or don't I?" "Do I choose this way or that way?" The closer you get to pure consciousness the more intense the choices are and the more you are drawn to the center even though your ego may fight all the way. In order to be able to choose God, or oneness, we have to have an experience of egolessness and taste the joy of it or be sick enough of the pain of ego attachment that we don't want it tripping us up any more. We have to have some feeling or deep memory of unity or bliss to remember that it is a superior state that brings us more happiness. It is very difficult to risk letting go of the ego and trust that something better will happen unless we have some experience of this process. This is why Creative Conflict is a nursery for saints. You learn which part of you leads to bliss and which leads to ego reinforcement and more pain.

We must want that bliss more than we want our ego position if the will is to be strong enough to overcome lesser drives or desires or the pulls, needs, gratifications and habits that keep tripping us up and keep us bound to ego. Until you reach a point in evolution where you have that will and the experience of a greater harmony, you will think that what the ego is craving will bring you greater happiness. But this is a false perception based on identifying with your ego, and it always leads to more misery, more stumbling over itself—until you learn. We call this choice "stomping on Kilroy" or "Killjoy". Remember the wartime cartoon figure who pops his nose and head and sticks his hands just over the brick wall and says "Kilroy is here"? That's just how ego gets hold of us. It sticks its nose over the fence, and that is our moment of choice, where we move toward self-mastery or away from it. As soon as you learn to recognize the thoughts that are going to lead you astray or make you miserable you bop them, tell that Killjoy to get down before it gets a hold on you and takes your thoughts into a downward spiral of negativity. The Creative Conflict process takes you to the place where your will is strengthened so that you can make decisions for individual growth, decisions that benefit your real Self. The group mirror, if you are willing to listen to it, can help you see those Killjoys, can help you grow faster to the point where your will is directed continually to the greater, universal will, which the soul of each person really does want, underneath the ego's misconceptions.

There are some people who resist letting go of their egocentric viewpoint to the bitter end. Convinced that their own perceptions are superior to the group, they persist in setting up an ego barrier and are closed to the group. This can only invite a battering ram type of communication where the whole exercise comes off like a threat to one's survival. Internal anger mounts and mounts and the defenses thicken like a brick wall. They get set in their ego position and nothing can budge them because they are not willing to look at themselves as they really are. To look would risk losing their self-image and everything they have invested in it. This type of resistance can only disappear by willingness to change, willingness to grow and a seeking of a breakthrough into new light. Group persistence may win out until there is a breakthrough, but if there is no free will to cooperate with the group mirror, send the person on his way and do not waste your time.

Coercion cannot be used and still have a Creative Conflict. Persistence must be distinguished from coercion and browbeating because persistence is a creative process whereas coercion is a destructive form of brainwashing and one-upmanship. Creative Conflict cannot be creative by the group pressure forcing people to accept something about themselves that they do not wish to own or acknowledge. At first, of course, every ego automatically thinks it is being pressured to conform, even when it is not. That is the way an ego perceives any criticism at all. But often beneath the initial stubbornness there is a real willingness to know the truth however uncomfortable. After a while the ego proceeds to have insights about its own egocentricity, and then progress towards a breakthrough is swift because the situation is not perceived as threatening, so the defensiveness dissolves.

The following is a personal narrative from one member of the University of the Trees community about her experience with Creative Conflict.

"In my own personal life, I have been in very deep creative conflicts, where the deepest thing in me that I didn't want to look at at all was seen by the rest of the group. They said, we all see this thing in you. We all see your ego feeling superior and looking down on others. They gave graphic examples to illustrate their feelings. I had to buy that they must be seeing something, even though I didn't want to and couldn't see myself like that. I had to come to a point of choice—to resist and deny their reality in order to preserve my own ego position, my own image of myself, or to say, "God, I have to own this and look at it. If it's there, it won't work to hide it or I'll just have more pain." I'd learned that from experience I needed to "try on" what they were saying in order to know directly whether it was real or not. My mind said no, but they kept saying yes and getting frustrated with me. It was me or them, and so I decided to let go and really look. I trusted that in letting go, some inner truth would come forth to tell me, and it did. I let go and opened, took it in and with the help of each person got in touch with what they were seeing. As I looked at their mirror intensifying that part of me, I felt I was looking from behind their eyes, and something incredible penetrated my soul. I felt like I was right in the Tao, right at the soul level of my being, in clear consciousness; my thoughts cleared away, the universe opened up; it was an incredibly deep meditation. I was beyond the ego; I let go of it. Now I have learned how to let go of it, by looking straight at it, but I couldn't do it on my own then. I needed the focussed, concentrated will and help of the group to see, and then the release came. I had to risk. It doesn't mean that I have completely mastered ego and can stay in that space forever. Your consciousness does slowly cloud over again as you go about daily life and as other patterns of thought reassert themselves, but it's never the same. It gets clearer the longer you practice, the more you can risk and open to a wider reality. In six months of Creative Conflict with a committed group I gained more insight into my deeper self and into the nature of reality than in many years of meditating alone. And for weeks after a penetrating Creative Conflict I have deep meditations because I am meditating on a deeper part of myself than I was in touch with before."

We always tape record our sessions so each time you hear the tape you are taken to that deep space again. And you always hear something new, something different that confronts another part and you look at it and it wears away another block, another defense. You miss so much the first time because it is hard to take it all in. Your ego is only capable of hearing certain things and you may find that in your first listening you twisted something up. But later on, when you listen to the feedback again, after putting all your argumentativeness, your ego, aside and getting inside the worlds of the speakers to feel their feelings and their viewpoint as you listen, you penetrate to another level. How do you know it is truth and that they aren't screwed up in how they see you? Sometimes they *are*, and you share that's how you feel about it and together you work it out. If you are both committed to truth then you get to the bottom of it and it feels real. You know it in your bones. To work in this way is a real commitment to truth. In order for it to take you to your real self, you have to know that you really want truth no matter what the cost.

There are many groups now functioning around the spiritual supermarkets of the 1980s. Most people move from one group to another, searching for something. Most participants in groups are always looking for that someone or something that will fill a certain part of their self, and they find it in the Creative Conflict experience. That part they wanted touched was their soul.

There is nothing more fulfilling in the process of Creative Conflict than experiencing that penetration of soul, yours or another's. The reality is that we are all going to be forced by life, by nature to look at truth eventually or be divided if we resist. This is the way the universe is structured. "A house divided against itself, against truth, cannot stand."* Since our natures, our souls and essence, are that truth, that clear reality, we have to eventually meet it or be living dead. Most people die before they ever face themselves in depth. As Christ said, to gain eternal life or the kingdom of heaven we have to consciously make that decision to do this work on ourself. Not everybody is going to penetrate deeply right away because not everybody is secure enough, trusting enough to look in the group mirror, or courageous enough to be a good mirror for others and really be open about what they feel and perceive. It takes awhile to be able to sort out when the other person or other people are projecting their own shortcomings onto you or when they are speaking a direct perception about you. It takes awhile to check your own words to know when your ego is speaking or when you are seeing clearly and speaking without your ego coloring what you say. Some people may think this process is learning to buy someone else's truth and that this woman was really giving up her inner truth and growing more deluded, but the proof is in the inner knowing and in what life mirrors to you. Being able to polish the mirror of life is worked out in the steps of the Creative Conflict process.

In the transformation of society we have to evolve together. Together we must probe our attachments and our images of ourselves, which are at the core of our separate identity or ego. Working on the ego is working on the very roots of self-identity, the drives that motivate us to act in separating ways. Those drives are causing ego pain at that deep level, that causative level which fosters our separation from life and distortion of mind. It is our ego-centricity which is causing the feelings that bring us pain and generates the way people relate to us. The conflicts and problems

---

* Mark, 3:25.

we have are born out of our ego. These conflicts bring us guilt and keep us perpetuating a cycle of fear, separation and error. We have to risk to break this pattern. Creative Conflict is a skillful way of probing as deep as you can go, together with others. If it is done with love, from the spiritual basis of oneness that we *are* one in essence, then the participants are taken as far as they are wanting to go and as far as the group can go, depending on how far the members themselves have evolved using the process of Creative Conflict. It doesn't matter if you begin as novices. Begin where you are, in your own situation, and life will lead you from there, because Creative Conflict is a process of life. The process begins as soon as you begin it and takes you as far as you are willing to go in looking at yourself. It faces you with yourself and, if you choose to go to the end, can take you all the way to that blissful nonseparate space of oneness with the whole, with everyone.

The process starts with real listening, learning how to mirror, in the first step. Getting to the basic motivations and discovering whether we have the will, the willingness to look at ourselves and to make evolution and change our purpose, is the second step. This second step leads us to integrity, that quality sorely lacking in society today. The Creative Conflict process fosters integrity and thrives on integrity. Integrity is not just saying anything you want to say. Many encounter-type groups degenerate into mud-slinging ego clashes. But real integrity is standing in the calm center and finding a creative way of expressing what you are feeling to another where you neither compromise yourself nor separate from him or her. You remain true to yourself in your actions and your words. And that establishes trust. How do you do this? Children are naturally quite integral, saying things just as they see them, just as they are, until they learn through the adult socializing process what is acceptable and what is not. Then they lose their integrity, their directness. Creative Conflict is *integrity training*. You begin by learning integrity with your group even if that is just one other person, and then it expands organically to more and more people.

Sometimes the most integral thing, the greater truth, is *not* to say anything, to be quiet. Integrity is knowing what not to do as well as what to do. It knows what is best for the whole situation.

When we are not integral in our communication we get just what we deserve. For example, if you are bored talking on the phone with a friend who keeps you chatting for two or three hours, you get just what you deserve, because you are not integral and are not saying that you are tired of talking and need to get off the phone. A person with integrity is a very magnetic and powerfully attractive person. When your family or business or group learns to be integral with each other, there you will find honest and deep sharing of feelings, and that is a powerful soul force for others who will want to join your group or who will be attracted into your orbit. As long as you are caring and communing with the inner world of the other, you will know how honest and real you can be without harming the other. So genuine integrity is not just bluntness but maintains the heart connection while it speaks its perceptions, and it is also humble enough to be checking out the reality of its perceptions in case it is seeing wrongly. This brings respect.

Something very electrical happens when soul communication occurs. It involves you like a drama because it captures your inner participation. It captures your being, even if you are not the subject of the Creative Conflict. There is a vibration that is very high because everyone is tuned in on the problem that is going on inside the person involved and on the total energy of the group. To achieve this soul contact in Creative Conflict takes commitment—commitment to practice the process and to set times where you actually sit down to be open—to share feelings and probe your perceptions with others. The consequences of not living up to your commitment to practice the process is that conflicts build up and psychic blocks build up and communication remains shallow and unfulfilling. It is no different from tilling the garden where you have to keep up the digging and weeding and tending in order to grow beautiful flowers.

Once you get the vibration of integrity established in yourself and in your group, then you can use that powerful force to look at the basic self-images held by the people in the group. Self-image is the biggest block to oneness, and a lot of problems boil down to that. When you really get down to basic motivations, underneath the motivation is often an underlying self-image, how you see yourself, how you want the world to see you. It is very threatening at that level to change that self-image, unless you can see or trust that something better is going to come of it. And that takes a long time usually. But if you stick to a group that's really working together on that depth of self-image, you have a very powerful group, because the next step after self-image is to confront the void, to become nothing, and to really become nothing is a real state of grace and humility. We get down to these basic archetypal patterns we cling to, the basic images we hold, subtly, of ourself, that condition our motivations and our drives, our fears and our hopes, and that is the real spiritual work when we get to that vulnerable, nitty-gritty level.

The group members serve as checks and balances for each other's perceptions because there is no coercion, only freedom to get in touch with deeper and deeper truth inside ourselves and to test it in the group mind. The group learns to hear the "ring of truth", something that is deeply penetrating and hits home, where all know that what was said is a direct perception. When someone says something that is "off", your inner divining ability says, "There is something fishy, something not quite right, something a little off in what you said," and the group may probe that to reveal the real, or to see if there is a projection or a twisting of reality. With the freedom to speak your deepest feelings and the support for sharing your perceptions along with having to be responsible for whatever you do say and not being able to get away with anything, you find that the group process becomes a pure channel for the spirit of truth.

One point I must raise is that some readers might fear that Creative Conflict may lead to communist collective life where people are always being brainwashed and always re-enforcing each other's commitment to the party doctrine. But the Creative Conflict process is vastly different from communist or cultist group coercion and self-confrontation sessions where people are confronting only how well you are in tune with the party "truth", the group line. In totalitarianism, there is no listening, there is no room for examining the basic assumptions of the authoritarian philosophy. That would be considered traitorous. This limit upon freedom amounts to a denial of soul, a denial of real and deep feelings when they conflict with authoritarian party statements or methods, and is coercion of the most psychologically manipulative kind.

Creative Conflict accomplishes the group union that idealistic communism and cults are wanting to achieve, but does so in a holy spirit of total freedom and without coercion. Truth is wrought out of the group process where everyone maintains the oneness in the heart and uses their inner divining ability to perfect their intuition and their perception. There is no partisan party "line" on truth. The only truth in Creative Conflict is the deepest truth that the group together is able to reach by probing and questioning and practicing the process. This is "group consciousness." When the group consciousness is focussed then there is an electrical energy, a soul energy, like you have in a high meditation. This is different from everyone in an audience being absorbed in a movie or a play on the stage. It is not a vicarious experience, but a real living participation. Everyone is on stage, and the whole group is participating in making this work. It is as real life as one can get. Group consciousness is when there is this dynamic energy and everyone is in tune, listening, vibrating and resonating on the same harmonic. Then you have group intuition, penetration and soul force—truth that no one can deny, as it is straight from the heart. When all your relationships are infused with this ability to listen and to have that mind penetration into truth, you will have a rewarding and wonderful experience.

If you look at nature, you see organic groupings. You see a seed growing into a whole forest of trees. But a seed or group of cells that has divisiveness within it eventually will break apart and destroy itself. Humanity needs to learn from nature to form organic, natural groups that can survive and grow to oneness together. If the underlying motivations, purposes or wills are different, there has to be conflict, then disintegration at some point, unless the conflict can be made creative. And this is what we see everywhere we look in society. People do not know themselves well enough to know what they are doing to themselves, that they are out of harmony with natural order, out of harmony with truth which is evolution. When the unconscious motivations and the conscious actions are at odds, then we are in destructive inner conflict and this leads to disease which takes its toll on the body. Certain cancers and other diseases are actually spiritual diseases, where the person is somehow split within his consciousness, causing the physical cells to destroy each other. So getting to the real core of being, to the nucleus, is what makes Creative Conflict a path to healing transformation and enlightenment, not just for individuals, but for society.

4

BLOCKS TO REAL LISTENING AND CLEAR SEEING
The Ways the Ego Works to Separate Itself—

To reach transformation we have to be prepared to go down into the thick of it, the muck of all our human abuse and misuse of consciousness; not to wallow and get stuck, but to understand it so that we can lift ourselves out. You can never master anything by running away or trying to hide. There is a saying in computer programing called "bootstrap" which is what you do to get the initial intelligence into the computer and ready to go. Mastering the game of life is the same. We have to pick ourselves up by our own bootstraps, which means we are the ones who have to bend down and find out what our own ego blocks are and lift ourselves out of them.

The most prominent ego blocks are:

basic assumptions	internalization
projections	emotionalism
negative identification	yes, but . . .
rationalizations	playing tapes/
expectations	self-obsession
judgements and	stereotyping
wrong perceptions	compliance

The work of all beginners in Creative Conflict is to discover when these prominent blocks are happening in your own ego. As you get clearer the blocks will come less frequently and you will find yourself able to penetrate deeper in the heart. Nevertheless, we always have to be on the lookout for one or another of the blocks spontaneously rearing its head and be ready to point it out in ourself or in another if we are to live in truth. See if you recognize any of the following examples in yourself first, then look for them in your friends.

BASIC ASSUMPTIONS

The human world is run on the collective perceptions of people. As we struggle through the evolutionary process we are confronted with our misperceptions of life. We make the *basic assumption* that our perceptions are true and then we make more basic assumptions based upon these perceptions. When we finally find out that our perceptions were off, our entire edifice of basic assumptions comes crashing down. Once you learn how to listen through the mirroring process, the next phase in Creative Conflict is to check out your perceptions. Any assumption we hold about ourselves, about life or about another person can prevent us from hearing life's real message and can prevent us from communicating in depth with other beings. Mistakes bring emotional pain. A typical basic assumption is the following: "You didn't take me with you so you don't really love me." You are assuming this is true, but until you check it out you just don't know. Often those kinds of feelings are not true at all, even though they seem so obvious and feel so real. We even want to believe them to be true to rationalize our feelings of hurt, and yet we are relieved when we find out our assumption was wrong. People make such assumptions because they cannot see how their egos are operating. They cannot see the real possessiveness or expectation that might be at the root of such an assumption. This blocks them from being able to get inside the world of the other person to find out what the real reason is. The antidote is to check out your feelings and thoughts with humility, which means *not assuming* they are true. Basic assumptions are among the first ego blocks to look for in Creative Conflict. Whenever you sense one you "call" it. You say, "Hey, that's a basic assumption you made about John's inner world. I think you'd better check that out." When you do check it out you find that John didn't feel that way at all. Gossip thrives on basic assumptions, most of which are false.

PROJECTIONS

The most common ego block in society today and therefore also in individuals is called *projection*. Projection happens unconsciously because we have no way of assessing others except by the judgements that lie within ourself. We judge the actions of others by first making assumptions based on our own value systems and unconscious desires. These then get projected out onto the other person or situation, and color it. Projections are quickly revealed in Creative Conflict if we look for them. In Creative Conflict, when we are projecting our own ego patterns, feelings or motives onto others, we are accusing them of something or seeing something in them that is really more true of ourselves. Projecting is nearly always unconscious. Remember, we see life through our own filters, through our own ego positions and basic assumptions which are often a misperception in the first place. For example, "Rick is a very moody person," says Jean. She sees him that way quite clearly. But in reality Jean is moody and so Rick's moodiness looks big to her. It looks big to her, but not to others when she checks it out. Life mirrors you in how you see and judge others. What you cannot stand in another is very often in yourself. Creative Conflict brings the projections out for you to work with them.

NEGATIVE IDENTIFICATION

One of the biggest hindrances in Creative Conflict is *negative identification,* in which someone identifies with the person who is being confronted, and feels embarrassed or hurt, or protective towards that person. This is a normal ego reaction. We all tend to identify most with loved ones or with the underdog. Children will especially side with loved ones who are having to look squarely at their egos. It makes them feel insecure about their own ego position to see a loved one feel threatened in the ego We have to watch how we negatively identify with others' egos and, in order to free ourself to stand in the light of clear truth, we must discover why we do that. Until we can see that ego reaction is a defense mechanism which separates us from our real self, we will find it difficult to let go of negatively identifying with others. There are two basic types of negative identification.

1. One person identifies with the emotions of another. The sympathy pulls him off his own center and into the center of the other person. He begins to feel the same feelings as the other and they both get stuck in the conflict.

One woman, Pam, has to keep close watch on her tendency to swing into everyone else's center. She can be talking to Robert about his perception of a situation and she will sway right into his point of view. Fifteen minutes later she can be talking to Norah, who has the exact opposite view on that situation, and Pam will agree with her. Pam's block is not due to mixed motives, but it is in wanting to be understanding and amiable. So she feels first one way and then the other. Her identification blocks her from seeing truth. She has had to learn to watch her pattern of swinging and to stay centered in her own feelings while listening to the other's motives behind the words.

2. One person identifies with the group mind or with another person and begins to act out the other person's role as part of his own self-image. The other personality becomes a model for the individual and his opinions are held only so long as that personality has an important relationship to him. The relationship provides identity and self-esteem. It blocks real communication with others because the role image is too strong.

In the second type of negative identification, Debbie tends to take on qualities and mannerisms of whomever she directs her love towards. It seems as though she absorbs their energies. When she was fifteen she took on the qualities of an admired teacher—his opinions, ideas and even hand-writing—all unconsciously. Others felt she was a bit strange. When she was twenty-one she became like her boyfriend. As if by osmosis his being became part of hers and she could feel his expressions come over her face, feel his strength and his ego as her own. In Creative Conflict she has been accused sometimes of "coming on like Christopher", but with an added flavor of superiority and not in a way expressive of her real feelings. She has to learn to watch the energies and roles she picks up and to see how she uses them and for what motive. This pattern is negative in that it blocks contact with her own heart. The worst examples of this type of negative identification are those in which people identify with a dictator or with persons in authority and take on their qualities, losing their own center. Even if you identify with or try to imitate a Christ or a hero, you have to still confront your own motives, your own ego, to evolve into that state of being.

RATIONALIZATION

Rationalizing away why you did something or said something is the easiest way to get your ego off the hook and avoid looking at your real motives for why you really did do or say it. Rationalizing can give you some relief from conflict or from doubt about your position. "Oh, I didn't want to go anyway" is usually a "head" rationalization, covering up the real feeling of hurt in your heart at being left behind and the deeper ache of self-doubt as to whether or not you are worthy. The ego rationalizes all its slights rather than confronting the cause of them, especially in relation to the family, the school, the business. It rationalizes its blocks when it doesn't want to look at them. If we could only look at our national leaders and societies and see the ego blocks that cut them off from clearer perception, we would be able to penetrate some of the seemingly insurmountable problems in world politics. If you can tune into how many times you have rationalized away a feeling, you can see why most communication and relating between people is shallow and from the head.

Fortunately, rationalizations are also one of the easiest blocks to recognize when you learn to look for them as they fall out of people's mouths. Rationalizations lack the depth of feeling that an "I feel this, I feel that" statement conveys. The vibration is very different. When people respond to statements too quickly in Creative Conflict, they are often putting out a rationalization. You need to tell them that their response is too fast and ask them to let in the feedback deeper in order to get more in touch. Children often recognize rationalizations quickly. They see that the reasons given by parents, teachers and even other children are often not the real reasons why they should act a certain way. The deeper, real reasons are coated with a veneer of rationality.

An example of rationalization can be seen in a young man rejected by a club he wanted to join. He tried to convince himself that he did not really want to belong anyway. "It is only snobbish people who go there, the tennis courts are never free and it's too far to drive in the first place." Another man asked a girl for a date but was rejected, so he went around telling everyone the girl was not very pretty. He even told the girl herself. Children do this kind of "getting back" when they feel rejected. We all rationalize in order to avoid the feeling that we are rejectable or to avoid the work of looking at ourselves. Rationalization is the easiest and favorite way of hiding actions and words from ourself which do not fit our self-image.

Our society encourages rationalizing, especially in advertising. Our politicians rationalize all their expenditures. And because most people are used to this cultural rationalizing in their lives, they accept the rationalizings of others. How many smokers and obese people rationalize their habits? How many diet books sell millions of copies by promising fat people that they can eat what they want and still lose weight? One man I knew dieted for years but never lost much weight. He would say, "Just one little piece of bread won't hurt," and "I never eat," but his finger was always in the refrigerator taking little bits of food. He died of a heart attack, still rationalizing, still not knowing why he was so hungry or what he was craving; he could not stop the rationalizings and the compensation long enough to get in touch with it. And all this rationalizing made him feel not very good about himself. On the international level we rationalize why we should not give aid to starving countries; we rationalize that to help certain people weakens their character, or we rationalize that if we give five dollars a month to charity or the Church then we can feel free to continue our greedy habits of overconsuming and wasting energy. We always have reasons for not loving, not giving, not serving, not sharing and keeping our old well-worn, unfulfilling habits.

EXPECTATION

Expectation is expecting someone to say or do something in the way you want. Desire is at the root of expectation. For a long time in our community, Ann would bring conflicts between herself and her boyfriend Robert to the group, always expecting the group to confront Robert and prove her point. They never did! They always felt there was something fishy in Ann's position, even though they knew Robert had responsibility in their conflicts too. Ann could never understand why the group feedback would always come back to her. Her very expectation that Robert should get the feedback blocked her from seeing her own unwillingness to look at her own ego. Her tremendous desire for Robert to change, to be more the way she wanted him, created her expectation that the group would tell him to change. Her desire also prevented her from seeing the insecurity and selfishness at the root of her feelings that were fueling her desire. She was afraid to even look at the desire lest she lose Robert in the process. We would try to go into it—the attachment and the motivation. She wasn't willing to look at any of it, not in relation to Robert. Yet she was one of the best people when it came to going into somebody else's needs. She saw their motivations right to the core. But she wasn't willing to give up her intense desire. She put a demand on the universe to give her what she wanted, no matter what! She had to learn the hard way. Unfortunately that is true for a lot of us; there is only so much pain threshold that people have, but it is incredibly deep for many people, before they are crushed enough to say, "Okay, I have got to make some change, there is no more bottom. I've got to open up." Through patient mirroring and her own meditation Ann was eventually able to see how her own ego was creating its pain and to release her tremendous attachment.

The greatest danger of expectation is having a strong feeling about how others should be or how things should be, so that you cannot listen to the real message which the cosmic intelligence is mirroring to you. Expectation can work in very subtle ways to destroy your peace and fulfillment. If you expect your husband to give you an expensive gift and he does not, then you will be disappointed, especially if all your friends receive expensive gifts from their husbands. You would then probably go on a big ego trip, fretting in your mind on how he can't really love you if he doesn't give you what you want. But really the universe is trying to show you that these desires have consequences that keep you miserable. It is only by not being attached to your desires or expectations that you can stay free of ego and pain. And when you learn to stay free of ego and let go of your expectations, blessings pour in; life works quickly to respond with gifts aplenty. Creative Conflict teaches you these rules of life. These rules of consciousness are the same for everybody. We all walk the same path and learn the same rules to successful, happy living. Creative Conflict intensifies the learning process of the rules of life's game. The mirror of life responds faster the more you get used to looking at it. Pain becomes a clearer corrective mechanism the more you understand that it is just a mirror saying that something in you is not in tune. Nevertheless people still cling to their egos until grim death, and you wonder why they can't see the obvious. But the obvious is always clouded by our judgements and perceptions. With practice we gain the skill to see the cause of our judgements more clearly.

JUDGEMENTS

Judgements are usually the result of thwarted expectations. You have certain ideas of how people *should* be or *should* respond and when they don't, you judge them for it. The answer is to share your differences in perception if you cannot let them go. Share your negative feelings with the person who has disappointed you so that you can get to greater truth together and purify your consciousness. The danger of not sharing the negative feelings is that they build up one upon the other, creating more judgements and misjudgements, more blocks and more painful ego separation. The realization comes eventually in Creative Conflict that although there are many "truths" there is only one roadmap to truth really, and we all have the exact same lessons to learn. The laws of consciousness which govern our pain or our bliss are just as "given" as the laws of motion, gravity and energy in nature.

As you learn to recognize projections, you also learn to discriminate semi-projections. Semi-projection is when what you are seeing in another person is both in the other and in yourself, probably in about equal amounts. We are often strongly attracted to or strongly repelled by people who have the same blocks we have. Semi-projection is usually more conscious than a projection, that is, we are more aware of the fault in ourself as we see it in the other.

A direct perception is where you are seeing clearly and not projecting, not coloring your perceptions with your own filters. During the group process in Creative Conflict you will learn to feel the difference in energy between a direct perception and a projection. You learn to sense the vibration of right-on truth, which has a different feeling about it than a projection or a semi-projection. The first few Creative Conflict sessions should be spent looking for these blocks to clear seeing and listening.

INTERNALIZATION

Internalization is taking on, internalizing, someone else's feedback as your own. It is similar to negative identification but not quite the same. When Lana was told she should not talk so much but learn to be quieter in order to hear others more, Kay took that feedback onto herself. Kay clammed up out of fear that she talked too much too, but actually her real need was to express herself and share more so that others could get to know her. Lana took the feedback well, but Kay's ego twisted her problem into the exact opposite of what she needed. Internalization then, is adopting a solution or an attitude because it satisfies an ego need; in this case it was Kay's deep need for approval.

Another example was Ary. Ary decided to take a vow of celibacy for a year as a reaction to being rejected by a man she liked very much. Another person in the group had recently decided to become celibate after much soul-searching. Ary jumped on the "bandwagon" for a different motive and woke up a month later with nightmares and a terrible feeling of loss and aloneness. The group helped her to see that her decision to become celibate was an unconscious power play to make the man she liked respect and want her, and to make him feel bad that she was now unavailable.

She had incorporated celibacy into her value system, but for the wrong motive. Nevertheless, she set forces in motion by her decision and she stuck to her vow to see if she could master herself. She has become a much stronger person as a result.

EMOTIONALISM

Emotions provide tremendous energy to help you achieve goals, overcome barriers and provide enthusiasm for work. They can also cloud your perception when you wallow in them and use them as a defense against looking at yourself. Negative doubts, morose moods, over-reacting—all these are *emotionalism* that block the light and therefore need to be challenged.

Whenever Wendy was confronted on almost anything, she used to start to cry. The result was people would leave her alone or try to rescue her with sympathy and her ego remained intact. One day she wondered why she was not growing and changing as she wished. The group reached a point where they saw through her defense. They confronted her on using her tears to ward off feedback and avoid looking at herself. Crying meant she did not have to change. By not buying the emotionalism and constantly confronting her with it, the group mirror presented Wendy with her real self, and not the image of the too-sensitive good girl she was used to projecting. Wendy has since changed considerably as a result of getting in touch with the motive behind her tears. She has mastered a deep pattern of self-pity that she had for over twenty years since childhood, in spite of years of psychology and years of meditation. She is now a much stronger person. This change came, not from group therapy, but from group integrity.

YES, BUT

Whenever you hear people respond, "Yes, but . . . ," you know they are not listening. A "yes butter" never listens to you because he is listening to his own opinions. As you are speaking, he is dying to say the next thing. So whenever you hear the words "yes, but . . " coming out of your own mouth, you know you have not been receptive. If you get a "yes, but" reply from others, all you can say is that perhaps they haven't really heard, and ask them to please mirror the thought you said. That is the polite way of saying, "You haven't heard me." Usually a "yes butter" cannot mirror properly. He will come on with something very different from what you have said.

PLAYING TAPES

We all have mental tapes playing unconsciously, and this block to real listening must be watched very carefully. For instance, if your friend says something to you and you hear it correctly, it goes into your memory where there are stored all kinds of existing experiences which you have had and valued, emotional experiences, truth experiences, horrible experiences, nice experiences, and if she is telling you something nice it will go into that area of your memory where you start to compare it with other things that have happened that are nice in your life and you may be thinking about them while she is speaking—so your own tape recorder is activated and you are not listening. You are listening to your own memories. Sense impressions coming in—the car on the street, the newspaper boy walking by, the wind on your shoulders—all stimuli can trigger your thoughts, preventing your listening by preoccupying your attention. You have to learn to be very conscious if you are playing any tapes in your mind while another person is speaking, or even while you are reading. How many of you are playing your tapes about what you have just been reading—reacting or agreeing, looking for examples in your own life? Even in reading we must be careful to receive what is being said completely *before* we begin to play with it in our minds. People who cannot turn off their mental tapes are self-obsessed.

STEREOTYPING

One of the biggest blocks in communication is labeling people. He's a professor, he's a yogi, she's a religious fanatic, he's a scientist, she's a this and that. He may have been a professor yesterday, but he could be a father today. When you fix people in your consciousness you cannot really hear them in their being. The mere fixing of an image in the mind is going to color and determine what you hear from that person. So many people react to race. He's black . . . (implying all blacks are a certain way), or she's a communist . . . (implying she must be mean and nasty because all communists want to take over the world). Stereotypes lead to many basic assumptions. Many famous movie actors and actresses have miserable lives because their public stereotype allows them no freedom to be themselves. If the image you hold of a person is not a true image of his being, then that person is not going to accept your vibration and is not going to accept what you say. You will not be speaking to him, rather you will be speaking to your private image of him. If you are afraid that people are stereotyping or judging you, your reaction might be that you will want to look good in their eyes. So you will do many things to please them. It may not be true that they feel that way about you. It may be a projection of the way you stereotype others, so you fear others will do that to you. We must always check out judgements and stereotyping of others before we try to communicate, or better yet, let them all go so that we can listen and mirror with an open heart.

COMPLIANCE

Compliance occurs when you adopt the opinion of someone else, or of the group mind, in order to go along with the crowd, gain a favorable reaction or omit something unfavorable in order to be liked. You may not actually believe in the opinion. You may be privately disagreeing while outwardly going along with the other person. This will block communication between your head and heart as well as with others. In the Creative Conflict process you soon learn to tune into the subtle vibrations that reveal this inner compliance and you can mirror it to the person who is complying. It is hard to do Creative Conflict with compliant people because they always nod in agreement with everything, even though you know that deep down in the unconscious they aren't feeling that way. The head and heart are split. It is important to share with the person your perception about his compliance to help him get in touch with it in himself.

A good example of compliance is the secretary who goes along with everything her boss says even when she disagrees strongly and bad-mouths him behind his back. Yet she puts on a sweet smile and compliant personality in front of him in order to feel secure in her job. Many spouses comply in marriage out of a need to feel secure, and many children comply unquestioningly to parental demands which they feel are unreasonable out of fear of punishment. Complying never builds trust nor does it build creative or truly productive relationships. It always backfires eventually on some level.

Another example of compliance is Ralph, one of the newer students at the University of the Trees. Ralph was the good boy. His self-image was to always try to make others happy, make their load easier. So whenever anyone asked him to do anything he would readily agree even if he had already scheduled something else to do at the same time. Whenever he received negative feedback on his work he'd always agree with the feedback. People wondered who the real Ralph was. His need to be liked was so great that you never knew if he had any reactions or real feelings underneath a suspicious mask of yesses. Trouble began when people told Ralph that he was more of a nuisance than a help. He would not complete the tasks he offered to do. Or he would do them sloppily and someone would have to always follow behind him, picking up the pieces. No one could trust him. He was afraid people would reject him so he complied even more, trying harder to say yes when he felt no, trying to be good and agree.

This vicious cycle was burst in a Creative Conflict where he was confronted on being false. By mirroring to him many examples of when his actions hurt rather than helped, Ralph's real motive became clearly revealed to everyone including himself—his desire to gain prestige and attention. This realization pierced his veneer of compliance and his self-image as "the selfless helper". Ralph got in touch with his own desire not to do drudge work. He comes from a wealthy family and is used to doing just what he wants to do. He admitted that he was comfortable being untidy and slobbish and he always got away with it as a child. The inner being was now exposed and there was nothing for Ralph to do but face it or run away from it. He chose to face it. "I know it isn't the best of motives, but my first reaction was, 'I'm going to show them I can do things well.' " Since then Ralph's manifestation has been an all-out effort to be honest and real and his work has been excellent.

RISK

The antidote to compliance and to working on all the blocks is to *risk.* Risk sharing your feelings, especially your negative feelings so you can open them up and see where they are coming from. Risk sharing your fears about what will happen if you do not comply or if you do say what you think. More importantly, risk sharing your projections and your self-image, your idea of who and what you are and how others are going to see you, in order to get to your own truth of being. Only when you can dare to risk that self-image will you build strength and character. Obviously there are some situations where you cannot risk and have to consciously comply, if the risk would cause you or someone else harm. But generally the rule is, if you hold your negative feelings in, then it only creates more blocks and increases your misperceptions, ego separation and pain. If you share these feelings with others who are prepared to get to truth too, it brings love, depth of friendship and oneness. Be persistent and you will find clarity and the truth that sets you free.

GOING DEEPER

Through watching these blocks as they come up we learn to risk pointing them out and probing where they are coming from. This probing of our blocks to communication takes us to the deeper next level of getting into basic motivations—the stubbornness, fear, doubt, guilt, etc., that feeds the block to listening or seeing. The process of Creative Conflict can only go deeper, to another level, if you are willing to look at the causes of your own blocks. People often say *yes* with their heads, but in their hearts they lack the motivation to look or to change. Only those who are ready for this next step in evolution will go with you. Usually for a resistant or stubborn person, pain is the only motivator to change, and sometimes it takes a long time and a lot of pain.

The desire to feel not separate, to feel one, to go beyond the differences and to improve relationships is the first motivation for most people wanting to be part of the Creative Conflict process. But practice of the process tests whether we are actually prepared to get our inner-fire going to do the deeper work necessary to attain oneness and harmonious relationships. If the group degenerates into just a job counseling, marriage counseling or therapy group, it will deal with short-term stop-gap solutions but will not generate that inner-fire and self-change that ego penetration brings. Probing our motivations for growth and for being together is getting closer to the real fiber of our egos. Most business, family or school Creative Conflicts will be content with the beginning stage of Creative Conflict, of merely learning how to listen and of looking at our misperceptions as a way of getting to deeper truth, communication and harmony. The next level of Creative Conflict is really only for those who have the will to probe the ego deeply, to be in the heart. And that *will* is a force that cannot be legislated; it must come from the free choice of each person. In reality there is no choice, because eventually life itself will teach you that you either freely choose to go deeper in the heart or face unfulfillment.

Once the will is firmly directed toward growth and change, then risk becomes a matter of integrity—of facing ourselves and each other as openly as we can and with a sense of responsibility. Through integrity we open ourselves to a vaster intelligence. Integrity is something we develop the more we know ourselves. It does not happen overnight but is evoked according to our commitment to truth.

COMMITMENT

Commitment is a big factor in the effectiveness of the Creative Conflict Process. Commitment does not happen all at once either. It is an evolving process. First there is the commitment to use the Creative Conflict techniques to discover where you are at in your own consciousness. Then there is the commitment to each other in the heart in spite of the differences in the head. The commitment to look at the first guideline of Creative Conflict, "You are whatever disturbs you" (see page 280), is a commitment to really consider life as a mirror and test out the validity of your perceptions and ego reactions. The next commitment is to stick it through when the going gets rough or when you are challenged on your commitment to truth. Sometimes you will feel like running from someone confronting a part of you or running from the group.

The ego is very tricky at justifying its position when it feels cornered. We say, "That's me, you're criticizing me, leave me alone." Egos get hurt, protect what they want to, try to get their own way and unconsciously hurt others, not realizing that they are not seeing clearly. The Creative Conflict process sorts this out. Children especially do not like to look at their egos until they experience what the process and the feeling of oneness can do *for* them. The delusion is that we *can* run away and forget looking or find something easier. In reality, life's lessons are harder to bear without Creative Conflict. The mirror is always with us, whether in a group or not. But it is more difficult to see into the mirror alone, even if we are working on our own growth. It is more intense, but more rapid and fulfilling to meet the challenge of life with a group of people who ask you to look at yourself, who care about you and who are committed to each other's being. This kind of group is a greenhouse, with ideal conditions for growth. The Creative Conflict process is a form of social enlightenment for everyone in the coming age, based on nature's laws of energy and of feedback. It is the foundation for the new order of a nuclear family based on commitment to spiritual growth, not to ego attachment. In the years to come families will again be the stabilizing foundation for society, but they will be spiritual families, not necessarily blood families. Up to now the family bonding and kinship has been an evolutionary tool of nature. With divorce and separation and poor communication with offspring, the next phase of evolution will come from the nuclear group or spiritual family life.

SELF-IMAGE

As we earlier stated, the hidden image you hold of yourself, your secret self, is the greatest and deepest block to real listening and real communication with others and with the universe itself. The image colors how you see everyone else, because it is coloring your Real Self which has no color, which is pure, clear, universal, with nothing in it. So when ego penetration gets to its deepest levels, it always hits the fundamental *self-image.*

When Ann was afraid to look at her motives, lest she lose Robert, she was really afraid that she might come out not looking good—her self-image would be tarnished and Robert might see that and reject her. It would not look good to others either. When we are afraid to express our real feelings for fear of rejection, it is usually a fear that we will come out looking bad. Our lily-white image of ourself will be tainted. This clinging to self-image as our security operates especially strongly in love relationships, where the admiration and love of the other is important to us. We also build self-images to give ourselves a feeling of identity and worth, for example, the mother, the teacher, the good girl, the he-man, the savior. All roles we identify with are self-images. Here is a portion of a Creative Conflict dealing with self-image.

Kay: I am so afraid to give feedback, because it might come back on me. I see lacks in the group but I have trouble sharing because people so often say that I come on self-righteous. The fear makes me feel squashed and then I can't get in touch with my feelings.

Robert: Is it a problem of trust?

Kay: I don't know. I feel like something is wrong with me. I've felt this from childhood, that something is wrong with me. Like wanting to be loved for the things I do because I don't feel loved for myself. So I'd always do things for my family. But I feel more secure now. I'm not so afraid I'm going to be trounced, but I feel a certain hardness.

Ann: I don't somehow get the last part. It's a contradiction. First you said that you *are* afraid of "being trounced". But are you aware of how you trounce on others?

Kay: Yes. (Silence. In the silence it is obvious that Kay is searching within herself. She gets in touch with a feeling but then cuts it off. This happens twice.)

Rod: Are you afraid to feel empty, vulnerable?

Kay: No. (But her feelings are now cut off, everyone can feel this.)

Debbie: Do you really want the group to help you to penetrate through this?

Kay: Yes. (a head response)

Debbie: Well, you're not letting anything we're saying in, to work in you.

Norah: What are the things you might have to let go of that are precious to you?

Kay: Control. (She's let go a bit and is crying a little but in a controlled way.) My buoyancy, my self-image and position. My image is, I'm the sheep dog nipping at the sheep's heels, reminding everyone to not leave their papers everywhere in the office, to pull up the weeds in the lawn, etc.

Norah: Who is Kay in relation to everyone here?

Kay: I'm buoyant, nice, cheerful, so people will want to be around me. I like contact with people. I want contact and good feeling, to love people.

Rich: Your preoccupation with yourself often blocks you from getting into my world or other people's worlds when we are in the heart space. So you don't get the contact.

Sue: You know, I experience you judging yourself for the heart space and judging others when they are in the heart space too. You see it as weak.

Kay: (This touches something in Kay. Something in her melts. She's teary. She's let go now. Everyone feels with her. She's glowing. After some silence . . .) That's what I have to work on accepting, that I can let go of it all. And that it's okay to be in this heart space. That I can trust I won't lose anything and I can love others and be loved just for being here.

Roger: (tenderly) Do you see how you drive yourself to perform just to compensate for your own judgement?

Kay: (nods, again it feels like it's real)

Roger: And do you see how *you* put people in cold storage? (Everyone laughs. This is a term from an old Creative Conflict months before where Kay said she felt that the group was putting her in "cold storage" when they told her she was refusing to be open, so the group decided they wanted to go into someone else's problems.)

Kay: (smiling) Yes!

The probing of another's personal self-image in Creative Conflict has always to be done with the finger pointing at ourselves at the same time. Only in this way can we stand on the razor's edge of direct perception without projecting our own self-image onto the other. This tuning to reality also means humbly pointing the finger at the group self-image, if there is one, which may be holding an ego position as a whole in relation to the individual. We have to be always on the lookout for group ego or a group self-image that the group members may be feeding, even unconsciously. The whole group consciousness must use other groups, new members and visitors as its mirror. If the group process takes on an energy of its own that is not pure, not in a state of humility and always open to a greater truth, it will become self-righteous about its own reality. This self-righteousness is what creates cults and turns group work sour. It leads group members to feel, "My group or my reality is better than yours." While having a conviction in your group or method is important for commitment, much divisiveness and separateness in the group ego will arise with self-righteousness. The danger sign is when there is compliance or conformity to the group consensus from the head, not an agreement from the heart. The group ego may then reject or not understand someone new who may be at the leading edge of humanity and has a totally new, more enlightened view. He or she may be seen as a threat to the group identity rather than as a vehicle for evolution. If negative identification of the members with "the group" becomes so strong that their own intuitive direct perception is sacrificed to some group ego or power perceived to be separate, then "group consciousness" is not possible.

Only when you *are* the group and there is no separation between your inner being and the group being do you have a group that is integral as a whole. In true group consciousness people are so much looking for the greater truth all the time, that they learn to be receptive to all signs from the cosmos. Even in a small or isolated group, if you are training yourselves to be receptive, when new input comes in and says, "Hey, you are missing something important," you will be able to hear it. Group humility brings grace. And this total openness actually bonds the participants instead of threatening their unity.

The probing of self-image is the deepest and most threatening part of Creative Conflict. The ego wants to preserve its idea of being somebody special and unique, and fears loss if it does not keep its image intact. The self-image works very subtly, shifting from one identity to the other if one is threatened until it eventually lets go and surrenders to nothing. Then the real Self can blend with the greater Self and become truly someone. Great sages have always said we must lose ourselves to find our Self. Usually there are many ego battles on the way to this deeper level before freedom is won. To get to the level of continuous penetration through the self-images as they rise is an advanced state of consciousness and takes a tremendous amount of commitment to Creative Conflict. When a group of people can help each other see where their self-images are operating and dissolve them together, they can work in higher group consciousness. Then through this clarity the group becomes a pure channel through which the cosmic consciousness is able to express.

How do we know what true spiritual insight really is? Do we read the teachings of a guru or writer who confirms our own rationalizations? Do we listen to someone who only writes words or to someone who has actually lived out their words in action? There are some wonderful word spinners, but if we knew their private lives we would know why the world is deceived by fine words which may not be true words. Christ is a perfect example of someone who lived what he taught, but he was a discomfort to be around because if you showed any hypocrisy he would point it out. You could get called, "snakes and vipers". People don't like a spade to be called a spade or hypocrites to be called liars and deceivers. They identify with the person and wouldn't want *their* deceptions pointed out like that. Christ was not all gentle and sentimental light as some people depict him. To some he was and still is intolerable!

In the spiritual training all these ego defense mechanisms we've been mentioning are often more visible than in ordinary people who live less intense lives or do little self-introspection. Frustration and conflict are always intensified whenever our goals, expectations and ambitions are high. People on the spiritual path will convince themselves that their motives are admirable and that they are living an exemplary life, but secretly many of them are hoping to get by without actually doing the work on their egos. As long as they can act out the role, wear Indian beads, dress in white or go to a priest and do church work or social work, they can rationalize that they are spiritual. Yet the nagging feeling within that something is not quite right, or that there must be more, is trying to tell them to search deeper, confront their self-image and open to new possibilities. In Creative Conflict these gaps between our real manifestations and our self-images are gradually eroded until we have a more humble or more realistic approach to our fulfillment and our motivation becomes more clear and pure. This then provides the basic consciousness which sees directly through the self-delusions so that the real spiritual training of ego annihilation can begin.

When you have penetrated the self-image, you reach the vulnerable heart that has been lying there under wraps, under the ego blocks all the time. This vulnerable heart, when it reveals itself, moves everyone in the group to love and the unity that only comes from heart. Advanced Creative Conflict is when a group of people who have opened their hearts and who have tested their willingness to be vulnerable and open together are committed to work together on what remains of their egos to surrender completely to truth and to the cosmic will. They form a nucleus, an organism on a higher level of being. Your ability to read the cosmic will and see with direct perception is directly proportional to the openness of heart. The advanced group is awesome and full of love as you hear God speaking through so many. Direct perception then is the order, not the exception, whereas in the beginning Creative Conflict, poor listening, projections, basic assumptions and other blocks to total openness are the order. You have to be patient enough to plow through the blocks, aware of what comes next in the process of ego-unveiling and to look for it to know how to guide the Creative Conflict to its ultimate potential as an instrument of evolution.

5

"I AM TRYING TO TELL YOU SOMETHING BUT YOUR TAPES KEEP ON PLAYING"

Before we plunge into the actual applications and the "how to do it" of Creative Conflict, it is important for you to gain a good feeling for the dynamic of the Creative Conflict interaction. The following excerpts are from tape transcriptions of actual Creative Conflicts. Notice the struggles of the people in the tape transcriptions trying to get in touch and feel the difficult, frustrating moments as well as the releasing moments of breakthrough. These are the crests and troughs—ever part of the dynamic of a Creative Conflict session. These excerpts deal with romance, love, self-image, responsibility, the willingness to grow and the challenge of living from the heart.

Romance is both the greatest trap to expanding human love and the greatest purifier of love. It can bind us in a cocoon where others appear to have no importance or cease to exist and we live only in the folds of two egos, or it can awaken the heart to the glory of love. A heart full of love will spill over to include the hearts of others. Everywhere people yearn for romance and find it sublimely attractive because they want to experience those intense feelings of the heart, while at the same time they fear it as the harbinger of attachment and pain. Romance is such a potent force and cause of conflict for most people—a conflict when you do not have it and want it, and conflict with the love object when you do have it—that we need to deal deeply with it. See if you can recognize yourself or your loved ones in these real people.

Editor's Note: As you read, notice how the group had to go around and around the same point for quite awhile before Ian could at last receive it. The points where the energy changes are noted in italics for you to better follow the dynamic of the session.

Creative Conflict example #1

Ian: Grace and I have been having a miserable time together. I experience our relationship as kind of dull and not exciting. Lately I'm feeling like old folks getting married; it's a bit ho-hum. About a month ago I started getting in touch with how frustrated I am on a sexual level with our relationship and that it just isn't zinging enough for me. Although I have highs and lows, the highs don't go very high and the lows get really low. I am in touch with the fact that there is something in my vibe that is turning her off, but knowing that doesn't help because I don't know how to change it.

About a month ago Grace told me that she still felt like she was being grabbed and I felt so awful about the situation that I just tried to do something in my consciousness to change it because I could feel what she felt in her heart and how it was frustrating for her. At times I was thinking that I didn't have enough zing myself. I have difficulty because when I try to put the zing in, I find my ego is there because I have a lot of insecurities playing inside. So it is very difficult for me to be zingy without being phony too. I decided that I'd go celibate for a month—minimum—to create a breathing space and to get in touch with my real self, my real heart. I took walks and tuned in, trying to come to terms, because I'm so used to handling these things by thinking, "What are other people going to think?" Not only Grace but other people in the group. 95 percent of the time I don't even know who my real self is.

For about three weeks I felt that I got in touch with my real self. I was more willing to go with it no matter how the chips were falling. I felt accepting. If Grace and I broke up, well, that was just too bad. I was determined to be real. My relationship with her improved almost immediately. But a week ago I got really insecure again and she got that same grabby feeling. The minute I have a vibe of insecurity or a need for affection from her, she immediately shrinks back and she isn't aware of it herself, but that's what happens.

In the last few days I've been trying to get to the point of not letting it bother me, but it still keeps rising up. The ideal would be to create a new relationship out of the old one, but it's hard, seeing how we wash dishes together, brush our teeth together, go to bed at the same time. Just in the last day or two we've seriously considered moving apart, living in different houses. Not so much to break up but to give each other breathing space so that if anything new wanted to happen we could give it a chance to happen.

(Deep breath . . .) I was real scared to bring this up. We've been talking about heart sharing and this is the deepest and hardest thing for me to bring up. Damned if I was going to share it with anybody because it was freaking me out completely. I've been unwilling to share it because my ego identifies with it a lot and I judge myself very intensely for the relationship not being better than it is. I feel that if I bring it up, all you guys will think that I'm a schmuck. The lowest of the low.

Ann: What is the insecurity connected with?

Grace: I shared one of my old hidden fantasies of walking the streets of Boston and that stirred up the insecurities.

Ian: I don't remember that the fantasy triggered the insecurity but it sure helped a lot. What that comes down to is that I see in Grace the part I want to relate with. I feel the womanly part of her soul that I want to relate to and in the last month or so I've gotten in touch with my masculine self and I want to relate in that way too. So I feel freaked out that I get attached to wanting that. I feel I'm going to lose her and somehow screw up so bad that I'll lose that possibility.

Richard: How does this insecurity manifest?

Ian: She tells me that I come on a bit like Hollywood. It's like I try to compensate for the feelings by being macho and grabby and it completely bombs.

Richard: When you come on like that, do any white lights flash on in your head?

Ian: Oh yeah. What happens is that I say to myself, "You're being fake again, this just isn't going to wash," and I know I'm feeling insecure and I want to go away and work on it. Nine times out of ten I just get more insecure, feeling like a schlep, because I start separating and laying my trips out.

Debbie: I feel that you are trying to relate to Grace's womanliness before you relate to your own manliness. When a guy's in that male center, the electricity flows automatically and the woman energy is attracted to you. You don't have to pretend to be macho. It seems funny to me that you are going to her first and avoiding yourself.

(Ian mirrors this back.)

Sue: So you're doing a phoney manliness instead of discovering your real manliness. You can only discover your real manliness by being real. Give up the game, no holds barred, no holding onto reason. Surrender is the only way out.

Ian: Yes, I see that.

Deb: Why not just become a schlep and be good to yourself?

Arlene: What does a schlep mean anyway?

Deb: It means just what it sounds like. So what am I saying Ian?

Ian: I think what you're saying is not to worry if I *have* attachment to worrying about whether or not I'm a schlep.

Sibyl: I heard her say something different, more like, "Look at the schlep in you and accept that part of yourself."

Deb: Like Jeff and his "country bumpkin." You know how Jeff used to be so self-doubting he'd get into a weird dumb space like a bumpkin. Now he's in a different new space because he somehow owned being a bumpkin as part of himself. No one ever sees him like a country bumpkin anymore, tripping all over himself. In the same way you don't need to fear that you might be a schlep if you have certain feelings or if you ask for certain things. Admit that you ARE a schlep. Then you're real.

Ian: Well, I've half-sat down and examined it, stared it in the face and half-felt that "that's really me." But, the thing that's changed me from doing that is a propensity for going into it and wallowing, feeling negative. I say, "Okay, I'm a schlep but I've got to identify with my real self, otherwise I'm always going to be a schlep."

Roger: What are the consequences of being a schlep?

Ian: Nobody will love you.

Sibyl: But that's not true. Everyone loves a schlep.

Ian: (Shaking his head strongly) Not my kind of schlep.

Roger: There's energy tied up in a fear of being that part of yourself. That would be worthwhile probing to see if the consequences which you fear are true. There's some basic assumption here. Who knows? When you're a schlep we may love you even more because you're not so cool. You're more human.

Dave: I'd like to hear him say just what a schlep is.

Ian: Somebody who's got this hanging-on-you vibe like "Give me some love! Hug me, hold me!"

Grace: God, I'd love it if you had that vibe. You act so cool, such the opposite, when really you're a little kid inside.

Ann: His cool vibe says, "I don't need any hugs."

Deb: Yeah. When you said "Hug me," I thought "How nice!"

because it's so strange coming from Ian.

Rog: So you see, Ian, you'll just have to be a schlep. (everyone laughs)

Deb: What else is a schlep?

Ian: (Slowly shakes his head, embarrassed) Well, insecure, awkward, can't communicate very well. When I'm in that space, I feel non-radiant, sucking energy. Scared. Hung up on feeling that I'm going to be rejected.

Deb: What are you embarrassed about?

Ian: I just had a thought. Everybody sure loves you when you're a schlep. I can't believe it!

Deb: Looks like schleps have it made.

Roger: So you come on to Grace with this insecure vibe trying to conceal it by being macho and she gets turned off. I wonder if you could be up front with her. Say, "Hey, I'm needing some love, but that doesn't mean that you have to take care of me, it's just a feeling." If you were more real about your softer side it would give her the space to respond. That wouldn't be sucking energy. It would be being a man about your feelings as opposed to being afraid of them and turning them into a schleppy, demanding, needy thing.

Ian: I feel I've done that, though maybe I haven't done it right. We'll sit down and I'll say "I feel really insecure."

Robert: But the real need is still repressed. The insecure grabby feeling is an effect of your deeper need and it makes her recoil and separate from you. What you just described to us about your simple need for affection was something she *wants* to cuddle, just the thing you're looking for. There must be some way that you come on to her that is different from what you're really feeling. Your needy vibe is amped up by your suppressing your simple underlying feelings which you can't accept. If you came on with the real thing and if she knew how you felt . . .

Ian: (mirrors, shakes his head as though he doesn't fully understand) I know what you're saying. There's a side that is afraid of being a schlep so I come on like a schlep. Or even worse, I come on all cool and want something to happen with big expectations from Grace.

Grace: It feels like a *demand,* like, "you better start responding to me soon because I'm desperate and there's something wrong with you too." I feel that complaint very subtly. A lot of times it's out of the blue. It's like you're denying that we've had good times. Then I feel inadequate and insecure myself because we don't know what's wrong or whose fault it is. We're both miserable about it.

Norah: You say that it has come in out of the blue, but if we get into Ian's world it's been building up for a long time and there's been no sharing between when his feeling starts and when it comes over to you as grabby insecurity.

Grace: You're so anxious to be a man and not show any of this, that any little thing will disrupt it. He hates it when I go, "Oh, poor baby," you know, natural little affectionate things. He is really watchful about his image. (laughter)

Norah: Don't you want to be a baby, Ian?

Ian: NO!! (in a loud voice)

Deb: That must mean that you *are* one.

Ian: Yep.

Norah: What are you afraid of *not* being if you were a baby? There's a fear there, isn't there? Is it not virile to be a baby?

Ian: Yeah, it's not virile, supposedly. One night we came back from Sunday chanting and Grace turned on this Clint Eastwood movie on TV. He is the exact epitome of super-cool. In the whole movie the guy probably says only twenty-five words and he's super-macho. She said that the movie got her in touch with what she really wanted . . . maybe I'm paraphrasing.

Grace: I said that I identified with his *magnetism*, which is missing in our relationship.

Robert: So Ian's not going to say anything for the next month?

Roger: He'll smoke cigars in the nude, right? (laughter)

Ian: The reason that I brought that up was that I identify with the cool role that I sometimes play.

Deb: But the thing is, Ian, that when the magnetism is there, that means that you've gone *through* the other side of this schlep thing, into the heart's magnet . . . that means going through the baby stage, not avoiding and repressing it.

Ian: It's a real deep pattern. Pam and I did an aura balancing once when she got me in touch with the part of me that wants to be Clint Eastwood all the time. I've done it ever since I was a little kid.

Norah: Has it ever paid off?

Ian: Only from an ego point of view with people who can't see through my image. It used to work before I came here, not in a real way but just enough to keep me going. I was in gangs when I was little and I used to face down kids a lot bigger than me without having to fight. I just put on an image and scared the other guy.

Deb: I feel that it's going to be real difficult for you to change. You mirror our points, but you haven't yet felt them. Unless you make a real effort to share the feelings you don't want to say to Grace, there won't be much of a change. Like, "I want someone to take care of me and I want the schleppy things I don't want to admit." You've got to share that part honestly to get the relationship going. It's not just a matter of trying to be in your heart with your ego desperately doing the trying.

Robert: That's a self-defeating cycle.

Grace: And the Clint Eastwood isn't real. Ian comes on with a, "Hey, baby, want to wriggle in the grass?" It's like a big movie. It just doesn't come off.

Ian: It's partly out of desperation. I know sometimes what my real self is, but a lot of times I find myself acting because I'm not in touch.

Deb: I feel that we can help Ian on this because we buy the cool guy vibe; I know that I do. When someone says something deep to you, Ian, instead of taking it into your heart and receiving it, becoming warm, you just shake your head and half laugh. We buy all your ego responses like that instead of challenging them and going to your being. I feel like we can help mirror that to help you be more honest about your real feelings.

Ann: Are you afraid that we won't respect you?

Ian: (No comment)

Pam: What are you afraid of, Ian? What do you think we're going to judge you as?

Ian: (still quietly contemplating)

Deb: I see you as a little boy under the "he-man" exterior, and he's not getting attention at all. If I would try to talk with that part of you I feel that you would reject it and put it down. Maybe you're afraid that being looked at as a little boy would be despicable to you. There's something you're not seeing about getting into the space of being a little boy; you have to do it.

Ian: Yeah, that feels right.

Norah: When you give us business reports, you're talking with people who are real dummies in that area, and you must feel that we respect you. That part of you is real. But there are other times when there's no harm in letting the other parts of you get space. They are both real: the competence and intelligence and then the baby, the boy who wants to cuddle, that's real too. Why can't you have the whole range?

Ian: I don't take notice of the other part.

Deb: I know, that's why I see that part of you so much, because he's always in need, always there. There's a little boy image that shines forth even when you're being Clint Eastwood. That's why Clint isn't quite believable. It's still a matter of you going through the baby space to the other side, not rejecting it. We keep coming back to it over and over.

Norah: As long as you're rejecting or denying it, we're not going to get anywhere tonight and you're not going to work through it.

Pam: Do you understand what people are saying about being a boyish person? You try to present Clint Eastwood—cool, virile, turning on women. What you're afraid of in yourself is the opposite. And somewhere in the middle is your real self. Somehow you're going to have to risk being what you're afraid of being in order to find out who you really are.

Ian: (mirrors)

Richard: It's like you're laying down there and she's patting you on the face and saying, "Poor little boy". That's a classic example of getting what you want and then rejecting it. If you could see why you're rejecting her love at that point, what it is that causes you to cut off right there, that's the example, that's it.

(Richard has brought in a new angle, zeroing in on the situation. Here the energy changes.)

Ian: That's not what I want. I want roomphy, sexy intensity. I don't want to be patted on the head.

Grace: But it could lead to that, why not have both? It could just merge into it.

Norah: It's only an opening gambit.

Stephanie: Sometimes that's just what a woman needs to lead into that space you're seeking. All that tenderness is what woos her in.

Pam: What do you think of Bruce getting so much attention? He's cute and a baby, and everybody just hugs him to death. What do you think when he gets all that attention? Do you think that he's unmasculine for getting it?

Ian: No.

Pam: "Damn my sour attitudes"—that's what I feel when I see Bruce getting the hugs because a part of me wants that, too. But I'm also afraid to let that part out. I play it cool, too.

Deb: How do you see Bruce, Ian?

Ian: He's a very warm and loving man. Kind, radiant and trustworthy and loyal. Seriously, I feel that he's solid. Does that communicate?

Richard: Is he a member of Schleps Anonymous? Somehow he gets hugs.

Ian: No, Bruce, you don't seem schleppy. Schleppy just doesn't feel so bad right now. I feel my attitude changing. It's just that if it's Bruce, it's okay, if it's me, it's schleppy. Lots of people are soft and tender.

Ann: Rather than reason about it, it seems that we just have to act differently with you to help you be more yourself.

Deb: Let's treat him like a little boy; then he'll have to be that way.

Norah: How are you feeling, Ian?

(Brings it back to the feelings)

Ian: Well, I'm getting in touch with lots of things. I feel happy and tearful feelings. I was just wondering if there was something in the tears that I should get in touch with.

Deb: You first started getting teary when you talked about what a schlep was, then you stopped it.

Pam: And also when you were thinking about the chance of losing Grace.

Ann: And also when you saw that the schlep was loved.

Deb: (softly) I hear a yearning in you.

Ian: (Teary) I don't know where to go with it.

Deb: Why not start by sharing how you feel.

Ian: (pause of 20 seconds or so) I just don't know.

(Ian again disappears into a fog.)

Dave: What was that trigger that Christopher used?

Ian: Christopher was at dinner and he mentioned about Grace's risqué side, her saying years ago she fantasized about walking the streets of Boston . . . I don't feel that yearning anymore.

Robert: You started this by saying that you had a yearning for cuddles and being soft. So you need to get in touch again with the yearning which wants soft things that you outwardly seem to detest.

Ian: I remember. When I see what I really want, that's when I get the yearning. It builds up to a lot of passion and love and intensity.

Dave: Do you want this passion and love to come from outside or are you going to bring it up and radiate it out yourself—the magnetism Grace wants?

Ian: I want to radiate it out, but I screw up everytime I try, and the yearning gets more intense.

Robert: So what's the key?

Ian: Just be myself.

Robert: Not really. When you're in this soft space that you're in now, just to be yourself is obviously the thing. But the feedback from the group is that you've got to go farther to the other extreme and let yourself be the schlep you repress. Then you'll be more yourself. If you try to be yourself without letting go you'll be too cool.

Victor: Maybe you can see how quickly you close the door when you get to the entrance to the sexual intensity you're seeking. Richard made the point that something inside you closes that door. We seem to have diverted from that. Can we go back to that point?

Richard: You brought up the example: she fantasized going streetwalking. That makes you feel insecure. Why does that make you feel insecure? Is it because you feel like you're not measuring up so you've got to play more Clint Eastwood?

Ian: Yeah . . .

Richard: Okay, so you play more cool Clint Eastwood and you get more secure. And all the time you keep repressing and fearing the schlep. It may be that the schlep is the key rather than Clint Eastwood. Isn't that what everybody's been saying?

Ian: Yeah.

Richard: Do you hear it?

Ian: Yeah.

Richard: Can you do it?

Ian: I see. The schlep is the way to go!

Richard: The thing I'm not so convinced on though is what your *image* of a schlep is, and what the actual reality of *you* is. When she says, "Poor baby," you're going "Eek, Schlep!" But she's not seeing schlep and you refuse to see that, so you cut her off and play Clint Eastwood and jam a cigar in her face.

(Richard succinctly and graphically speaks in a way that puts Ian in touch—gets to him.)

Ian: That's right! When she gets motherly and warm and says, "poor baby," the word schlep pops in my mind. Weak and sniveling, not respectable at all.

Victor: A little light should go off in your head the next time she goes, "poor baby". *That* is the doorway to *Passion,* love, ecstasy. A little wine and a little cuddling and you're through the door! (laughter)

Robert: And for you, Grace, if he comes on with Clint Eastwood, you say, "Okay, Clint, get your horse and saddle up!"

Ann: It seems like what schlep is, is a willingness to be vulnerable and that's your heart. Grace is probably starving for that.

Creative Conflict example #2

(Editor's Note: Rose and Larry are just breaking up after being together for three years. This session follows a previous Creative Conflict with Rose about how she was dishonest with Larry during the break up. The group asks Rose how she is doing this week. Christopher is trying to show them both the deep nature of their

attachments throughout this trying time for them both. His comments are given here so that you can use them to reflect upon the nature of your own attachments.)

Rose: I feel really much better, much more in touch with being open. I really heard a lot in what Christopher was saying in his last talk about attachment and love objects and I really identified with that and saw that I have this image of myself as a free and independent God-centered person without a relationship. And then I see myself on the other side looking for a love object, someone to put my love into. I'm trying not to be sucked into either image of myself. I want to just get into a more God-connected space. I've felt that way this weekend, these last few days, like God's going to help me to see what is really needed for me and that getting into sharing and being more open is just the way. Robert said to me last week, "If somebody comes up and asks me, 'How are you doing?' and if I can say really what I feel, 'I feel lonely' or 'I'm feeling a little sexy' or however I feel, I've seen the caring that comes back to me when I've expressed my being. Not only do people share but they suddenly express something deep from their world too, what they're feeling, and I get out of myself. Just feels lighter." I haven't felt that ability to get outside myself in my relationship with Larry. I'm feeling better about Larry. I felt really good about him recently. He's shared some things about himself feeling less attached to me and meeting other ladies outside of our relationship, sharing more intimately and that made me feel very free. I feel a little funny about sharing this. (to Larry) I don't know how you feel about me sharing this.

Christopher: Does it relieve some of your guilt?

Rose: Yeah. I guess so. But it also makes me feel that part of his own being that was left unexpressed in our relationship is now coming out, kind of feeling new things and expressing them. I don't know. A kind of joy welled up in me when he told me. Am I being too vague?

Norah: Well, why don't you talk about your own new relationship with Mark and leave Larry to talk about his?

Rose: (squirming) Well, *his* is affecting *me,* and it's . . . (long pause) . . .

Debbie: Why are you feeling so embarrassed?

Norah: She doesn't want to mention names.

Rose: Cause he's been opening up new doors in other relationships with other people.

Rich: You make it sound like a love affair.

Larry: Yeah, for God's sake!

Christopher: The thing is, Rose, you might be misperceiving the things Larry has been telling you, making more of them than he really means. Do you get that impression, Larry?

Larry: I felt that the other day when I shared with her. I don't know exactly how you perceive it now, Rose, but what's going on with me is not a love affair.

Rose: I'm not saying it's a love affair at all.

Larry: Somehow people are getting that impression.

Debbie: Yeah, especially if you're embarrassed. If you can't mention names because he's just developing a friendship with somebody it means there's something touchy about it.

Rose: Well, okay. Maybe because it's more intimate than a friendship. I mean there are levels of friendship.

Sue: I'd rather you shared about yourself, Rose.

Debbie: Wait. I'm still confused even about what she's implying about Larry.

Christopher: Rose, you're talking second-hand about Larry's relationship. Why not talk about your own relationship with Mark.

Rose: How I feel? In relation to Mark? I feel very warm, loving, and I want to see what's there. I want to be open. I've been feeling a little funny because I don't quite . . . Well, I got some feedback from you, Christopher, that I'm attached, that it might not be the right thing to work out the attachment with Mark, that maybe I should not get so involved with him. But I felt sticky about not seeing him because there's already a relationship there, so I find it difficult to cut off and not be flowing.

Christopher: Why is it difficult to cut off?

Rose: Because it hurts.

Christopher: That's what I was trying to show you. But when you were talking to us on that morning a few weeks ago when we had that session, you were saying it was just a little relationship where you talked with each other deep into the night and you got excitement from it but it was no deeper than that and why should Larry react so much. I said very clearly that in order to find out whether you were attached to Mark or not, whether there was something more going on than you were speaking, then the ideal thing would be not to see Mark again and you'd discover just how attached you were, but the first thing you did was you went to see Mark to tell him all about what I said, and you've seen him several times since. And you have been deceptive about it with me and with Larry and everyone.

Debbie: I thought you were going to stop seeing Mark in order to get yourself clear from your relationship with Larry?

Christopher: You see, first you weren't open with Debbie. You drove the whole day with her and she asked you how you and Mark and you and Larry were doing, and you didn't mention that the previous day you had been with Mark.

Debbie: You were? I'm really flabbergasted. I thought we were having a real open conversation. You gave me the total impression that you were trying very hard not to see him and that you *weren't* seeing him, but that was hard for you. So I said, why don't you talk to Christopher about it since he was the one who challenged you not to see him. You were struggling, but the impression I got was you were not seeing Mark and it was real hard.

Rose: Well that was only the second time I had seen him.

Debbie: But I asked you point blank and you didn't tell me that you had just seen him the day before. Why did you need to be dishonest?

Rose: (no comment)

Christopher: Thursday night you went for a long walk with Mark. Right?

Rose: Yeah.

Debbie: I just feel really funny that you felt you couldn't be open with me.

Roger: Rose, Could you mirror?

Rose: (mirrors, no response)

Christopher: This was the impression you were giving us that other morning too, when I challenged you and said, "Look, what you're giving us is skating over the surface of your relationship and you're not really telling us the truth. You're glossing over so much that we're getting a false picture." In fact Norah confronted you, too, about when you went to see the film and you created the impression that you'd gone on your own, but there you'd been on the beach with Mark and gone to the film with Mark, and you never even mentioned it, so it looks like there is some kind of deception in your words. You are not being integral.

Debbie: I thought we'd been through all this. All last Wednesday evening session we confronted you on this same deception about Mark and the hurt your dishonesty brings to Larry. It still goes on. God, I thought we went into this last week and that we'd gotten somewhere, which is what you said a while ago. But what I hear your being *really* saying is, "Larry is off my back now and I'm free to develop my relationship with Mark, 'cause Larry's got someone else."

Robert: Could you mirror that?

Rose: (mirrors)

Robert: How do you feel about that as being reality?

Rose: (Long pause) Part of that's true . . .

Rod: What part?

Rose: The part that Larry is off my back now. I wouldn't have put it that way. And now I'm free to develop a relationship whether it be with Mark or somebody else.

Debbie: That's the part that's been hard for you to own, that you really want to develop a relationship with Mark or you wouldn't have had to be dishonest. If you would really face the mirror then you would be struggling with a part of yourself that makes you grow and you could go to Christopher for help and say, "I'm working with what you said, but it's hard. What will help me?" You're deceiving us as well as Larry and yourself and you're not listening at all to any of us. You're trying to fudge it. "I'll do a little bit this way and a little that way" is what your actions say.

Rose: (mirrors, then is quiet)

Christopher: Another aspect is that unconsciously you're twisting things because you told Larry in your sharing with him that Debbie was the one who said you shouldn't be seeing Mark, not me.

Rose: Originally that's what Debbie had said to me that morning of the talk—"How do you feel about that, if you couldn't see Mark?"

Debbie: But I said that only after Christopher had already challenged you to test your attachment and not see Mark.

Rose: What you're saying then, Christopher, is that you said it?

Christopher: I said it very clear.

Debbie: It came from him. I barely remember even saying anything.

Larry: When I raised it with you Rose the other night, you accused me of being nit-picky. You said, "Well, Debbie gave me the feedback that I shouldn't see Mark, but I really couldn't understand it," and I said, "Wait a minute. I got a very strong impression from Christopher that he had said it twice very emphatically in the meeting with you and it was meant so that you could look at yourself right now and not get sucked into another attachment."

Pam: Geez, we discussed this last Wednesday night at the last Creative Conflict too!

Norah: In fact Christopher's last words to you in the center of the room here were if you did not see Mark that it would really show you where your attachment was.

Rose: I didn't hear it. Didn't want to hear it.

Christopher: Why did you twist it when you talked with Larry saying it wasn't me who said it but Debbie?

Rose: Some part of me doesn't want to hear it.

Robert: That response is too quick. He's asking why does some part of you not want to hear it?

Rose: Because I love him.

Christopher: Is it love or attachment? And how are you going to know unless you get yourself clear. Your twisting of reality shows that you are very attached. But is it really love? Your aura has been looking so dark and withdrawn lately. Do you think I would ever suggest you stop loving someone? Why would I say not to see Mark? Only for you to get in touch with your need, your attachment and look at the quality of your love. Look at the tremendous attachment you had when you were with Larry. I wanted you to now look at yourself and what you are doing with both Larry and Mark. Where are the feelings really coming from? Is it real love? Your dishonesty with everyone shows you cannot face it, cannot face looking at that part of yourself. Do you know why?

Rose: (mirrors) I'm afraid I won't get what I want. But I can see how this is causing me to block out others.

Rod: And block out truth.

End of Excerpt

(Editor's Note: The ego deceives itself and deceives others when its deeply felt needs are at stake. This portion of the Creative Conflict is printed here in order for you to get a feeling for the intensity that sometimes is required for the mirror to get through. The session with Rose continued for another hour. Rose felt genuinely remorseful for her dishonesty when she finally owned that her attachment was the cause of it. She expressed for the first time to everyone that she wanted to have a total relationship with Mark to discover where the relationship would go, what the potential might be. She wanted intense passion and love and said that Mark opened up a new part of her. The group acknowledged her openness and her feelings. They also asked her to keep looking at what was love and what was ego attachment and to be honest about her feelings. It finally became clear to her that her dishonesty was due to both her own doubts and to a fear that the group would not think highly of her if she went with Mark, and that the deceptiveness with herself is what caused Christopher to challenge her to not see Mark.)

(This next excerpt is from later on in the same evening when the group focussed on how Larry was handling his attachment to Rose.)

Christopher: Can you get in touch with the point when Rose said she was in love with Mark and Mark was in love with her? At that point something happened in you. What happened? Your words were, "I said to hell with it." I'm asking what is "it", what is going to hell, what did you consign to hell?

Larry: Rose's . . . well . . . what was going on was . . . you're free to suffer, almost . . .

Christopher: What was "it", though? You said to hell with it.

Larry: My attachment to working on the relationship.

Christopher: You were sending the attachment to hell, were you?

Larry: That's what I thought.

Christopher: Is that where it belongs? Isn't the attachment itself hell as long as you cling to it?

Larry: That's for sure.

Christopher: Rose has got a huge attachment right now. You're just sending yours to hell, but she's actually hoping to go to hell, I mean to the attachment, where it is. It doesn't seem like hell to her or to most people, not when you get to the front door, or when you get in and go down a few roads. It all looks paved with gold. But the deeper you get in, the deeper the attachment becomes. Then you find a few more. Of course, that's where attachments are— they come out of every door. Attachment keeps you bound there, in hell. So you have sent your attachment to hell to reinforce the other attachments that are there? What have you learned by sending your attachment to hell? Does it still hurt?

Larry: No.

Christopher: Is it huge surgery that's taken place, leaving a big gash, a hole?

Larry: It was like a wart at that point.

Christopher: Oh, you mean you whittled it down to wart size?

Larry: Yeah. It felt like, oh geez, get rid of it.

Christopher: You whittled the attachment down that tiny?

Larry: (nods)

Debbie: I have a hard time believing that, Larry. I think you've been doing valiantly, really, but I know what it feels like having been so deeply in a relationship for three years, to suddenly have the person that you're with and have been committed to in the relationship, suddenly fall in love with someone else and out of love with you and want to leave you and not want to be with you and all the unspoken messages beneath her words. That hurts, you know. It hurts the ego, and somehow I feel like you're not owning something to really be able to go through the other side of it.

Larry: I don't know what I'm not owning.

Debbie: Well, you say it's just a little wart that you just tossed off.

Rod: To hell, you sent the little wart to hell.

Debbie: When it felt to me like you're *repressing* your attachment, your big ego attachment.

Ann: Last week you did say you'd get rid of it one day and a couple days later it would be back again, huger than you thought. This may be one of those.

Debbie: This is what I am saying. You're going to keep going flippity-flop until you can reach the whole thing on a deeper level or own it on another level and go through it. The struggling you're doing is valiant. I'm not saying it isn't.

Pam: She's just warning you not to assume you've just tossed that one little wart off, that there's more to come.

Larry: (mirrors) That's what I felt initially when Christopher was asking me. I felt like I wasn't just completely throwing my attachment away. I felt it was an ego reaction too, so I wasn't quite clear. It didn't seem that what I felt had gone away that easy. It was clear that I hadn't got rid of the total attachment.

Debbie: We're trying to ask you now to get in touch with something deeper.

Pam: When Brian left me I was so relieved, after the pain and all these unspoken messages for so long. I said, "Oh what relief, fresh air again." It took a lot longer before I got in touch with the other feelings. Maybe it will take you more time.

Christopher: What I was trying to say when I asked, "What were you sending to hell?" and you said, "It was a little wart," is that it was a huge wart really, because you had a huge attachment. You may have worked on it until it became a little smaller each day till you were able to send it to hell, but it was a huge attachment. My point is that actually nothing of your free will caused it to go to hell. You had to wait to hear the real crunch point—from Rose—Rose is in love with someone else and he has confirmed that he is love with her. And all this time you knew it really, but you were doing what they called in Shakespeare's time, playing cuckold.

Larry: What does that mean?

Christopher: It's when the wife is with another man, but the husband is being really nice while knowing something's going on, pretending to be the gentleman, without saying what he really feels. In your case you wanted to say "to hell with it", because you've felt to hell with it for a long time now, but you've stayed in there because of the attachment. And you've been hanging in there to the last ditch, to the last thread, until it was cut for you by Rose, not by you. Although you've sent it to hell, the ego that created the attachment in the first place has not really done the work on itself. Because it finally had to be cut by the other. If you'd done the cutting of the attachment you wouldn't have needed to send it to hell. It would have just dribbled out and become nothing, no energy. While that wart is still in hell, something's still there.

Larry: (mirrors, is thoughtful)

Debbie: I remember you challenged Larry a couple weeks ago to do something strong to cut the attachment.

Christopher: Right, the same as I challenged Rose to do the same thing. Both of them were just clinging. He to Rose and Rose to Mark.

Larry: That was the morning of the session with Rose.

Christopher: I knew you weren't going to do it, Larry, that you would not be able to take that action, and you didn't.

Debbie: You said to me, Larry, that morning, that you were relieved that Christopher had told you to cut it and was bringing out in the open the things you were feeling but couldn't say. I've experienced your ups and downs the past few weeks. The ups have all come when the group or someone has confronted Rose, and that lets you off the hook so that you can ride feeling like you're conquering the attachment. And then the downs come when that external energy is not there helping to tide you over and you get in touch . . .

Larry: (nodding) that it's still there.

Debbie: So I feel you have to be careful not to whitewash yourself and make light of that, because the real deep soul-searching is still there to be done. You're glossing over it.

Larry: I hear what you're saying.

Christopher: The point is, when are you going to send for that wart, and get into a compensating relationship that will heal the hurt that you feel? The wart will come back with full force and grow into a huge big one in a new relationship.

Richard: What's he going to do, how's he going to get around it?

Christopher: Well he still has to do what he just nearly did that morning but didn't. If he could have cut the attachment before Rose cut it for him, then he would have done the work on himself. But as it is, he's only done the work on himself after it's too late. So the pattern of attachment is still deeply there. It was a fantastic opportunity that you missed there—to really cut your own attachment. You would have grown with the knowledge of your own ego. You would have really had an insight into that trickster. So let's hope the next time it comes around . . .

Debbie: Oh, that sounds awful.

Christopher: He had the power to cut the attachment three weeks ago when it became very clear where Rose was at and what she wanted. I challenged him to do it, because I knew what was going on. That's why I called for a session with Rose that morning, to find out directly and bring it into the open. But she was being deceptive and her aura betrayed it already. I challenged Larry to be ruthless with himself then, but he dragged and dragged, hoping all the time that things would be different. Rose had to cut it!

Larry: (mirrors and then responds). I had so much trouble relating to the way you were asking me to be strong. You were suggesting I say to Rose, "Look, it's either Mark or me." I couldn't see it that way. A part of me has felt through this whole thing that if I were on the other end, I might be saying to Rose the very same thing that she was saying to me, because I felt like leaving at different times, to be free of the relationship. There had been such attachment and insecurity, and yet it felt like it was mostly a phantom I was latching onto. It didn't feel like I really wanted the relationship in my heart, in a sense. But there was still a real strong attachment there, an insecurity.

Christopher: I challenged you to say to Rose: "It's either me or him" for you to get clear. But you daren't say that, because you were so clouded in your attachment to Rose that you were hanging onto every thread you could. As long as there could be any kind of relationship at all you were begging along, cap in hand, for even a few crumbs.

Larry: (mirrors, but no response)

Debbie: It got to the point one Friday back then where Rose said she really didn't care. Remember? It really broke you up. But she never has changed her vibe, in her being since, and you know that. Somehow your attachment was so strong it blinded you to that, especially when she said point blank she didn't want a relationship with you anymore.

Christopher: She wanted to move out, she wanted her own life, but that was unacceptable.

Larry: (mirrors, is teary)

Christopher: I said the same thing to you that I said to Rose, for you to find out where you were really at. If Rose is not going to see Mark and is truly in love, it's going to mount into a fire, which she can't do anything about. That kind of human love is there for us to purify the ego, where the love needs a love object for the ego to go to, relate to. You think you're following the heart when you feel attached, but you're following a great teacher who's going to teach you the hard way because you can't hear any other way. You're deaf and blind to your own ego attachment, right? So when the ego speaks inside you and says, "This is what I want, this is what I crave, now, not next year," the ego says, "go on, eat, have it, it's good for you." What do you think the Garden of Eden is all about? "Go on, eat the apple, eat this fruit; it will tell you everything, you'll know everything. Just eat."

Whatever you're attached to eating is pulling you. Your ego has to say, "No, I've been told that's hell. Eat of the fruit of knowledge, that's death and suffering." This is what Adam was told. Up to that point he was free of death, he was in bliss. He was not touched by comparative knowledge, but he had direct knowledge. Once he fell for the temptation of the ego, then he was cast out of the Garden of Eden, the cosmic state left him and he became blind to himself, to his own guilt. What I said to you and Rose was the same pattern. To Rose I said: "If you don't see him you'll grow in knowing yourself." If she runs to see him the very same day, she'll know the extent of her attachment. Actions speak. But to the ego that doesn't know what it's doing, it's falling into the pit. And I knew it would be very difficult for you, Larry, to cut your attachment, because you were clinging. And long after I challenged you to cut it, I heard from Rose that you were still hovering around her, wanting to touch her. If you could have left on your own steam, it would have required enormous force in you to rise and say, "I will not be attached; I am master of myself." But something was cloying and your master was Mark. Everything Mark thought, did, or didn't do was your master. Your pain and happiness depended on whether he came or went, whether he saw Rose or not, or whether she was in love with him or not. So your whole reality revolved around him for some time. He was the threat to your love object, to the possession of the love object. So you'd get up in the morning and look out your window and see if Mark's motorcycle was there outside the camper. "Is it there this morning? I wonder what time he left?" Your ego is being governed—dominated by that awful situation. Horrible isn't it? Just unbearable. But bearable to the point where the ego is squirming, even trying to hide it all, push it all down, but it's really hurting because it's a feeling of rejection. So what I was trying to say to you was almost identical to what I was saying to Rose. In order to cut that sort of thing, that kind of attachment, you have got to get into the spirit and generate some real power, and you grow by that. Because it's a big challenge and you'll only grow according to the challenge that's set.

Larry: (very vulnerable and teary)

Christopher: Having to separate from someone you've made yourself dependent on for your ego confirmation is for you a hard thing to do. But if you could have done that—done what I suggested—you would have been master of your ego rather than whittled it down to the size of a wart. Actually that wart is very potent, because it's got all the concentrated ego power in it. It was actually cut off and sent to hell by Rose in not caring enough in her actions whether you were hurt or not. Maybe she's been dying to tell you she no longer loved you for a long time but couldn't muster up the courage. Or maybe she was saying the reason she couldn't be open about it was there was some fear there in her; maybe *her* challenge is fear. Your challenge is to cut the wart yourself rather than always wait for circumstances to do it. Because if you had done it yourself, you would have been strengthened immeasurably.

Editor's Note: (three months later) From this session both Larry and Rose received a profound mirror of their inner psyches and their own attachments. Larry did as was predicted—he sought out several compensating relationships and became attached to a lady who again did not want him and he had to look at his need. And Rose has been living in constant push-pull relating with Mark—a hell of intense ego battles, until they finally broke up. Both Rose and Larry are much more serious about looking at their patterns now and, with the group feedback, are confronting these very deep attachments and the motivations and insecurities feeding them.

6

IN SPIRIT
AND IN TRUTH

(Editor's Note: The next two chapters are a series of tape transcriptions which form a poignant discourse by Christopher, including some of his personal background on how Creative Conflict began, a sharing on the attitude to maintain while going through the process, and answering questions from new Creative Conflict students at the University of the Trees.)

HOW CREATIVE CONFLICT CAME INTO BEING

When I retired from business in 1957 to write a book, I wrote a very idealistic book about how the world ought to be and how I would like to see it, but I realized very quickly that there was only one person at that time who was prepared to put any energy behind my own idea and that was me, since I hadn't really been out in the world to find if there were other people willing to invest their time and consciousness, love and care to do somebody else's idea. I realized that not only was I in that situation but that most idealists who try to change the world first get an idea and then get some kind of symbol or flag, and they go around waving it, saying, "Follow me, I've got the answers," and so either they get people who have no critical ability who follow—followers—or they attract to themselves leaders who go out on their own trip and use their ideas, and so the world gets more idealists, more people who think things can be changed through ideas.

I rapidly came to realize in life that, looking at the world with its many thousands of years of civilizations that have come and gone, it doesn't matter what ideal a society is based on; there will always be conflict in putting it over, getting it manifested or running it. As long as there are people there's going to be conflict, whether it's Christianity, Hinduism or Buddhism, Marxism or any "ism". As long as we have people we will have power-seekers, we will have egos, people looking for fame and name, we will have people searching for wealth and all the other things that humans do. And in the pursuit of these many things that we want, we come up against others who are either competitive or put us down or don't like our ideas or in some way create so much conflict in the society we live in that we cannot ever get anything done. Nothing ever seems to happen that is perfect and society often seems to be just a mess, a mess of people seeking different goals on different trips. The conflict that results from the competition between various people is destructive and divisive. It does not bring unity to people, and so as long as we have humans we are going to have conflict. As long as we have conflict we are going to have division and separation. As long as we have people around, there will be strife unless we suddenly find something which can make conflict creative instead of divisive and destructive.

So I saw that I would be wasting my time to write a lot of books or to try and put an idea over. Instead, the idea must come from *within* each person. And it really did not matter how different people were in the head if they were united on one thing in the heart, if they were united in arriving at the best possible solution in spite of all the different individuals involved. That meant that we had to find a way of allowing everybody to be completely unique, not requiring them to think like we do, or to think only one philosophy—Marxist or capitalist, this or that, or one man's thought. We had to find a way of saying, "Well, we're all supposed to be different. Let's be as unique and as different and individual as we can be and still have this resolution of conflict. Let it be our aim to create unity, not by forcing people or coercing people or trying to persuade them or sell them a trip or whatever, but let the unity come as a by-product. By the interaction of all the various egos and ideas and individualities and so forth, let the result be something creative that emerges out of all this interaction." What would that result be? Growth.

If human beings are not growing, they are as good as dead. If human beings are not growing in spirit, vision and awareness, they may as well just be walking automatons, robots in the flesh. So I saw that if growth came out of conflict, then there would be some hope for this world, because as long as people grow, as long as people become more refined human beings—whatever the pain involved—they are alive and dynamic. I saw that the pain that accompanies growth, growing pains, was not something to be afraid of, not something that needed to be pushed under the carpet, but something perhaps even to welcome in order to see why we are pained by growth when we are stretching ourselves to the limit to face somebody or someone who doesn't agree with us, doesn't even like us or think at all like us. How can we use this growth, this pain, to become a bigger person, become a finer person who can help the world by knowing what is right action?

It is no use getting power over others or even getting monetary power if we do not know how to use it. And if you look at most politicians who get in the seat of power, whether it is President this or President that or whether it is a dictator, you always find that when in power he is subject to the same pressures that the previous person was and so he never fulfills any of his promises, or very few of them. So you see that the power, unless we have the grace to know how to use it, is not much use. It is like trying to do good without first becoming good. I saw that what Creative Conflict could do was to make people good before they tried to do good, because if they are not good and try to do good the net result will probably be that they screw up somewhere because how can they know what is good if they themselves are not good? And I saw also that good people did not need to try to do any good because they automatically do good just by being what they are. I saw that all the do-gooders in the world are wasting their time. They are trying to help the world before they have got the right insight into what the world needs.

The question arose: how can we get people together so that

they get a better look at themselves in this growth process? I saw that they could get many more mirrors through Creative Conflict than they would get by belonging to a do-gooding group which goes out and supposedly helps others and often interferes with the lives of others without quite knowing what the others really need. I realized that there are so many people running around society who *think* they know how to help it, and thousands of years go by and it does not seem to get any better. So, this is how the Creative Conflict method emerged.

I wrote a book, what I thought would be an ideal constitution for a group of people living together and governing themselves. They would not be governed from outside, but governed from inside themselves through free will and yet in such a way that they did not have to be coerced by an outside authority, a government. Why do we have government? Because we do not govern ourselves. We have not been self-governing creatures. We do not know how to govern our lives. We appoint others to govern us. I saw that until communities, whether the community was just like a family or whether it was like a small community like we have here, a village, or even the entire world, could come to this realization, we will have government by pressure. We pressurize those people, we lobby them, we appoint representatives, we put clout behind them if we can, if we have any. So then if we pressure enough we get some changes. So I saw that government was not really like that in nature at all. Nature achieves change and growth and things grow rather magically. They transform from one state to another, one energy system to another and all are interlinked—whether it's clouds dropping rain on the earth and evaporating from the sea— it's all cyclic. Can we learn to govern ourselves the way nature governs herself?*

In human affairs something is missing, even between two individuals. Even if you are married to a person for twenty-five years there are certain things you can't say without bringing a lot

---

* See *Rise of the Phoenix, Universal Government by Nature's Laws* and *The Living Constitution* by Christopher Hills, University of the Trees Press.

of conflict, and if you are in love with someone, it is even worse, because you do not want to lose the love of that person. So how can you say certain things about that person that you see and do not like or that you don't quite think are the way they should be? Can you go up to that person and say, "Hey, look at this part of yourself?" Usually they don't want to look at that part. So Creative Conflict has to do with looking at those parts of ourselves that we don't really want to look at. You may say, "That's crazy— attending a group of people who are looking at those parts of themselves that they don't want to look at!" Well, this is the whole point. Unless the world looks at its blind spots, there will not be any New Age or any fantastic improvement in the human situation.

Where do you begin? It's no use going out there and buying advertising space or writing books. You have to begin with small communities, like a seeding process, just as in nature.

The whole idea of Creative Conflict is to get into the kind of vibration or the kind of feeling towards others where we can tell them anything we feel and think without their getting hyper-reactive or angry, or at least if they do get angry they see the anger and are able to get a clue as to what makes them angry from the various mirrors in the group. Then we can use it to find out how to control our own minds, how to control our own selves. If we can become masters of our own emotions and the way our thoughts work, then we can walk out there into the world and can be people who are centered and at peace with ourselves to such a point that nothing out there which is in conflict is going to affect us. So it's one way of creating a master of yourself, to enter this experience as a golden opportunity, not to get only vicarious excitement by hiding behind your ego, but to say, "Okay, I'm going to *heighten* my individuality by being part of a group, not lessen it. But in order to become a greater individual I will have to look at my ego, the self-sense." By ego I really mean that psychic skin which separates us inside from what we think is outside. It is really an imaginary skin because there isn't anything separating us from anything else, except our own minds. We have an idea that we sit inside this bag of skin; we say, "This is inside and that is outside," and we believe that outside things affect us and make us miserable or present us with "outside" situations to which we respond, but it is not true. Most of the outside situations that affect us and that we respond to are self-created; we all have the power to go almost anywhere we want to go and to be with whom we want to be. Strictly speaking, wherever we are at this moment is the right place, even if it is painful, even if we came by "accident" seemingly. But is it an accident? Something in us, in our mind, our soul, our being has brought us to a situation and the way we respond to it is going to determine whether we are happy or miserable.

So the whole object of Creative Conflict is not just to sit around and have a good time throwing dirt at each other or criticizing each other, but to see whether it is an instrument which can have a lofty vision of not only changing ourselves but of changing the situation in which we live. If we change even a little bit of the environment around us—whether it's a psychic atmosphere that we give out or whether it's a whole community we infect with our being, or whether it's the whole world—that is the only way we are going to create real change in people, instead of imposing it on them from outside and forcing them to toe the line. They themselves do it spontaneously from within. So that is the whole concept of Creative Conflict, that we change our environment by changing ourselves. Once the group has helped us to change ourselves, then the group itself is changed, and in this way society becomes transformed from within.

All organizations, what are they formed for? What are groups of people for? Only to achieve things that individuals don't have the power to achieve. So individuals group together in some form of union or group in order to become more powerful and effective. You find that in the organization of groups, whether in companies or in the commercial world, there are also groups of people who are banded together as political parties or shareholders to achieve some economic purpose because individually you couldn't do it, but as a big company you can buy ships, railways and telephone equipment, you can do something big. The same thing applies when you're in a Creative Conflict group like this. You can do something much bigger than you can do as an individual. By Creative Conflict, the growth process can be intensified so powerfully in a group situation that in effect we achieve immense spiritual growth in a few short years.

GETTING TO KNOW YOUR EGO

The first thing that happens in Creative Conflict when you start saying your two cents worth is that the whole group seems to spring on you and say, "I don't feel that's the right motive," and "What makes you say this?" and you feel attacked. You feel you are in a corner wondering what move you can make next, or you decide you'd better just be quiet rather than risk getting pounced on. These are natural reactions of someone who is trapped inside the self-sense, the ego, and we all have an ego. You eventually learn how to look at your ego directly, see why you did say what you said, without taking the question as a personal slight. The concept of Creative Conflict is not necessarily to get rid of your ego, at least not to squish it and force it down, but to bring it out so it can teach you. Your ego reactions are a way you can learn whether you are right or wrong, whether you are able to take right action and say a thing in the right way and do something in the right way.

So we don't mind the ego in Creative Conflict. If you have got one we had rather you had it out up front, not because we are going to tear it to shreds but because you are going to learn more about yourself if you are honest and open with your self-sense. If you think you are the greatest thing in the world, like the boxer Muhammed Ali thought, then why don't you say so? At least people will relate to you as someone who thinks he's the greatest. And they would probably say, "Well, you're just an egotist." And you would say, "Well, I can prove it, there are a few great things I do." And you say those things and they say, "Well, we all do those things already; that's nothing." So you see, you get a picture of whether you are justified in having a self-concept that is so high without any extraordinary manifestation to prove it.

This is usually what happens to human beings. These people with such high opinions of themselves have very zig-zag paths through life. When you point to the track left through life, it's very crooked, it's very zig-zag. They don't really steer a straight and narrow course. The people with the highest opinions of themselves have very little to show for the opinions they hold. The most humble people, the people you would never suspect, who have achieved all kinds of things and are quiet and never talk about them much, are the people who are skillful in action. They go direct to the goal and they create very little wake behind them because they move so skillfully nobody notices.

It may be that in the Creative Conflict process or in the group process that you will remember these little extra ways of looking at yourself, so that when you are in the corner and your ego is out there apparently being torn to shreds, you realize it is not something destructive that is going on, but something tremendously creative and you will be able to see how your own demon works. That is all the ego is; it's a demonic separator. It is the thing which says you are separate from everybody else, says everything is out there and I am in here. It does not create union. It is the divisive part of ourselves. It is the thing that makes us schizophrenic—the ego. It makes us separate from everyone and separate from everything "outside".

So the whole process of Creative Conflict is to find out that separate one, to find out the tricks it plays on us, because it's a deceiver—a self-deceiver. If we're self-deluded we never can act skillfully in the world. So the objective of Creative Conflict, ultimately, is to see our self-delusions, whether the delusions are grand and fed by ego-food or over-confidence, or the opposite of that. Some of us walk around with a concept that is much below our true potential and some self-concepts are far above what's real. And it often happens in the group situation that you walk out feeling ten feet taller instead of a snake on the ground.

Now most of the people residing here who have been practicing Creative Conflict for a number of years probably don't notice the growth in themselves because having the ego confronted many times over, you get immune to it in the end to the point where it doesn't matter any longer. But there are certain dangers in ego-confrontation, that it might even reinforce your secret ego and chase you even more behind the battlements of your own private castle so that you begin to look out of narrower slits than ever in a protective way. Now you see, that only happens if there is no willingness to change. If there is a rigidity in a human being who says, "I'm not going to change; that whole group out there is all wrong and I'm right," and there's an unwillingness to look at the nitty-gritty which we have to change, then what happens reinforces the ego and that person usually leaves because he doesn't want to change, and you can't really stay in a Creative Conflict group unless you want to change and accept the pain of change.

Now it doesn't always mean that change is going to be painful. Sometimes it is a great joy. It depends on how resistant you are to it. If you like change and welcome it, you can absolutely be in a bliss at having made a fundamental change in your self. People who are very sensitive to criticism are called ego-sensitive. They are concerned about their self-image, yet this very concern makes it much easier to do Creative Conflict with them. Those who are not that ego-sensitive are not used to looking at themselves and it is harder for them to really change. They often need to experience a tremendous amount of pain before they will look at themselves. One woman, Sylvia, refused to look at herself and just kept blaming people in the group for seeing her wrongly. Eventually people warned her that if she did not listen and look at herself her husband was going to get pretty fed up. She felt the group had a lot of nerve saying that and that they were programing her husband's actions. She wrote the group off. One day her husband said he had had enough and left her. She was completely crushed. She had to lose everything before she would listen or see. She came running back to the group after that, kicking herself for being such a fool. Although the motive is not the highest, a more ego-sensitive person would have been more likely to listen to the feedback in the first place out of a deep desire to be accepted. Eventually this motive of wanting approval will not be sufficient, because there are always times when we have to stand alone and act on the promptings of inner truth regardless of what others are saying to us. But initially ego-sensitivity can be useful to spur growth.

One problem that comes up in Creative Conflict is that you can learn certain skills of how to fend off criticism, to transfer all the things that people are saying back on other people by saying, for instance, "That's a projection." You learn these skills and can handle yourself in the unsuspecting outside world, but in Creative Conflict a skillful intellect can be used to create division and protect oneself. It is sometimes very difficult to tell a person in a group that he's using the rules of Creative Conflict destructively and rather cleverly. It's a one-upmanship show. He says, "Well, that's your projection," instead of looking back at himself as to what was said. We find such a person is one who cannot take much feedback and you will find that the feedback he takes in is proportional to his willingness to change.

You can always find one person in a group who is not willing to change. It's important for groups to always know that there is going to be at least one negative. As long as there is a positive there must be a negative. So in most groups the negative usually settles on one person. In Creative Conflict what happens is that the negative shifts from one person to the next. One week it's on this person and then it's on another. It is creative sometimes to be negative, to see things that are negative about ourselves and to make mistakes, get our feet wet. By opening our mouth wide we get into hot water. But if we're creative about it and we learn from it, then the next time we share we find the negative is not us, it's someone else. In Creative Conflict we are learning to handle that negativity. In nature there must be a negative as long as there's a positive; the two can't exist separately—they exist within us. That's the important thing to understand—that even if we're seeing all good in front of us and everybody's lovely, in the back of our head we've got to keep the negative thoughts from jumping up and coloring the vision.

We don't ask you to drop the negative or say that you must come here without negative thoughts. We are not looking for total compliance like some instructors. Good students ask awkward and difficult questions and only followers and feebleminded people are seduced by arguments which hand Truth down from a high authority. If you join some movements they say, "Oh, you can't come unless you get rid of all this questioning or unless you believe this." We say, bring all your differences because in Creative Conflict we agree to differ. That's the one creative thing that you begin to say from the very outset: "Well, you're supposed to be different from me. You're supposed to think differently. Why are you trying to make me think the same as you?" What we do is we use all these differences. We are not afraid of them nor do we get defensive if others lay trips on us. In Creative Conflict we get feedback from everyone in the group. The members of the group looking at us are like TV lenses, and we look at ourselves through all those TV cameras and see a different shot of ourselves. We don't have to buy any of it. In Creative Conflict you don't have to say they're wrong or right. You just have to look at it. Before we point a finger out there we point it inward too, to see if we've got the same thing wrong with us that we're accusing others of. That's what makes Creative Conflict a growth experience. That's what gives it the dynamic for using it in everyday life, like when you're talking to your husband or you're talking to a group of people or even if you're a member of a union and you're on strike with the boss. You can even have Creative Conflict come into union disputes or disputes between politicians, like Americans and Russians. It is possible to have conflict that turns out in the end creative if everyone understands the process. Creative Conflict can change the entire world, because people are involved and it's only people who will change the world. Organizations can't change the world because organizations are made of people.

Misperceptions of reality are so constant and large-scale. Hitler and Stalin are examples of the demonic mind. No one could believe it, so they let them get away with their misperceptions and mis-actions. Stalin killed with a silky white-gloved hand, so no one perceived him as evil while he was in power. Yet 60 million people died to keep Stalin in power. We allow twisted perceptions to rule. They are the problem of the world we have to conquer. The root of the problem is the twisted view of man's nature that most people hold because they do not know themselves well. Minds are molded to accept the cultural dictates as gospel. In totalitarian societies everyone is coerced to be the same mind. It is not done through probing the different viewpoints and welcoming dissension in thought. In communism all dissension is worked out in the upper strata of the Party, and the best plan possible is brought to the people in "Pravda"—"The Truth". This is what the people are told and they are not allowed to threaten this process with conflict, questions or dissension. So they do not learn to think for themselves, and they do not get to know themselves because they do not have the freedom to err and to learn from their mistakes. Only through the freedom to make errors and suffer and then re-think our state of being can we come to the humility to see the truth and beauty in everything, to stand in awe of the cosmic intelligence and its ways and really see it.

Actually, everything that is negative is really helping the world and is a positive in disguise. People are all getting back what they deserve, brought upon them by their own level of consciousness, their own misperceptions causing misactions and reactions. The scales will have to fall from the eyes of man even if there is a huge global catastrophe that destroys a lot of life. But this is not important in the cosmic sense. Life is for the purpose of refining our perceptions, refining consciousness, and sometimes it takes a catastrophe to accomplish this. Eventually, those in an expanded state of consciousness will see it, not as a negative but as a purification. If you surrender your life to the cosmic plan, its ways unfold before you. Direct perception is in you, but you have to become it. A person with this understanding doesn't need to read the scriptures. When you see with direct perception, your life is the scriptures, and the way you live your life, in righteousness and truth, mirrors beauty all around you. This is the ultimate goal of Creative Conflict.

DISCOVERING A NEW YOU

When we examine ourself with the help of the group we see that the group is not there to put us on the hot seat, although we might find ourself on the hot seat, but the actual function of the group is to help us, and that's one thing that we have to keep in the upper part of our being, because if we keep thinking that the group is all against us, then there's something wrong with our ego position. It doesn't mean you have to buy everybody's opinion, but you have to look at everybody's opinion. Otherwise you're not listening. With the whole group saying the same thing to you eventually you have to ask yourself, "Am I really like that?"

Now, one problem about Creative Conflict is: how do you listen to another being? This is what you are really learning. How do you listen to the being of another? It is not to listen to what they're saying, not to the intellectual garbage of the mind from the culture they live in, the family they're born into. We're all programed beings. We've got to wash all that stuff out of our brains. There is no use for it. If there was any use to it we would all be enlightened. But if we cling so hard and so possessively to our own experience in life up to now, then we'll not be able to learn anything new. So in Creative Conflict, what we do is temporarily take all this junk and put it on the shelf. If we love it we can always get it back again, it's easy to get back. But unless we put aside all that we know at this moment, we can't effectively listen to the being of another speaking. It is the opposite of brainwashing because we are deliberately not putting anything in, only making it more clear.

The main technique in Creative Conflict is the mirroring process. You have to be able to put yourself aside to be able to mirror what a person is really meaning, not just what they're saying. Often they might say with their mouths the opposite of what they mean, so you mirror back the way you received the communication. And then he or she can confirm that that is what was actually said. Once it's confirmed that that's what was said, then you can answer it. But if you haven't properly received the communication, how can you answer it effectively? That is the whole secret—to get rid of our own investment in our own opinion so that we go beyond opinion-making altogether. In a Creative Conflict group we're into the nitty-gritty of our true self, not just the ideas, the things we've been told and the books we've read. That's all brainwash, which is why we have problems, because we tend to think *that* is us. It isn't, and what we're trying to find in Creative Conflict is the you, the real self, that thing, wherever it came from, that is a spark of the original creative universe—your consciousness—indestructible, immortal consciousness. It's taken many curves. It's sitting in a body right now. How many bodies has it had, how many will it ever have? You see, sitting inside each of us is the same stuff: consciousness, streaming out of our eyes, lighting up everything that we see. It's the same for all of us but we're all doing different things with it. When we come into the Creative Conflict group, that's when we sit back and say, "Hey, that guy's got the same stuff as me but he's doing a different trip with it," and that is his freedom, and everyone has that freedom in Creative Conflict to be who he or she really is.

So this is the way that Creative Conflict can change the world; it can re-make everyone and it can do this without any coercion, without forcing people to be docile or setting down regulations or anything. A minimum number of rules are required to create peace on earth; in fact the minimum number boils down to one rule of which the outcome is bliss. If each person were ultimately responsible for clearing up his own mess physically, psychologically, emotionally and otherwise, then we wouldn't need other rules. This is a major rule: "Everybody clears up their own mess."

You may have questions that you've come with, difficulties or something that you fear might happen—loss of ego, or loss of individuality or being swallowed by the group—that's the usual fear to begin with. "Are they going to take me over?"—all that stuff. If there are any questions or fears or anything that we can answer before you go into this deep experience, you should voice them at the beginning. It can be a very profound and deeply threatening experience if we don't approach it in the right way. But it also can be an enlightening experience because we probe areas of our being that we never knew were there. We're all so much richer than we know. There are depths to us. And I like to use an analogy which is not too favorable to human beings, but I always like to say that we have a lot of manure deep down inside of us and that manure is very fertile soil for growing things. We shouldn't really reject it. We should thank our lucky stars that we've got some good manure down there because the most beautiful flowers grow in the richest manure.

We don't try to forget that manure; we try to use it so that it is creative and helps us to see what sort of person we are. It helps us to change more effectively because the worse you are now the more of a challenge it is for you to change, and once having changed you'll see how much better you've become. So that's why the greatest saints were always once the greatest sinners. They see how much they've transformed themselves. So they don't reject other people who are naughty; they don't do an ego trip and say, "Oh, look what you're doing, all that evil." They say, "Yeah, but for the grace of God there was I when I was twenty-one or thirty-one or fifty-one." They've been through those trips and so they have compassion for others who are still going through the Dark Night.

So Creative Conflict brings this experience to us and we're able to have compassion for others who still have got trips to go through.

7

QUESTIONS FROM MY STUDENTS

Question: I have a question about Creative Conflict, how it can be used to help a person who isn't willing to change. Is there a skillful way of doing it without "hitting a person over the head with a hammer"?

Answer: I think the best sort of thing *is* probably to "hit him over the head", metaphorically speaking. Not even God can help a person who doesn't want to change. He's against the universe. The universe only exists because of its ability to change. Everything that doesn't change perishes. The secret of death, if you want to know it, is rigidity. Not stability, but rigidity—mental rigidity, emotional rigidity. Now, rigidity is not the same as stability. Stability is only achieved by adaptability, by the ability to switch between the positive and the negative at the slightest fibrillation. You see, the whole universe is quivering, everything in nature is quivering and vibrating. Why? Because it is hanging between the balance point of positive and negative and when you're perfectly balanced, God is sitting on his throne and everything is at peace, eternally stable. But if you have rigidity, you're dead already, you're going to be crushed because the universe is against you. There isn't anything in the universe that survives in that state of pressure.

So whether they are people who are rigid or things, they are going to be crushed by life if you don't crush their illusions yourself. So you don't need to worry about crushing a person's feelings who is unable to change. You can only hold up the vision of life and the living waters and say, "This is yours when you change. You have a perfect right not to change." And you must give him the right not to change as well as to change, otherwise it's meaningless. Freedom is meaningless unless you have the right to do wrong. Sounds funny, doesn't it?—the right to do wrong. But you have to give people the right not to change; that's their choice. You can't communicate with a person about life if he is spiritually dead. Anyone is able to change if he is willing. The will is the heart. If you have the will in your heart you can change. But don't waste time with those who are unwilling. You're wasting your time with the dilettante and half-hearted. You can take all the forces in the universe and you're plunking them down the bath hole when you're trying to change someone who doesn't want to change. No matter what you do for him, you can love him as hard as you like, he'll take your love and turn it around and hate you more. So you're wasting your time going against his real nature. Love him, certainly, but leave him be. Love him and leave him to himself because life will teach him how to change much better than you. Life is the greatest teacher.

Now if you are determined to communicate with such a rigid person you will probably find that feeling like hitting him is the end result and that's what's happening in the world, violence. It's just the lowest form of communication there is, but it *is* communicating. The stage beyond hitting is not caring at all and ignoring the person completely. That's the ultimate form of communication, ignoring a person totally, because this doesn't leave any options. Even if you had all the power of the universe and offered it to help such a person, it would be no use. There would be no receptivity. And he is getting that power anyway, don't forget; every person is subject to the same cosmic light. They're all receiving light the same way but what they do with it is all different. What they do to it determines how they are living. But everyone here is receiving the life force from the cosmos. I'm not getting any more than you. I might be using more of what I'm getting; that's a different thing.

So everyone is favored equally; no one is favored more than another. The sun shines on a rat or a blade of grass or a human being, favoring none. So it is with the cosmic life force. You cannot say to that fellow, "Hey, you must get more life force; you must change." You have to agree with him and say, "Okay, you're right from your point of view, but I'm not going to help you stick there in your smugness. I'll let life teach you."

Question: Yes, what if a person is consciously willing to change, but he's not changing and he can't seem to get a hold on what to do. Then what?

Answer: Well, if your unconscious mind is going in the opposite direction from your conscious mind then you have internal conflict which will definitely come out in Creative Conflict. That's one of the purposes—to bring out your unconscious, because what is unconscious you can't know. That's the whole problem with human beings: ninety percent of their lives is lived unconsciously, not consciously.

How do you get to the unconscious? If it's unconscious it means you don't know it's there. So most of our motivations, our emotional reactions, things we do, things we like, things we don't do are all coming from our unconscious. Creative Conflict is a better way to get in touch with your unconscious than going to a psychiatrist and lying on a couch and paying him so much money. In a matter of one week or two weeks you can get in touch with far more about yourself than will ever come from association or interpretation of dreams. If you really use Creative Conflict you'll find out more about yourself than you can ever find out by any other method. If you're truly using it as an instrument for self-examination, then the will that is in your head unites eventually with the will that is in the heart. All that Creative Conflict is doing is creating a union between head and heart, for if your heart and your head are going in the same direction you're in tune with the universe. Wherever your heart is, there you are. Eventually your heart is going to decide what your head is going to do, you see. And if you fall in love you know your heart always gets you into trouble. It doesn't matter what your head is saying.

If your heart is loving, it will put you through the refiner's fire your head walking one way and your heart walking the other. You're in for trouble, but if you want to know what love is you have to walk into that trouble and face the fire. There's no other way to get to know what love is than to go through the pain, the refiner's fire. Maybe that is even the purpose of love, who knows? The true lover, even the cosmic lover, must be pained as well as joyful. He wants to share himself with everything and nothing will let him. You want to love someone and he keeps giving you a hard time and won't let you love him the way you want to love him, keeps twisting your love up and making it something different. So it's just a matter of the level that you're looking from, the head or the heart. If your heart is as big as the cosmos, then your head is inside your heart, you're exploring your heart with your head.

There are certain kinds of research you can do, right? The mental kind is where you put bits together and become a scientist and look through microscopes and do analysis and you tear things apart intellectually and you have concepts and models and theories and this and that and you have just one big head. There are such people kicking around the earth—huge heads—nothing but head, no heart. So they create all kinds of monstrosities with their heads—rockets and bombs that kill people, all kinds of things. They have no heart or they couldn't do those things. They're just huge, encyclopedic brains that know everything. They can't even love properly; they're all screwed up in their emotional lives. Now there is another kind of research you can do with your head by analyzing yourself, your own heart, by probing your heart with your own intellect. You can use that analytical faculty for finding out what is the structure of your heart.

What does it mean to live life from the heart and to think from the heart? That's a long trip. You can't expect to come to a few Creative Conflict sessions and bridge that gap overnight because the gap has been created, perhaps, through many years. It means ultimate fulfillment. If a person says they want to change from the head alone and not from the heart, the group mirror is that there is no enthusiasm from the person. The mirror is, "You are not helping us. There is no willingness to risk that vulnerable space inside, and without opening to your vulnerable heart you cannot grow." That vulnerability is what you look for in Creative Conflict.

Now it is possible to bridge the gap quickly, but that's what is called going through the Dark Night of the Soul—complete loss of the self-sense and ego. Not everybody's willing to let go of ego. Very few. We feel more comfortable hanging on to that which we know. That which we don't know in the unconscious is rather dark and fearsome. It's frightening. In the depth and core of the heart, which is what we mean by Nuclear Evolution, there is that black unknown self. I call it Black Night, not because it's evil or anything but because it's like the Dark Night of the Soul where you don't know what's there. It's what a scientist would call a black hole. There's no way of knowing before you get in there what it is like. You have to trust it and most people don't like to trust the annihilation of what they fear most—themselves. They would rather sit down and cry with self-pity or shout at the universe with anger than change even one small bit of themselves.

Who is your worst enemy? Yourself. Yourself, the self-sense, is the worst enemy. Why did I say that? Because you really don't know your true self, the one who sits at the seat of consciousness watching this whole thing, because everything you see is re-created in your mind and your consciousness, experienced inside, not out there.

We think it's out there! Actually it takes place inside our consciousness where we make sense of it all. That's the important part of our unknown self, to understand who is re-creating the whole universe inside of us. That is the process of the nuclear self and the vision of its fantastic evolution. As I say, if you want to find that One, that's a big trip. You have to give up everything else in order to get there and you have to trust that this big, black, unknown self there is really worth becoming. This is frightening. Some people cop out or drop out from such an enormous confrontation with themselves, and when they do they will blame you or anyone else for their failure and their egotism.

Now we don't *need* to go to that point in Creative Conflict. Creative Conflict can deal with ordinary matters of living. It can be a nursery for saints but you don't have to be a saint or want to be a saint to get some benefit from it. But if you want to bridge your heart and your head, to answer your question about the conscious willing of change, then you have to become a saint. That's the only way you can resolve the conflict between the world of space and time as you see it and the love which you feel—to get the two going in the one direction so that they're flowing with the cosmos instead of trying to make things happen according to how you think they *should* happen. When you're flowing with the cosmic energies, then everything happens magically. Everything happens as it is meant to happen. Even what's wrong is right in disguise. But to get to that point is a big number. You have to take up the spiritual life and get serious about it. Even with this many-splendored thing called love, there are different kinds.

The deepest love is finding your true Self. You can have a conscious will in your head but if you haven't got the will in your heart to change you're going to be miserable. That's the whole reason for pain; there isn't any other reason for suffering. And if you can understand the way your human consciousness works there is no suffering. Even suffering which you see and experience is not any big trip to enlightened minds because they see it as a teaching and so it is welcomed. Now you say, "That's a strange, weird trip to welcome pain and welcome suffering!" But a wise person learns that what is painful is not necessarily bad. It is really just the squeaky wheel that needs some oil. If there is any pain in any of our lives and we can look at it honestly and openly we will find that we are doing something inside that is not in tune with the cosmic plan. We learn to flow with the cosmic plan. That's the whole purpose of Creative Conflict. How can it save the world? How can it transform society? How can it have use everyday in our life? Can it change politics? How can it change the way we live and the quality of consciousness we put out in society which causes all the mess?

Human beings are a mess not because society's a mess. The mess out there is only a result of human beings not having their consciousness in tune. They are drugged by self-delusions even more powerful than dope. In fact it is these delusions that turn them onto dope, and they are equal to the delusion of the dope dealer who thinks money will make him happy while he helps others ruin themselves by supplying their destructive addictions.

So the origin of all peace begins with the individual. Nations are made of individuals. If individuals don't have peace at heart, if there is uncertainty and conflict in them, then there will be no peace in the nation. So the first prerequisite is for each individual to attain peace for himself. Then he will interact with others peacefully. Then the society will be a peaceful society. It will interact with other societies and there will be international peace when individuals have peace. You can't have peace by super-imposing it by military might or legislation or by trying to coerce people; it has to come from within. That's the whole object of Creative Conflict.

Allow people to be unique and have the right to see things through their filters and be different. Eventually through Creative Conflict you will come to see things as One. Eventually everyone is at the deepest truth together and everyone sees the same when they penetrate the heart. It's a lofty vision, but you don't have to go all the way, just as far as you want.

Question: I have a hard time knowing when I'm in my ego and when I'm not. How can I tell?

Answer: Most people can feel when their ego is resisting. They tend to make judgements in order to get their ego off the hook—or they rationalize all the time and think it's always "out there"—the problem's always with him and him and her—it's *their* fault and it's *their* ego at work. It's also a way out for the ego to say, "I don't really have to do it because I don't know how. Please forgive me for being such a dummy or a worm or whatever, because I really don't know any difference between an ego and a non-ego. I'm such a kid at this whole game and I'm really not going to be very successful at it, I'm afraid. It's going to be a very heavy trip for me," says the impenetrable ego. Sure, the ego's going to get a very heavy trip—it's going to have to look at itself—but if there's willingness to look at the ego it isn't a heavy trip. It's a joy to have your ego pointed out if it means you're growing. This is a mark of a truly advanced person. If you're doing something wrong and you really want to do something right and six people come up to you and say, "You're doing something wrong," you will feel better if you really want to do it right. You say, "Oh, thank you very much. I nearly would have done that wrong. Thank God you just saved me in the nick of time. I was just about to do it and I really want to do it right, so thank you for giving me that feedback." Another person comes up to you and gives you the same thing, then another person and another person, and you listen instead of having six ego shocks and going into depression, "No, no, no I don't want to listen. I'll put a thicker skin on myself so I can't feel a damn thing. No, no, don't tell me anything. I don't want to hear it. I've got my own tapes going on like crazy and I'm not going to hear anything."

That's how the ego makes it a heavy trip because it does not want to change, it does not want to listen, it does not want to take advice, it does not want to be pointed out as being in the wrong, it does not want to be told anything different from the way it is perceiving things. It is so arrogant in its own estimate of what's real that it refuses to hear anything from anyone else. You're fighting the universe when you're in your ego, and the universe will eventually destroy you. That's the way it gets rid of human beings who are not fit or up to scratch—it destroys them. The ego is its own worst enemy. It destroys by pain and disease. The origin of all disease is from the ego, because ultimately it's a sense of separation, a divorcing from the cosmic impulse, a misunderstanding and a misreading of the life forces and a usurping of God's power for oneself. That is ultimately what the ego is—it is running on a collision course with the universe, with the One, because it is separated. An ego is fighting the universe—that's why it's an ego. An ego is the self-regarding sentiment raised up to its highest potential, instead of the *universe-regarding sentiment* which is a projection of self into everything—meaning that whatever you're hearing from nature, from people or the environment or from your life style, is some kind of message.

One way you tell when you're in your ego is whether you're suffering from any feelings of separation from others, any frustrations with yourself or others. If you are the slightest bit disturbed about anything, then the ego is reigning, because the only thing that can be disturbed is the ego. If you're centered in God or in the One, every ripple on your consciousness is self-caused. If you can't handle a disturbance or something that is threatening or not pleasing or something that's not giving you peace, then it means that your ego is somehow out of touch with the cause, the totality which is our ultimate teacher. So it's very simple to know when you're out of touch. If you're angry you're out of touch with the situation.

Now there are certain kinds of anger or irritation or impatience or intolerance that can develop even in a selfless person in the sense that it's not selfish anger, because you've not been slighted. It may be anger at the world situation or the blindness or greed or certain attitudes of people which, by our being tolerant of them, only help to prolong a self-perpetuating situation where there's no change going on; so one has to become righteously angry in the same way that Christ was an angry person, which you can see if you read the Scriptures. From that point of view with that in mind you'll see there's a lot of anger in what he's saying. Even to his own disciples he was angry when they didn't understand. He more or less said, "Hey, look you guys, if you can't understand simple earthly things, what the hell am I wasting my time talking about heavenly things for?" He talked like this. "You bunch of country bumpkins—wake up man, this is big-time stuff I'm telling you and here you don't even understand small-time stuff. Wake up!" That's just translated into modern language but that's what he's saying word for word in the Bible. "You bunch of hypocrites standing around looking so holy with all these prayers you've said written on your shoulders and all your tassles and religious garments and offering sacrifices and making the house of the Lord into a den of thieves. You snakes and vipers. Hypocrites, the lot of you." That's not peaceful talk. He's making their egos squirm like hell inside them. He knew what he was doing. He knew they were going to hate his guts, didn't he? He was wise enough to know that if you start telling people where their egos are at, you're going to get some heavy feedback. They're going to start scheming to get rid of you. Because that's what the ego does once the ego is trapped or disturbed or insulted or whatever; instead of changing itself it says, "We've got to get rid of him."

So there is always a time for truth to marry with intolerance. There are limits to tolerance because if you're totally tolerant, then the world never changes and nobody grows. The universe itself is intolerant of certain things. It's ultimately intolerant of egos. The universe is one whole nucleus. It's one big thing and it's all interconnected and interdependent and there's nothing separate in it. Humans are not separate from the earth they live on. They live by the laws of the earth, by the laws of nature. Everything on the earth obeys the laws of nature. If humans don't obey the laws of nature they suffer. Eventually they finish up with pollution in the water they drink or fall-out coming from the skies or too many car exhausts that poison the cities, and so forth. We take our human laws from our own minds and our own perceptions but they're not natural laws. Many of the laws of man are utterly stupid because man doesn't understand the natural law of the planet. But even the planet has to obey heavenly laws. We take our laws and the laws of nature from the earth but the earth itself is part of a wider scheme, the solar system, and it has to obey those laws or it will suffer. If it gets too close to the sun it will burn, and even the sun has to take its laws from a wider galaxial rotation in which it's imprisoned in the grip of those natural laws. It cannot get off on its own ego trip and say, "Tomorrow I'm going to another place in the universe." It cannot do that. It's part of a totality, and so it is the same in the universal sense of our ego thinking it's IT—the one who is doing everything—saying MY life, MINE, whatever I've got. How can we say it's MY life? That's just an ego trip to say MY life. You had nothing to do with it. The ego had *nothing* to do with it. It didn't even know it was being born. You say, "MY body, me, mine, don't touch MY body, don't touch me, *mine.*" But it doesn't belong to you at all. What do you have to do with it? You don't even know how to run it. You didn't make it—you just got it. It's a gift. And it's not yours either. It can be taken away tomorrow. It's only loaned to you by nature like a friend lends you a car. You've got to look after it—feed it and keep it in running condition and return it hopefully in the same condition you got it. It's not *my* body; it belongs to the universe, it belongs to God, and the minute we think its mine-me-mine we're already on an ego trip. We had nothing to do with its incarnation nor can we control its passing away. Only if we're centered in the cosmos, the One, do we have any control or will over the important events of life, such as death. Only when the whole cosmos is working with us and behind us do we have any real power over the world, ourselves, the situation we're in. Anything else is just an ego thinking that it has such powers, and just look at what happens all around you in the world out there—the most surprising things that make all the best-laid plans of mice and men go astray.

So for you, personally, it's very easy to tell when your ego is in control. Your sense of separation from your husband is the first indication. Your sense of separation from your children. Do they really communicate with you, do they really tell you what is in their hearts, or are they afraid that you might be impatient with them? We also have a sense of separation from the group. These are just the immediate surroundings, small separations compared to the big, big separation where the ego is looking out at the universe and thinking it's all going on out there instead of in your consciousness. A good way to know whether your ego is in control is if you think that it's all going on out there. Then you know you've got an ego—a big one—because as long as you think that the events you experience are not happening in your conscious-ness—that they're somehow happening to you from out there—you're separated and you're living in uncertainty. You're living in a universe which is hazardous because you don't know what's going to happen tomorrow, nor do you know what's going to happen in the next five minutes. As long as you are in that state you are separate from the causation of the events which are in you. You could say, "Well, I couldn't help coming here. My husband came and I just tagged along. I'm here because of something quite out of my control." That's not true. You tagged along with him because of something in you that you wanted from him. So you've got to look at that. Why are you here if you didn't come of your own free will—if you're only here because your husband is here or wants to be, then there's some attachment there with him that you've got to look at. What is it you want? Is it ego confirmation? Is it security? What is it you expect to get that makes you follow him against your will? You haven't wanted to go to any of the places that he went to. List them off, one, two, three. You wanted to stay at home with your parents, and the first impression you had of any place you went to when you arrived was that you were depressed at the thought of being in this place. Why is it you don't have that thrill of expectation with new things? Do you know why you aren't content just being with the one you love without feeling that separation that you're in the wrong place? That's ego that's making that separation, ego that's making those distinctions. If you really love someone it doesn't matter where you are—you can be in a shack. It wouldn't matter whether you had all your furniture or drapes brought from England, why is that important? You know that can all be taken away overnight. There are people in Cambodia right now swarming to escape even with only their heads. They're leaving gold and houses and property. They're leaving everything behind just to get away with their lives. None of all that possessiveness is important and they feel lucky, grateful to get away to begin life again. What is important is, are you living a life which is peaceful inside? Painless, not frustrated? In other words, are you doing what you came to this earth to do? Because if you are, then you'll feel fulfilled doing God's work, and anyone doing God's work is fulfilled. If they're not being fulfilled, they're not doing God's work.

It's as simple as that. ABC. Logic. Anyone who is not doing God's work cannot be fulfilled. And it may be God's work for some people to first do a big ego trip. I don't know. It may be to first become the super ego so that everyone can see their ego. For every person the way is going to be something different—God's will, God's work. What is God's work? God's work is to get rid of the ego. It's very simple. And as long as we're not working on that we're not going to be happy. Because we won't feel much real growth. We'll feel stuck in a rut, stuck in our own perceptions, in our own conceit. We have ourself for a guru, we don't listen to anyone, and a man who has himself for a guru is a fool because it means you can't learn anything from anybody. It means you don't have the right attitude towards the teacher, and the teacher is life. So it's very simple to know when you're in your ego or not. And you can bet your bottom dollar it's most of the time, so you really don't have to worry about *when*. It's no big choice of yours. No need for you to have supreme powers of perception. It will be ego 99.99% of the time. So there's no need to worry about it—when you're in and when you're out. I hope this removed your difficulty.

Question: You were saying that the purpose of the group is to show you that side of yourself that you don't want to see. To do that they exaggerate that side and they don't talk about the positive things, just that one thing, and make it big enough for you to see it. If you have a person who is self-doubting or not on center during the Creative Conflict, he can hear that in a funny way and feel very depressed and do a long trip. Are there any safeguards against that happening or anything that we could build into the Creative Conflict so that you can spot that happening and make something else more positive happen?

Answer: I don't see that as necessarily a bad thing in growth—to be depressed or even to have a nervous breakdown. I think if we really understand a nervous breakdown it can be a blessing if we learn from it. Most psychiatrists will tell you the same thing, that people have so many insights about themselves and situations they're in during a nervous breakdown which they would never get in their normal state of consciousness. I agree that there should be some positive feedback at the same time, not all negative. And the whole object of Creative Conflict is for you to get the growth feelings, that you are able to see things about yourself that help you to feel positive. Now for you to be able to live with your own negative and feel right about it is important. You don't *have* to feel so perfect, everyone else is living with a whole load of manure too, as well as you, right?

This makes it a little easier but not much good to your self-image. But your self-worth grows from your certainty about the way your ego and mind works. People are vainly striving for ego food, recognition or praise, but self-worth does not work that way. Only humility works. Anything else is not worth anything, because if you get positive feedback and it just adds to your vanity and your self-concept is just mere conceit, then you'll be tripped by life even more by thinking you're somebody you're not. The emphasis of the negative in Creative Conflict *that is placed on where you're not seeing correctly* causes you to see correctly. And the only way it makes you feel depressed is if you're hanging on to your ego, proud and possessive about your opinions or your way of seeing, and refusing to see any worth in what other people are saying. Then you find it's only an attitudinal rigidity that makes you feel depressed. If your ego is very strong and you're hanging onto it and feel that you're really somebody special, it might make you depressed to find that other people don't feel you're that special. That in fact, you're rather arrogant. That can be disappointing, but I see that as very positive because it's humiliating. And what does humiliating mean? It means becoming humble. I think humility is a very rare quality, and even at the cost of being humiliated, I think if you can acquire humility which is such a rare thing, it's worth it. The Bible and many religions predict this ultimate humility of humanity through violent humiliation, but I believe it can come to man another way through Creative Conflict.

Another way of looking at it is that if you're a really humble person you can't be humiliated by anything. You're already as close to the ground as you can get. Isn't that the way of the cosmos? It lowers the mighty and raises the humble up? So all of the things that people look on as bad I look on as good. My world is totally upside down to ordinary people's. Everything that is up for them is down for me, everything that's down for them is up for me. So it makes life very interesting. What makes other people unhappy makes me glad. What people see as foolish I see as wisdom, what they see as clever I see as foolish.

Reverse everything, turn everything in the world upside down and you'll be enlightened. Human beings live upside-down, don't you know? They think they're separate from God and everything else. God's out there and they're in here. If they reversed it they'd be living in Truth. There isn't anything that's separate, that's just a mental trick we play on ourselves. How can we find this out? Only by having the mirrors come back to us with what we're really saying and thinking and feeling. It helps us to communicate with the world and with our environment and with others because the Creative Conflict process teaches us that as long as we have something going on in—between our ears that we think is so important, we become self-important and as long as we're self-important we're not communicating.

So the best thing is not to go on listening to knowledge *about* Creative Conflict but to go out and try it for yourself. Practice it all day and every day and once a week you come to the University of the Trees for a refresher class. It's something you can live by everyday. Having the courage to conflict with someone creatively, you'll find it enriches life and takes away fear. Not that you should go home and tell your husband what you think of him, because after twenty-five years he's gotten used to you hiding a lot. There are ways of doing things skillfully that you learn in Creative Conflict. You learn to say things you would normally never say to anyone, and have it received without rejection.

I also wanted to tell you what I feel is the ultimate vision that you can use Creative Conflict for, so that it's not just some little thing you come for once a week but something that can be totally transforming of your entire mind and soul. *It is refining your consciousness so that you will be able to be a light unto the world—where you'll actually transform the society and go out from here as leaders. Not as followers but as leaders where you will actually be masters of yourself.* If you want to take it to the ultimate, or as far as you wish to go, there are courses here at the University of the Trees that can turn you into a leader. Everyone who lives here will eventually be a leader. They don't know it yet, but I only welcome strong egos because they have to be that way to stand up to mine. The problems of today's world will not be resolved by renouncing them, or by traditional religious practices of avoiding them. They will only be solved through confronting them squarely in the strength of self-mastery. The people here come with strength and that strength will eventually make them want to be their own boss and form a center and do their own trip. And they'll do it out of the freedom of their own hearts. No coercion, only for the sake of their own self-fulfillment.

The greatest thing anyone can get is to be fulfilled. Ultimately Creative Conflict is the fastest method for fulfilling yourself.

PART II

8

CREATIVE CONFLICT
IN SOCIETY

Some people see the past twenty years as a series of social trends: first in the '50s it was breaking out of the old stereotypes and molds culminating in the activism of the '60s; then there was a retreat into discovering human potential and the introspective self-growth period of the '70s which embraced the flower children and the drug culture along with various cults and guru followers at one end and the transpersonal discoveries in psychology and physics at the other end. This introspective trend gave the '70s the label of the "me" generation of narcissistic people avoiding social service and social change. The "me" orientation in the new decade of the '80s is now supposedly changing away from introspection toward a felt need to express socially. Some even say that all the interest in meditation in the '70s was a passing fad. Hopefully, though, the pendulum swing to social consciousness now beginning in the early '80s is actually a higher turn of the spiral—to a spiritual activism that can be the leading edge of human consciousness in the '80s.

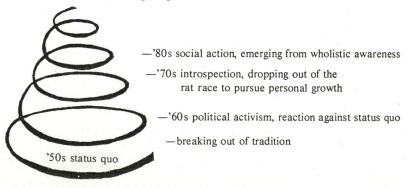

—'80s social action, emerging from wholistic awareness

—'70s introspection, dropping out of the
  rat race to pursue personal growth

—'60s political activism, reaction against status quo

—breaking out of tradition

'50s status quo

Creative Conflict is a form of social activism at the spiritual level. The potential of the new trend of the '80s towards spiritual action is actually a synthesis of the best of the introspective period of wholistic thought and the best of social activism. It is the dynamic hope of mankind's future! Spiritual action can no longer be reserved for churches, fund-raising or even do-gooder projects to feed the hungry. It is concerned with causes, not the effects. Spiritual activism is cross-cultural and multi-religious, and its supreme goal is to resolve conflict.

But realistically, there is a tremendous amount of conflict in all aspects of society today. Not that conflict hasn't been with us throughout history, but the alternating periods of relative peace and conflict are again entering a new cycle—this time on a global scale. The vision of potential in the decade of the '80s begins with a grey aura of general pessimism about the future in contrast with the bright optimism that has been with us in previous years. A few people have foreseen the limitations of the material, technological age and have for a long time glimpsed coming events of intense conflict, but as this bleak future approaches, the vision becomes less abstract as it crystallizes into a more concrete here and now reality. The lives of everyone will be touched on many levels. It is one thing to foresee the coming conflicts as they are *out there,* in the imagination, like a distant war or famine being brought to you on television, and it is quite another thing to experience the world's conflicts affecting your own life drastically as they concretize into your everyday reality in your physical environment. We all share in the world psyche and whether we know it or not now, by the end of this decade that fact will be brought home.

The decade of the '80s will reveal much about our ability as a society to evolve consciously to a higher global awareness. There will be much suffering. Few will escape unscathed. All will be touched in some way, yet those with clarity in the heart will remain centered. The challenge will be to not get pulled off center by the untold misery and suffering of those around. As the heart expands, so does compassion, but as we discover in Creative Conflict, compassion is not negative identification with others. You may be already emotionally secure in your family life, but not financially secure. You may have invested all your finances in gold or some stable store of value upon which you feel you can depend. But if your home is near an atomic plant where radioactivity is released or if there is an earthquake under your feet, then where will your security be?

Whether your attachment and investment are physical, social, intellectual, financial, familial, religious or spiritual, you are vulnerable to suffering in the unpredictable times ahead. The only real security is in developing spiritual fiber—placing your strength in the cosmic intelligence and tuning yourself to its vibration. It is not sufficient to study intellectually about the intelligence in nature; only by directly experiencing it can you attain spiritual security. With spiritual security, suffering is minimized and you gain the understanding of what to do to maximize your security on all the other levels of consciousness as well—from the financial to the physical. With spiritual security if doesn't matter if the body dies or not, although you will make every effort to live and do your best to reach ultimate fulfillment.

You may think that you would never be able to get to such a state of mind, that this kind of thinking is for saints or crazies. This is because you have not yet experienced the joy that springs from subtle places in your consciousness when you live by cosmic laws, and you have not yet tasted that deep feeling of total security that actually does dwarf and minimize the importance of physical life in the body. Once you start to walk in tune with the cosmos, your security and survival is rooted in the higher will of the cosmos and the universal love which flowers within your soul. Behind all the acts of fate and destiny are the universal laws of cause and effect. By tuning to the dynamic of Creative Conflict we tune to the consciousness behind natural laws, and in that state we become spiritually free.

The opportunity before each of us is to do the work *now* that will give us the evolution and the understanding we will need to protect us from suffering caused by human ignorance and wrong action. What is right or wrong action? Only you can determine right or wrong in yourself. No one can tell it to you. Wise men and women have given humanity the laws of righteousness for all ages, but the world mess continues no less now. Creative Conflict is not Sunday School lessons, but the realization within yourself of what the cosmic laws of righteousness are. In every aspect of society, in your work, in the home, in school and in politics, you have the opportunity and the necessity to realize and apply these natural laws of success, not only by following religious commandments which were handed down from on high that you may have read in a book or learned from teachers or parents, but through discovering in and for yourself what kind of behavior brings you fulfillment and success and what brings you pain, misery and failure. You tune to truth, direct. The discovery of righteous living in all aspects of daily life happens quickly with Creative Conflict, because Creative Conflict speeds up the cause-effect rhythm of life so that *you become aware of the effects and consequences your words and actions are going to create before you even cause them.*

The call to discover what the immutable cosmic laws of consciousness are is the call of Creative Conflict. By not making an effort to put ourselves in harmony with natural law, we have failed to conquer the present global suffering, and we are on the threshold of disaster. What can save us from human chaos? All the present answers available to mankind have failed us and we have failed them. What must come now is a social and spiritual activism which transcends politics and doctrine, surpasses ideology and idealisms. There is little democracy left in the world today. Most countries are controlled by ruthless power cliques. And even in the democracies there is no vision to unify society, no goal to strive for, that captures the spirit and the hearts of the masses. The revival of Islamic fervor in Iran, where formerly a despot ruled, is a desperate attempt to rekindle some spirit and vision. But going back to the belief systems of the ancient past does not serve the evolving spirit. Despair and unrest are the inevitable consequences when the vision for the future is nil. The creative nature of the human spirit must eventually come forth to fill this void or die.

Creative Conflict enables us to discover the vision for the new transcendent society, not by setting up a new set of rules that everyone must abide by, but by providing each person with a vehicle to discover for themselves that the furthering of human evolution on all levels of consciousness is what will bring fulfillment. This vehicle of self-government and self-mastery is worth striving for in groups but this furthering of social action can only be achieved by spiritual attunement on the part of every individual. Through direct investigation and realization of the cosmic laws to pattern our human laws after, we involve everyone in responsible self-government, and only in this manner will we come to our next leap in evolution. If only a small percent of humanity can make this conscious evolutionary transition to begin with, the process will spread when others see that it works!

The teachings of the great spritual teachers of the past are eternal truths that live on; only the forms change. Christ said he came not to change the old law but to fulfill it. He did change many of the forms which were the mores of his time in order to allow a freer expression of spiritual truth by flaunting the thousands of restrictive codes of living which the rabbis had imposed. Christ was constantly accusing them of laying a great burden on the people. He was criticized as immoral by traditionalists, but we now know that he cracked the nut of tradition to show people the life in the seed, the kernel of love which they could water and grow; yet so many were attached to the shell. Christ had a new message of the Kingdom of Heaven which few could listen to, and he admonished that you cannot put new wine into old wineskins. New wine is still fermenting and expands as it matures, and the old forms are not able to expand with it. They have served their purpose. Similarly the new message for this day is a message of conscious evolution, spiritual growth and cosmic consciousness which cannot be put in the old wineskins of our outmoded forms of social living. We have to realize the spirit anew within, the new vision, and then new forms of social organization will evolve naturally and spontaneously around our realization. Can we bring to birth living forms, not forms which are rigidly established and therefore destined to one day collapse, but natural forms which can be modified or shed as we grow—forms which we change to fit the spirit? By being so attuned to the cosmic will that it eternally evolves us according to its universal design and intelligence, we can discover the new cosmic program for humanity which some have glimpsed. Then our human laws and constitutions can become a living body, housing the spirit of humanity as one entity. And then human beings can see the one spirit in each other, reflections of the divine creative force which brought us all to this planet. Without this spiritual vision or sense of a greater destiny to which we can aspire, the human species is doomed to extinction.

Let us work towards the vision of union with steady, clear hearts that we who do Creative Conflict and get in touch with the laws of consciousness may emerge as the stable force and the new leaders in the years to come, as humanity learns from collective suffering the real purpose of conflict.

So what are the new social forms that Creative Conflict can now take? And what new social actions might we be able to glimpse arising from Creative Conflict? Let us look at how we can bring Creative Conflict into business, into the schools, into the family and into politics. Let us see how we may practically merge the inner, introspective life with the outer, social or collective life.

What follows can only represent the bones which have been constructed during years of trial and error, years of interpreting nature's ways of resolving conflict. The flesh can only be added to these methods by our own creativity, by feeding our ability to adapt, modify and experiment in a living ,dynamic situation of real grappling with our conflicts. The method itself is not fixed, but a living, evolving, organic system of growth techniques. You are as vitally involved in their evolution and survival as we are. Creative Conflict cannot be designed for passive listeners or readers, but it is the best thing for such passive people to do to shake themselves free of their spiritual apathy. Spiritual poverty and apathy are closely related symptoms of a deeper cause. The vision of a new unifying form of human relationships, where truth and openness replace fear and deception in social intercourse, will proceed directly out of the practice of Creative Conflict.

9

CREATIVE CONFLICT
IN BUSINESS

(Some of the following material has been excerpted from *The Golden Egg,* by Christopher Hills, University of the Trees Press, 1979)

National polls taken over the past decade show ever-increasing job dissatisfaction among Americans, regardless of whether they are low income, middle income or upper class. Why is this? And what brings satisfaction in a job? In order for people to look forward to working, there has to be a feeling of motivation to achieve a goal that feels worthwhile. And there has to be a feeling that you are being challenged in some way that brings out more of your potential. This challenge has to be within your capacity in order to give a feeling of growth and progress. In mechanical or chore jobs which require little skill or creative thought, relationships between employees supply a large part of the job satisfaction. However large or small a business, if employee relationships are sour or if the employees have the feeling of being worthless cogs in a huge machine or mere automatons, then morale erodes, tensions build and dissatisfaction and frustration slowly kill the spirit of the people. Job efficiency drops and so does business productivity. In most communist and eastern socialist countries, where the sense of purpose is low and the feeling of being a cog in the wheel permeates the work force, job productivity is far below that of the western countries. In the People's Republic of China, where the people are optimistic about more material success and more intellectual opportunities, productivity is rising. In the West millions of wage-earners have grown placid in a life-style of rote work and coming home to hours of television viewing.

Creative Conflict is designed to turn around this whole dismaying trend and to penetrate the cause of the despair in order to provide fulfillment in work life. It brings worker enthusiasm, motivation and increased productivity and creativity. The positive results of Creative Conflict for business are dynamic because they offer solid evidence that creative resolution of conflict can bring a spiritual revolution to business. Large corporations today spend considerable sums on bringing in facilitators to increase communication and job satisfaction simply because of the huge expense of having a great attrition rate in trained employees. Regimented jobs, such as those in banks, suffer as high as thirty percent turn-around in employees because there is no growth or feeling of accomplishment in the lives of the people. Owning the business will not make this work experience any different if there is not a conscious awareness by the management to turn the whole operation into a dynamic opportunity for individual growth and satisfaction so that work and the job itself becomes the means of developing meaningful relationships as well as providing economic support.

Routine jobs have to be done. But they can become fulfilling if we can feel we have a share in the decision-making process and if we can feel a sense of responsibility for the whole which comes as we build deep friendships with our co-workers. To become an owner of a business by buying shares or being offered company shares as a bonus will not take the place of feeling part of the decision-making process which gives you the feeling that the business is yours. Even being a partner in a business can still be misery as we can see from the many legal partnerships which are dissolved through the partners being at loggerheads and unable to resolve their conflicts. The fact is that in the majority of work environments, hidden or open conflicts between people abound, sapping creativity and inhibiting the potential for work to be an emotionally rewarding experience. Family-owned businesses have the highest job satisfaction because everyone feels responsible and because communication is deeper between the people involved. When people commit themselves to creatively solving their conflict and to deepening their relationships with all company members from the president to the janitor, then the business becomes like a family business and all the ingredients for rewarding work life can be present. Work then becomes love made manifest.

HOW TO MAKE CREATIVE CONFLICT PAY

A good example of how Creative Conflict works in business is an incident that arose in our fulfillment and mailing department at the University of the Trees Press. We had been losing money and time in shipping out to customers. The man in charge of that operation could not organize the department or handle the job adequately, so he stepped down. The man who had been his back-up was the logical choice to replace him. Several members of the company held a meeting to ask this man if he would accept the job. His reply was practical and a little cautious, "I will do it on one condition—that we get some new equipment." Everyone at the meeting was relieved to have the job filled, because there was no one else to do it, and they felt he would have the operation running smoothly in no time. In most companies the matter would have ended right there. But with Creative Conflict as part of your life you do not decide business matters at the matter-of-fact level only, but include anything your deeper feelings and intuition pick up on. So one member spoke up, "I have to say that there is something a little funny in your attitude. What are you really feeling about this move?" Because the man did not fear for his job security he was able to share his deeper feelings with a little more inquiry.

It turned out that this man who had been asked to accept the job as head of mailing really felt that mailing and packing books was beneath his talents. He wanted to hire an outside firm to handle the book packing and other mailing duties so that he could be part of the more glamorous team in marketing. No one denied the fact that his mental abilities did qualify him for a more challenging job, but each member pointed out that our work here is not as separate individuals but as a team, and at this moment the need of the whole was to get the mailing department streamlined because it was the weak link in the business and he was the one most suited to the job. He would be free to go on to more challenging work once he put the mailing department in order so that someone less gifted and capable than he could take it over and run it efficiently. His response was to feel that perhaps this really was not the need of the whole, and he clearly had some fear of surrendering to the viewpoint of the others who knew it was; he placed his trust only in his own view, yet could not offer any other practical alternatives. This led the discussion deeper still, into the whole question of trust and the way his ego separates from others and how some others felt that he didn't care about them. It revealed the way his ego splits his perception of the whole in many of his personal relationships too.

Deliberately developing methods of expressing feelings to make unspoken conflict creative within the company structures has succeeded in creating a more fulfilling atmosphere, a more meaningful reason for working together, not only here at the University of the Trees Press, but in other businesses as well. Emotional encounters in business are frequent and usually negative and then quickly repressed, whereas they can be made growth-producing and positive.

Roche Chemical Corporation, a Swiss company with a large American affiliate, began to use some of the Creative Conflict methods in the formation of small groups within the company, using a facilitator rather than a leader, letting the Creative Conflict methods determine the leader or the authority. Small groups of people from different departments were brought together to share their frustrations, and the company encouraged them to criticize their higher-ups without fear of being ostracized, because certain members of the managerial staff believed that to know of these undercurrents would enable management to better deal with them. Using such techniques as the "love seat" (see page 293) as well as the basic mirroring, the facilitators were able to bring much better communication between departments, which resulted in more efficiency. However, as some people began to thrive with the opportunity, other people entrenched in authority felt very threatened and discontinued the sessions abruptly. If, however, the whole idea had been made company policy instead of being regarded as an experimental fringe activity initiated by a few, then everyone would have been required to look into the dark places of their own character and performance. High-level communication within the company structure and the greater efficiency that goes with it would have developed. There is always a risk in exploring deep patterns for some people who can only relate as egos. Yet we must form companies or groups within companies, with those who do want honesty, integrity and real communication in order to make an evolutionary work environment really work.

In normal business, people are continually self-conscious— watching their egos or watching the reactions of others, especially their superiors, and they are afraid of expressing themselves in case they should receive some sort of put-down. Creative Conflict eliminates put-downs and rids the participants of these typical deep-rooted fears so they can be themselves, although the time required varies from individual to individual depending on their sense of inner security, their previous background, etc.

Most work relationships occur on very superficial levels, and thus the real depths of being where the creativity lies are never released. In the normal business world today there are no means available for making conflict creative, for evolving integrity in words and actions, and so we have the present world mess. If you worked in a local factory or computer firm and you were to tell a co-worker how you felt about him in what he might call a negative vein, you'd lose a friend, even though you meant it to be constructive criticism. As you have to work with him daily, you can't risk that bad feeling between you, so you say nothing. And if you were to tell your boss or any of the people up the hierarchy what you thought, you might be fired, because people automatically fear this kind of direct feedback. In business one quickly learns what one can say and to whom. The pecking order is soon established. Only when you are president of the company can you afford to go around and level constructive criticism at people. Everyone else is pleasant and cautious, climbing his or her way up the company ladder. This conservative, two-faced vibration permeates the entire atmosphere of most companies. You can hear it in the interactions, the gossip and other conversations, and even in the vibrations of people who are silently working. Employees with resentments against the boss will mumble them to the safest person they can find. An old hand will say to an eager newcomer, "Don't work so fast; if you finish these forms before the due date, you might get laid off." The newcomer's heart sinks, because the only interesting part of the job was trying to be more efficient.

Conventions are set up as a substitute, and it is the same with working relationships in business as in politics, where human feelings are put aside in order to get the job done, and consequently the business loses its soul. Some practical-minded businessmen and women will ask the very obvious question, "How do we keep from going to the opposite extreme, where we communicate so much and have so many meetings that business becomes inefficient?" To initiate time-consuming dialogue is not the purpose of Creative Conflict. The real purpose is to provide space to probe into our unconscious reactions and see whether we're looking at others or at our own situation blindly, and to foster deep integrity in communications. Most people are totally convinced that the reality they know is the only reality there is, and this false perception is what causes most of the inefficient operations and problems in business. Sometimes to clear up one five-minute goof that Creative Conflict could have prevented takes many hundreds of hours of other people's work time. Lack of care and lack of precision in communicating correct information and repeating messages with accuracy comprise much of man's production difficulty in addition to the expense of it. Confused communication causes the perpetuation of most social problems. Yet efficient communication skills are not taught in business schools.

Creative Conflict sessions in business cannot completely succeed if those in positions of management insist on maintaining an authoritarian hold that refuses to take feedback. Neither can they succeed if one's frustrations are allowed to turn into personal spite or one-upmanship by pointing the finger of blame at others before we have pointed it at ourself. Usually in a business the strong people run over the weak and the weak resent them but say nothing. With a whole group of people to arbitrate and with the impartial rules of Creative Conflict, the shy person has a chance to speak. One bashful person in our business, given the opportunity to talk back to someone who had confronted her heavily, told him that he did not investigate the facts but always castigated her. After mirroring, he responded by explaining that for several months he had tried to gently point things out to her that were wrong but she would not hear, and that even though she might in fact know what was happening in her department, she would communicate it either too quietly or not at all, and no one would know that a matter was urgent. Thus the conflict between them was taken to its deeper cause—her own reticence and timidity. She felt better for having been able to speak her feelings, even though she had to look at the fact that she had brought the confrontation on herself by frustrating others. Her communication is very clear now when she makes a presentation to the group and the memory of the past Creative Conflict is a goad for her to remind her to speak out.

The same man she confronted has also been confronted many times for being too hard on people and for forgetting his own mistakes when he is confronting others for theirs. One of his mistakes is a habit of unconsciously manipulating other people. At one time a situation arose when he wanted to move out of the manufacturing department but didn't want to lose control, nor did he fully trust the man he turned the operation over to, so he hovered over him and meddled and tried to boss him around. This stifled the new man's creativity and made him angry. The new man brought it to the Creative Conflict group and confronted his "boss". "You say, 'Here, go to it, the department is your baby,' and then you turn around and snatch it away and interfere." The group, which included the whole crew, encouraged the new man to take full responsibility and commit himself to the job, and persuaded the old foreman to surrender his control over a project he really hadn't been able to totally organize and to give the new man a chance at it. The added responsibility cost the new man some of his free time, which he valued highly, and cost the old foreman some pride in his personal image. But the whole community evolved as a result of this decision because the old foreman went into the sales department and did a beautiful job, while the new man, when left on his own, totally revamped the whole manufacturing department with an efficient flow it never had before.

In the examples just mentioned, the whole group served as an impartial arbiter so that each person could be heard, and they could see their own faults as clearly as they saw the other person's. One of the greatest skills that comes from practice of Creative Conflict methods is the ability to communicate unpleasant perceptions and difficult feelings without anger or malice or an accusatory tone. The mirroring technique dissolves the separating feelings between people and creates a feeling of trust where individuals can be confronted with facts or embarrassing questions without reacting. Then they can safely probe their own unconscious world and see a mirror of their inner life in the company environment and in their relations to other people. In quick communications, many people do not mean what they say and are always horrified at how they actually come across when the group mirrors their statements back to them. Once these actions and words are challenged and mirrored, people can get in touch with the deeper, underlying causes, as in the next example.

Excerpt of a Creative Conflict session in a business:

Greg: I'm feeling bored and unfulfilled. I hold back from stepping forward and taking charge like Richard had done in book production.

Wendy: Are you jealous of Richard?

Greg: Yes.

Diane: What do you think about during your workday?

Greg: About how I'm always left out. Roger was talking to Jack about something new and exciting in the business but he didn't share with me. I'm in the financial department too, and I was only a few feet away. Aren't I important? I feel like I'm the hired hand who's supposed to just do posting.

Richard: There's a creative aspect to posting. It's a link to seeing where and who our business is. You could get an overview and come up with some ideas of your own.

Jack: You know, when I do share with you, you usually respond in some negative way instead of responding with excitement or creativity.

Greg: (Greg is asked to mirror and does so but does not comment)

May: Your mother is quite similar, Greg. When we stayed at her house during the business trip she negated everything you or anyone said. (trying to probe deeper) Greg, you seem to be so sluggish with so much inertia it doesn't give anyone the feeling of wanting to share with you. You would dampen the enthusiasm like a wet blanket.

Greg: (mirrors) I go around with pent up feelings and I feel frustrated that I'm so blocked.

Michael: Do you have any feelings towards anyone here now?

Greg: I'm judging you all for going on with me in this meeting when we're not getting anywhere. I'm reacting to May for being "out to get me". It bugs me . . . (silence) . . . I just flashed that it's like my brother sitting in front of the TV. He gets real irritable if I ask him questions. He just wants to be left alone. I too, just want May to let me be.

May: (mirrors) So you can just read the sports page all the time and ignore everyone else. *(Greg's fetish is the sports page.)*

Greg: I guess it's vicarious excitement. I know I need to generate more excitement in my own life.

Richard: You know if you watched your negative thoughts and put in a counter effort, even a slight one, to turn them positive, you'd feel a lot more energy and you could get your own creativity going.

Greg: Well, I'll start by going on a fast from the sports page. I won't read it. Maybe that will give me more energy to get myself turned on.

Sue: How do you feel about Jack?

Greg: I feel he doesn't care about what I do or how much work I have.

Jack: I was challenged in the last meeting on shuffling work off on Greg. What we got to was my executive attitude. I didn't know Greg was overloaded. He doesn't communicate.

Greg: It brought out my resentment to Jack which I wasn't in touch with. I also contributed by not communicating because of pride.

Sue: Does Jack sit at his desk doling out jobs?

Greg: He does with both me and Nancy. He doesn't see his role as doing any drudge work—only mine. He thinks of me as a naive, enthusiastic boy, an employee. Yet he rarely looks over my shoulder to even check what I am doing.

Jack: (mirrors, then responds) Greg, do you feel I'm in my imagination, spaced out a lot?

Greg: Yes. You're not here with me who's doing the heavy paperwork.

Wendy: That's Jack's same pattern at home of not doing the dishes. Jack says, "Not important."

Jack: Yes, that's true.

Sue: Greg, I'm not satisfied. You've been so peeved. Is there more resentment left?

Greg: I get angry when Jack resists the feedback. (To Jack) You took advantage of my initial enthusiasm and just kept letting me do all the drudge work, and we're supposed to work together.

Jack: I can see it in my vibe, in the attitude, but I can't see it in the daily work level, the drudge level.

Greg: I chase the accounts all day. Not one hour is free to do the creative work I see you doing. And we're supposed to be a team! You get exciting work to do. I don't see you doing drudge work, frankly.

Jack: I do feel there is something definitely fishy in my attitude.

Carl: (The company president) It's the same thing I've been trying to point out to you, Jack, isn't it? Self-importance. Like stashing the $4,000 in the drawer. Keeping checks in the drawer and not depositing them until days later, even though you knew you were supposed to deposit daily. You were supposed to also come to me with a daily plan or schedule. But nothing has happened. You do such good work in other areas, but you like to hang on to the control.

Jack: (mirrors) I can see my ego in this. I want to do it all myself, wheel and deal, be in charge. (To Greg) It would help me if you would tell me what I don't know about your job.

Greg: Someone could owe us and you wouldn't know. I could be posting all wrong all this time. Since you trained me you have never double-checked me. You think you know the accounts but you don't. You don't know some of the stores aren't paying.

Jack: It seems like I check.

Richard: Greg is saying, "Hey Jack, you made me feel crummy by treating my job as unimportant." This is what Greg is really feeling, really trying to say.

Jack: I can buy that. I don't want to do that anymore. I know it's a drag.

Wendy: There is some self-image we need to get to in Jack because he's missing business meetings too.

Jack: It's being the big shot. I see I've been separating from everyone, being super-cool.

Richard: I feel you are repressing something.

Carl: What keeps you from communicating what you are doing to me, and getting yourself double-checked too? You never come to me. I always have to run after you to find out what you're doing. Is it pride? I feel you are hogging information from me. You need to communicate more what's going on, take the initiative more and everyone will feel a lot better.

Jack: (mirrors) I guess it is my pride. I feel I'm the one doing it all. I can see how it trips me up.

Carl: We had a plan for communicating. Can we get it going again?

Jack: I'll start tomorrow.

Lying beneath all business problems and economic success or failure are these deeper, more real, more frustrating but unspoken problems of *people*. If these problems are not communicated, disaster can result. Creative Conflict begins to tackle the evolutionary tasks facing each individual by dealing first with the deep *inner motivations* of people. Anything else is cosmetic face-lifting and does nothing to the person inside. When we solve the people problem, we will have solved our economic problem. The social answer to the people problem is to study the "match" between people and fulfilling work, and determine the balance of interests between people and self-government systems. Whether that work and self-government is at the level of the company, church, school, national group, or community, the answer to fulfillment is the same, i.e., small groups working in social experiments which give first-hand decision-making powers back to those who do the work, or those who are the members of the churches, or the parents in the schools, and back to those who are the real owners of the government public services. Small groups are always the training ground for self-reliance and self-responsibility and large groups are always the hot-bed which germinates egotism, self-aggrandizement and the irresponsibility of playing to the gallery. Dynamic small groups must assume the task of training themselves, then re-educate larger groups until the whole mass of society is restructured on the basis of self-government, self-knowledge.

When special privileges are claimed either physically or mentally they should only be granted with the will and unanimous loving consent of the entire group. In business, a common promotion system is instituted throughout the enterprise so that staff may work freely and flexibly with the shop floor and not alienate those workers who have menial jobs by creating job distinctions which prevent collaboration. The working arrangements between members of a group are open for discussion so that members do not build resentments against each other, and differences and disagreements are talked through. Members of these workgroups should include a cross section of people with various levels of skills. In other words, management, owners and workers, from the president to the janitor, should be intermixed in the Creative Conflict groups. Specialized groups based on common interests can also spontaneously form to decide departmental matters or other common issues.

In the practice of Creative Conflict we do not confront as a superior talking to an inferior but as equals, even though our tasks and capabilities are not equal, and some carry much more responsibility than others. At the University of the Trees Press, the workers in the facilities department do manual labor, but their feelings and perceptions are just as important as those of the people in marketing or as important as those of the president. Creative Conflict dissolves the destructiveness of hierarchy in the commonality of people's beings. A natural leadership emerges through merit. No one person lays down the law. Rather, there are certain standards which all commit themselves to, so when we fall short of our own commitment we expect to be confronted on it. If anyone decides they do not want to live with Truth, they are free to leave and find work with another kind of truth elsewhere. This creates a very different work dynamic than you would find in most businesses. Contrast this kind of work life with the following description written by a member of our group who experienced this:

"This fellow Paul was a thin, wiry construction worker who worked on the commercial jobs. He was a very agreeable fellow in the morning but as the job would proceed during the day he would 'foam at the mouth'. He would get so excited sometimes in the din of the concrete trucks and the frustration of steel poking in his ribs, trying to form columns thirty feet high at the same time hanging off a safety belt, that he would become obnoxious. This had a grating effect on some of the other men, but because one really couldn't say anything without fear that such friction might cost you your job, we all chose to remain quiet.

But as the days wore on and the same old job of buttoning up columns for the concrete truck to pour kept repeating, tempers grew short. The pace was often gruelling and one had to constantly be on the move or expect to see the foreman with a check in his hand saying, 'Well, it's been nice knowing you.' The thin wiry carpenter seemed to get frantic at times trying to get his part of the work done and he became so pushy and foul-mouthed that at last one of the men exploded! 'Don't you call me a son-of-a-bitch, you son-of-a-bitch.' 'I'll call you what I want,' roared back the aggressor disdainfully. The other man was beside himself with helpless rage. He would have called the fellow every name in the book but what he really wanted to say was inexpressible. . . Inside himself he probably wanted to let the man know that he was a human being with feelings too, and that to be ordered around like a dog on a leash hurt him and made him feel outrageously angry. The supervisor soon walked up, fortunately perhaps for the squared-off carpenters.

'Cool it,' he ordered. 'Get back to work. Paul, you go over and give Manny a hand lifting those braces onto the forklift. Joe, you come with me and get a load of stakes for that retainer wall down by the shed.' Joe said, 'Just tell that guy not to call me names like that or

I'm going to bust him.' 'You bust anyone, son, and you'll be bustin' paydirt somewhere else,' said the supervisor firmly. He spun on his heel and that was the end of the conversation. But for years afterwards, whenever Joe saw Paul, he steered a clear path. Paul was not a bad person. No one knew what was happening in his family and no one knew if he had financial problems. All they knew was that he was there in the morning first before everyone else and that he was one of the first in his truck to go at the end of the day. And as for Joe? Who knew his feelings? Weeks later at a union sign-up of laborers, a little Chicano came up to Joe in the line and said, 'Hey Amigo, I remember you. You are the one who almost stomped Paul that day, eh, remember, eh, eh? Ha, ha, I remember, I thought you were really going to get him, eh? He was really nasty, that guy Paul, eh?' "

Creative Conflict could have exposed the real causes inside both these men who were ready to fight each other. Instead, they only related to each other superficially.

Of course, not every business can commit itself to Creative Conflict one hundred percent right away. People have to have time to get used to it and want it. The president or manager should begin by starting a program where small groups of employees would hold special Creative Conflict meetings so that each could share what he or she likes best in his work life and what most bothers him. Ideally this sharing happens with everyone in the business doing it together. Otherwise there will be no feeling of wholeness, no feeling that it has reality, that one can actually be open about one's feelings, be they right or wrong, and that one's deeper being can be shared. Creative Conflict would probably seem utterly strange and foreign to those long used to communicating in the way Paul and Joe did. It has to be gradually introduced to most businesses through time set aside in a quiet place for sessions specifically designed for integrating Creative Conflict methods into the day-to-day communication. When the methods are adhered to strictly, progress is assured. If your management in your company is unaware or wary of Creative Conflict, start with a few of your co-workers on off hours, or if possible, get your manager to agree to an experiment for a month of one hour per week of company time. Have everyone in the group report to him on the effects, and if possible, invite him to join a session.

By practicing Creative Conflict in small group sessions for one or two hours once or twice a week, the rules and process quickly become integrated into the working environment. The few hours spent in doing Creative Conflict each week will add years to the effectiveness of the business in terms of increased worker dedication to the company and the benefits that come from giving each other feedback on job manifestation. Much of the polarization between union and management disappears and much of the motivation for disputes dissolves as communication between all company members deepens. Using Creative Conflict, for instance, between union leaders who are striking for more money in a company which cannot pay higher wages without raising prices or losing customers, one can avoid the usual facing-off between sides in a battle array, where one side insists that it doesn't care about the view of the other. Many of the statements which pass between such opposing camps are not even completely heard by either side. Only when they agree to mirror each other's points until the other is satisfied that he has really been heard can real communication be assured. Union action, instead of bringing *union*, is so often destructively divisive. I am including here a first-hand perspective of a local carpenter's union, narrated to me by a union journeyman carpenter.

"Each Monday morning at 7:30 the carpenters out of work begin filing in through the door of the local labor temple to sign up for work and get the stamp on their unemployment cards so that they can get their money from the state unemployment insurance fund. But on one particular morning there was much more activity than usual. John, a journeyman carpenter, was busy handing out 'Vote for Chuck' leaflets, and Chuck himself was busily accosting every member he could get his hands on to come vote for him to be business agent tomorrow at the big election at Local #829. 'Don't vote for that new guy Tom,' he exclaimed. 'He's controlled by the other district. You don't want your union run by outsiders do you?' he asked forcefully. 'Tom is saying stuff about me that the outsiders are trying to use so that they can get control. They're saying I've been overpaid and I've offered to pay back anything at all that is improper and they can't even tell me how much it is!'

Tom, his opponent, was busy inside collecting dues. He was the acting financial secretary and he wanted Chuck's business agent job as well. He felt Chuck was not being honest about the union business. While Chuck was talking outside Tom was telling everyone inside, 'We know he's been overpaid and we're very close to finding out just how much he got . . . ' and so on. The sad thing about this is that hostile feelings, polarizations, factionalisms, split memberships, and divided leaderships were aroused in our union. Here, two members of the same labor camp were becoming embroiled in a struggle for power for union leadership in such a way that an aura of mutual antagonism was created for all the members, thereby separating us into two opposing camps which by their very nature were noncreative in the conflict. That is, in order for truth to emerge, one truth had to conquer the other, and what was left, by majority vote, thus became the truth. Or, as we nowadays say in the democratic process, 'the lesser of two evils'."

Had Creative Conflict been used in the dispute, the local union would have been able to resolve the conflict so that the points Tom had on the work Chuck was doing could have been made available without necessarily having to stoop to the mud-slinging that was a basic undercurrent of their interactions. And perhaps Tom could have heard Chuck's concern about preserving local control if there had been a system of conflict resolution that not only allowed for feelings to be expressed as well as facts, but which also had as its basic structure the idea that *conflict is not bad but healthy when it produces a synthesis of view through diversity of thought.* This synthesis of opposing views goes way beyond a debate and is the creativity that emerges from Creative Conflict when people listen and respond to each other's beings and not just to their words.

In the Creative Conflict sessions for business we focus only on communication problems that are directly related to work life. Upon probing we may discover that the business problems are rooted in family or deeply personal conflicts with our own egos. By setting a time limit on the Creative Conflict sessions to deal only with ego patterns affecting our work and by arranging time after work hours for one or two company members to follow up in the Creative Conflict sessions with more personal problems, there is no waste of company time. You cannot really separate many work problems from personal problems, but neither can you turn the business into long therapy sessions and still expect to meet dead-lines. The group will have to maintain the balance between the personal needs and the business needs and discriminate through the practice of Creative Conflict what is the priority for the good of the whole.

The same rules apply for Creative Conflict in business as in any other Creative Conflict group; just the focus is different. The environment must always be included in the context of the Creative Conflict. In the school the Creative Conflicts would be slanted toward the learning process, in the home toward family living and personal growth, and in the general Creative Conflict group toward group consciousness which would draw examples from all our daily living environments. During the business Creative Conflict process the different levels of consciousness are evoked and brought to bear on business matters. Eventually the Creative Conflict involves everyone in company policy-making and responsibility for decisions. More planning from workers is initiated and is synthesized with the vision and planning of management. As their strengths come forth from each individual, job positions naturally change so that the person is placed in the job he or she can do best. This transformation happens naturally as hidden resources are tapped and as communication and integrity grow.

Without awareness of differences in the levels of consciousness, businesses are often unable to pinpoint their shortcomings or discover their gaps. Managers frequently suffer from tunnel vision and the lack of ability to ask the right questions. As a result, prodigious resources of business are wasted getting right answers to wrong questions. Knowledge of the seven levels of human consciousness (physical, social, intellectual, emotional, mental, intuitional and imaginative) is essential if business is going to become wholistic and patterned after nature.

The great secret of nature is that each part of creation is whole and organic, and only the organisms which are sick are divided. The sickness of the business world today is that the workers get caught up in the work and do not really know why they are working or how all the parts fit together, and they do not feel the inspiration that comes from seeing the overview. If all the inspiration comes from the top-down, the bottom is just hard work. To reorganize the structure of our businesses to be evolutionary, we have to involve the workers in the planning and involve the planners in the shop floor manifesting. Then the inner life and inner needs and the outer life of work activity are brought together in one harmonious whole. This result is the true transformation of an organization into an organism.

With the Creative Conflict process the group intuition and imagination are activated as is the sense of security. The intellectual perception of each person is sharpened and so are his social skills. Thus every business becomes, in effect, a continuing business "school" as well as an evolving free enterprise. The end result is growth for everyone and growth for society. The only test of this growth is in the manifestation, in the improved results in the business itself. We look at business success as a mirror of the collective skill of the participants involved in the company. We look to see where further improvement is needed and then we draw on the group consciousness and those who are strongest in the needed levels to help give direction to fill the lacks. This is the nuclear model applied to our work life to make it a fulfilling part of the natural order.* The nuclear model is not something abstract or theoretical but comprises an aspect of your own being, your own perceptions and desires. Without the direct caring for the health of the whole business there can be no such thing as group consciousness. It is caring for individuals and their difficulties in expressing themselves in a group situation that makes Creative Conflict creative.

* See the chapter on the Nuclear Model in *The Golden Egg*, for a complete account.

10

CREATIVE CONFLICT
IN THE SCHOOLS

The breakdown of public education has not really hit our society yet in a big way, although it is general knowledge that most public schools are incapable of dealing with the needs of our younger generation. And because parents are disenchanted with their children's schooling they are reluctant to vote more public money to it, so it is falling apart. A deep sentiment is growing that any additional tax revenues to schools would only go to waste, to perpetuating rather than solving present problems. The feeling is that no one has any real answers and there is a lethargy about finding any.

The swing of the pendulum went from rigid authoritarian education prior to the '60s to too much "free school"-type education in the '70s where disciplines in the basics of math and reading were lax. Emotional and social problems also complicate teaching. Nearly half of all children under ten years old in 1980 have experienced divorce or separation between their natural parents. Conflicts in schools are getting worse; teacher "burn-out" is spreading like wild-fire, and parental apathy is a sickness affecting every large city. Creative Conflict in schools is only one answer to these intense problems in education, but it is a fundamental, root answer. An entire wholistic curriculum stressing the well-being of children's psyches is as important to our future as is the revival of teaching the three main basic subjects of reading, writing and arithmetic (the 3 R's).

Here at the University of the Trees community we have started our own private community school with the first truly wholistic curriculum that we know. Creative Conflict is a basic part of it, and it has fostered a feeling of openness, honesty and love that all who visit our school experience. We begin by building love and trust between teacher and children and among the kids themselves through centering activities and awareness games to supplement teaching the academics through creative methods. As much as possible in classes of twelve, we have individualized programs geared to the child's own developmental needs. But we have found that the greatest contribution to the success of our curriculum has been in the ongoing teacher training and Creative Conflict for the staff. The teachers' Creative Conflict and brainstorming sessions have built a bond of sharing and caring for each other through trials and triumphs. These sessions provide the teachers with a sense of community and, most importantly, a chance to get feedback for improvement in a loving environment. Learning how to draw each other's reality out has taught our teachers skills that they now use to draw out the children's inner worlds. When any problem arises the teachers work as a united team to zero in on it and do whatever is needed to solve it. Only Creative Conflict, where they have learned to be *real*, has provided the motivation to work so closely together so well.

Opening up these lines of communication also opens doors of creativity in productive planning sessions. The children are the ones who finally benefit from the creative planning and preparation and from the good vibrations generated. The classroom takes on the feeling of a large family. It is so important to establish this close rapport among the staff that we find it is even worth sacrificing some school time to accomplish having these staff sessions if that is the only time the teachers can all be together. When the teachers' hearts are one, the strength of each is infused into all and the children experience the harmony, the unity and the inner space. It rubs off. Next to the influence of the home, the teacher's state of consciousness and the collective state of consciousness of the entire staff in the school has the greatest influence on the psyche and the attitudes of the children in their school learning process. Both the teacher and the student must be excited by what they do, or learning becomes merely rote learning and boring.

A wholistic teacher training program incorporates each of the seven levels of development. We must dynamically weave together physical education, social education, intellectual, emotional, conceptual, intuitive and imaginative education which are all equally important. These must all be tied together in interdisciplinary studies. It is not a question of theory, because educational theories are useless unless translated into practice. To be dynamic the teacher training has to help the teacher implement the methods. We use Creative Conflict as the release valve to allow all the levels of being to express and unfold their full potential. When emotional scars or turmoil churn within, students find learning very difficult and stultifying. And when the ability to relax, get centered and get in touch with what is happening in the depths of being is blocked, there is very little imagination or intuition—the basics of creativity. Instead what you get is turmoil and dullness in the class life.

A teacher who is in touch with him or herself can automatically help a child get more in touch by the teacher's own psychic vibration and understanding. Because their ego patterns are not as long-standing, children are more open and responsive to positive vibrations than adults. It is impossible to list all the benefits that Creative Conflict used in education can bring to children. In terms of understanding each other and being able to enter each other's inner worlds and care what others are feeling, we see tangible results the first day. As with all groups of children there will be periods of defiance, reaction and negativity as well as times of joy, peace and responsibility. But with Creative Conflict children begin to release their ego defenses. In such a setting they are freer to express their negatives as well as their positives, so Creative Conflict is essential to direct the energies constructively and creatively.

In many ways the forming egos of children seem rather "crude" material to work with. Even in the best environments you will have a wide variety of personalities, some of them destructive. The miracle of Creative Conflict is that both children and adults can change overnight once they know that someone cares about their real beings. Here are a few Creative Conflict experiences as told by two of our teachers at University Community School. The first two are simple everyday types of squabbles. The third example deals with a much deeper area of sensitivity. It is important to realize that in all these little conflicts, which may seem so insignificant, lie the seed patterns of much larger conflicts that will blossom in adolescence and adulthood if they are left untended when they first arise. The seeds of alienation, rejection, repressed hostility and fear are all sown in childhood. In small classes of children the ego is less inhibited and expresses itself more frequently, creating a greater challenge for the teacher, but a greater opportunity for growth for the children.

Creative Conflict example #1

"Karen, 7, and Leah, 9, have had an ongoing dispute since school started. They often get into verbal fights before and after school hours. Since they both live in the same housing complex they have a lot of opportunity to encounter one another in the times they are not at school. I have overheard their disputes a few times which usually involve name-calling and put-downs. We have a rule at the school of no put-downs, but after school time the rule evaporates for these two.

"One morning Karen came to school upset because Leah had called her names and stuck her tongue out at her. Usually the disputes start in this way with Leah deliberately doing something to upset Karen. At noon break Jim, Leah's teacher, and I got together with the two girls to do Creative Conflict with them to see if we could lick this problem once and for all. First Leah expressed her feelings about Karen. She explained that Karen really bugged her because Karen was "weird" and did things like carry her lunch bag on the top of her head on the way to school. She also was disturbed that Karen played "making love" games with Leah's sister in a room shared by Leah and her sister Brenda. In the "making love" games Karen pretended she was the wife and Brenda pretended she was the husband and they spoke in sweet mushy voices to each other. Leah also expressed that she did not like the fact that Karen was mean and hit her, and that Karen lied to her at certain times.

"As Leah spoke, Karen often tried to interrupt, to defend herself or to get a point across. Jim gently reminded her that she would get her turn soon. When it was Karen's turn to speak her first response was to defend herself and claim that she didn't lie very often. She was encouraged to express her feelings to Leah. She told Leah that she didn't like it when Leah called her names and stuck her tongue out at her. This seemed to be her main concern. Often during this discussion Jim or I would ask the girls how it made them feel when the other did one of the things which disturbed them. If we felt the girls were not listening we had them mirror each other's point.

"The fact that the girls had a safe space to express their feelings towards one another and be heard by the other relaxed much of the tension between them. At this point in the Creative Conflict it became clear to me that the reason Leah was so upset by Karen and often taunted her and started fights was because Karen mirrored Leah's own problems. In other words, the things that disturbed Leah about Karen were also in Leah, even more so. Leah was disturbed by Karen's pattern of lying, but Leah is a notorious liar herself. Leah did not like Karen's "making love" games but Leah herself has a pattern of telling sex jokes and being obsessed with thoughts about sex. Leah complained that Karen hit her and was mean to her. Leah herself has often been uncaring and mean to other students in the school.

"We pointed out to Leah that perhaps she was so disturbed because Karen was a mirror to her and did some of the same things that Leah did. Jim and I brought up each point, one by one, in which Karen's behavior was a mirror for Leah's behavior. Leah was receptive by this time and was able to see how she did the things which disturbed her in Karen and to gain an insight into how she projects onto Karen her own patterns. We used mirroring to make sure she really heard us and understood.

"Next we asked Karen if she also did the things that disturbed her most about Leah. Karen claimed she never made faces at people or stuck her tongue out at them because her mommy taught her not to. But in this example we did not pursue the idea that Leah was a mirror for Karen, although in other areas it may have been quite true, because we did not feel we had enough examples to show Karen.

"Both girls were much relieved from tension and conflict and expressed to one another that they would like to be friends. Jim and I gave them the option of coming to us if another conflict should ever arise again. Both agreed they would like to do this. They have been friendly ever since."

Creative Conflict example #2

"One afternoon after lunch eleven-year-old Ronnie came in and expressed to me how unfair it was to allow several girls to eat on a nearby grassy field while he and his friends were prohibited. I told him I didn't know the girls were eating on the grass and that indeed they were forbidden from eating on the grassy field because of the numerous student messes left there from previous days. After hearing my comments, Ronnie began to scold the girls in a very unpleasant manner. Not surprisingly, the girls really reacted in anger. They said they didn't know of my special instructions, that they never heard them, and they especially disliked the bossy way in which Ronnie was coming across.

"With both Ronnie and the girls there was a lot of emotion. I felt it was important to deal with the issue, although in my former public school teaching I would have told them in absolute terms that there was no eating on the grass and there would be no more discussion about it. Then I would have sent the girls to the principal. Instead I wanted them to deal with their emotions. I began having them mirror each other's points. First, the girls mirrored Ronnie's point about my instructions stating not to eat on the grassy field. They correctly understood the message but they still maintained their innocence in never having heard it. I intervened here to challenge this professed ignorance. I went into the circumstances that led to the decision in the first place and even mentioned the day I told them. The fact that Ronnie and his friends heard the instructions and the girls didn't was also thrown in as evidence of their nonlistening. They now began confessing to having heard the instructions in the first place but twisted their argument a little more, saying they thought it applied only to the first day. They still were rationalizing and not buying the feedback.

"It was becoming very obvious to me at this point that their objections and nit-picking were not so much a defense of their point but instead more of an angry reaction to Ronnie's arrogant manner. So I switched subjects here from the girls' nonlistening to Ronnie's bossiness. I figured that by having Ronnie agree to his contribution to the conflict the girls would more readily admit to theirs, especially since Ronnie was still looking at them with his nose in the air. I capped the final communication to the girls saying I basically thought they bought the feedback and that if Ronnie would admit to his bossiness, they could let their defenses down. It is hard to humble oneself before someone very critical of you.

"We then went into Ronnie. The girls said they really reacted to his haughty and proud manner of speaking, and said that he does that all the time as though he is perfect. Ronnie, of course, was getting quite upset at this feedback. He first denied it and then when I pointed out to him several other examples of this same attitude he got very angry and wanted to retreat in a highly emotional space. He seemed to be hoping that his angry emotion would somehow pacify or dilute the feedback he was receiving. He was able to use emotional blackmail at home and thought he could use it at school. He seemed so resistant to looking at this part of himself that I tried to balance the picture for him a little. I told him he was admirable in pointing out injustices like these for he truly has a genuine concern for order and things being right. However, there is a lot of self-righteousness in the way he comes across. I then did an imitation of someone acting in a self-righteous, critical way.

"At this point Ronnie broke down and started crying. He shared how this pattern showed itself before in other schools and how much this upset him. Ronnie then bought the feedback and was no longer throwing his previous tantrums. Instead he was depressed at himself for having this pattern.

"Obviously, the class had to help him get out of this depressed space. Here's where the girls reentered the picture. In a remarkable contrast to the hostility they were experiencing ten minutes ago, Ronnie's vulnerability opened up the floodgates of the girls' hearts. They empathized with Ronnie and told him how they appreciated his positive sides. Sure, he had to work on this Achilles' heel part of himself just like they had to listen better.

"The girls' love and support was tremendous. It could have only happened by Ronnie reaching that delicate heart space. Ronnie began responding now. His self-pity and withdrawal left him. The coloring in his face became brighter and a real sense of peace came over him. This was a very special moment."

In both these examples the children began to openly experience the unifying dynamic of Creative Conflict. In the first instance the Creative Conflict was done privately between the teachers and the children involved. In the second example the Creative Conflict included the entire class (in this case 11 children). In a very large classroom of 30 children it is more difficult for the children to open up to looking at truth in themselves because the size of the group is socially restraining and can be frightening to the self-image of a child on the spot, especially if the child does not trust all the other children. In large groups children are more constantly tuned to the "pecking order" and the peer group relationships. Small groups are more intimate and bring more security, which allows children to be more naturally themselves, thus their self-image is not as threatened. There is something to be said for the inhibiting social restraints that larger classes bring as far as discipline goes, but personal growth and learning on all levels of consciousness are more enhanced by the family-like experience of the small class. Deep issues especially take skill, sensitivity and time. The more children involved, the more emotions and different inner realities you have to deal with.

A good rule for Creative Conflict in school is to use only general issues that concern the whole class (such as in Example 2) before the whole group. If the problems are between only a few of the children it is better to take them aside and turn the rest of your class over to an aide or to a quiet work assignment while you deal with the Creative Conflict in another room. If you take aside only those children involved in a personal conflict and follow the rules, especially the mirroring, you will generally get to the cause and to peace. Of course your own constant love and helping suggestions along with the mirroring and sharing of feelings is important for a good result.

Creative Conflict example #3

Our last example occurred in the first-second grade class.

"Three of the girls like to chase the boys on the playground to try to kiss them. The boys both like and dislike this little ploy for their attention, so they send mixed messages. (This game is now off-limits, but the children pick up these messages from TV and our society and it is a challenge to redirect this energy.) One little six-year-old, Tony, decided he had enough of this kissy chasing and said so. But the girls, not satisfied, wanted him and another boy, whom they had been chasing, to take a turn and to chase the girls. Tony said he didn't want to chase the girls but the girls kept on chasing him, insisting that he must take a turn. This went on periodically for days until Tony came running in crying one recess. I was assisting the teacher and we decided to resolve this issue with Creative Conflict. We asked all the children to gather in a circle on the floor. We used what we call the "power stick", a three foot long stick passed around from person to person and only the child who holds it has permission to talk. We had one of the more aggressive girls state how she saw the situation and share her feelings first because Tony was unwilling to speak. Tony refused to mirror and instead ran in a corner saying, 'They're just blaming me, I'm going to beat them up.' I said, 'Tony we're trying to work this out, I didn't hear them blaming you. Cindy just said her point of view—that you wanted to play first and then wouldn't take your turn.' It was difficult to keep the other six- and seven-year-olds from piping up out of turn with their opinions. But Tony kept insisting he was being blamed and that he was going to beat them all up and he did *not* want to work it out. It was obvious that the whole issue embarrassed him very much. Three other children piped up, 'me too', and ran over to Tony's side. Tony added, 'These are the only ones who are my friends, and even if those others say they'll let me be, I won't beat them up but I won't be friends.' 'Yeah', the three other supporters chorused. The room had polarized into three camps—the clique of girls and boys who enjoyed chasing each other, the group who sympathized with Tony and a third group who were not involved and were wanting to mediate between the two opposing sides. But Tony was adamant in his refusal to discuss.

"Andrew said, 'Hey, love your enemies, you know, Tony.' Tony retorted, 'I'm going to beat you up if you don't leave me alone.' We decided to let Tony experience the consequences of his unwillingness to discuss. It was lunch time and the children all went outside into the sun to eat their lunch. Quickly the sides again polarized with Tony and his three supporters getting more and more upset, and a few of the other children taunting them. It was a very exciting drama for the rest of the kids. Tony kept spouting off angry words until he was so frustrated that he finally started to hit one of the boys. We teachers decided it was time to step in at this point and I took Tony by the hand and brought him into the room. Two of his supporters followed. Both were very upset. I held Tony on my lap, my arms around him as he shouted invectives and tried to struggle away. His teacher and I both talked to him quietly about what his words and actions were creating.

"Suddenly Tony said, very bitterly and violently, 'I don't care about love, it's all snotty stuff,' and desperately tried to get away from my grip. I kept holding him until he relaxed finally and started to cry a little. The three girls in the kissing clique came in and this time we asked Tony to share how their actions made him feel. He was now willing and shared that he felt that they were blaming him for not playing when he didn't want to. He was being open now and kept fiddling with my ring as he spoke. I asked one

of the girls to mirror back what Tony had said. She did. Tony
seemed more at ease.

"Then I said, 'Girls, will you be willing to give Tony the
freedom not to play with you when he says he doesn't want to?'
'Yes', they each said, subdued by now. 'And his word is law,
okay? If he says he doesn't want to play you will let him be?' I
asked again. 'Yes, we will,' said the ringleader. 'Will you please
mirror what we just agreed to, Cindy?' Cindy mirrored that she
would let Tony be free to play or not and that whatever he said she
would respect. The girls were very sobered by now. Tony rubbed
his eyes, all relaxed in my arms now. He fiddled with my ring
some more and said, 'I won't beat you up now, but I still won't be
your friend.' His teacher quickly responded, 'Tony, you don't have
to be their friend, but they are going to leave you be when you say
you don't want to play. Whatever you say is your word and you
are responsible for it.' 'Okay,' he said. The girls ran back out to
play. Tony's supporters seemed pacified by now too, and they also
ran out to play. Tony didn't want to go out. He wanted to just be
alone. But soon it was time for a field trip and everyone piled into
the cars. Tony started crying. One of the mothers who came to be
an aide took him to her house where he happily played the
afternoon while the rest of the class was on the field trip.

"The next day Tony's stepmother called. 'What happened?'
she said. 'Tony has never been so happy. He came home and
kissed me, which he never does, and he has been so sweet and
loving all evening, so happy. Something must have happened in
school. He wouldn't tell me anything.' We were relieved because
we didn't know exactly how Tony would react to his first Creative
Conflict on such a sensitive subject to a little boy's ego—kissing
girls—especially when Tony came to the school in the fall with a
very low image of himself, frequently saying, 'I don't like myself,'
or 'I hate myself.' Tony had now met a deeper part of himself. He
had been held and loved when he thought love was 'snotty'. And
he heard other children agree to listen to him and to respect
whatever he said, that what he said would be the reality he would
create. But Tony had needed the space of being in an intimate
group before he could open up. The whole class at once had been

too threatening to expose this very deep part of his being."

In a very short while with Creative Conflict, children learn what integrity and being responsible for what they are saying and creating means. Integrity should become the highest value in the classroom, and experiencing it in each other helps children let go of the games they play to get their way, to get attention or to reinforce their egos to feel secure. Bad and good are relative value judgements that we do not use in Creative Conflict. Things *are* just the way they are, neither bad nor good. But actions and words create effects and effects have good or bad consequences. We always point out to children the consequences of their words and actions—how they affect others and how they rebound back onto their creator. Children learn that they are choosing to keep creating their reality the same old way or they can choose to change it. In this way they feel love and acceptance for their real self. They take responsibility for their actions. Since good, bad, right, wrong are not in question, your love is not dependent on a child being good.

Taking responsibility for their own feelings and actions regardless of age allows every child to feel worthy. Self-worth and a healthy self-image are not a matter of praise or giving ego food. This would only build a false self-image that reality will eventually expose as unreal. At the same time as we confront a child, we recognize the child for his or her real beingness, for having something deep to share, and to know how to give to the whole class. Especially with children, it is necessary to keep the Creative Conflict issues clear and direct. You confront the words and actions that hurt or infringe upon another's space or that hurt the child, and you affirm at the same time the real self which is capable of loving and of doing well. As this process is done day by day, children discover that they can be honest and that honesty will bring joy and make things better instead of worse as they normally fear. The most important thing they learn is that to be responsible is to discover who they are!

As with adults, the effects of how children use their consciousness are always evident in the manifestation of their life. One way we can see ourselves is to look at the wake we leave behind our ship as we sail across the waves of our life. A Creative Conflict exercise for children can be to keep a journal where they chart their own track record. They look behind their boat of life as they sail across each week and they write about what kind of wake they see, what consequences they have created from what they have done or said. Younger children will need help in seeing their creation. They can draw their wakes if they don't feel like writing about them. The symbolic representation is just as important as the verbal to them as long as they express it. The mood in the picture will reveal the same track. Another step is to discuss with each other in the group the real meaning of what they have written or drawn.

Children come to realize that the more they give of the richness of their inner lives, the more they can communicate and share their innermost thoughts, which are so sensitive and tender a place for us all, then the more will other children, adults and life itself, give back to them. Nature smiles and the mirror of life speaks positively. In a loving atmosphere, when one child is real the other children will often become very real too as though it were contagious. The teacher's job is to be real first with the kids and then create the space for them to be open and real too. Being able to be open is vital to feeling secure, to tapping the inner dreams and the inner desire to love, to learn and to celebrate life in school.

It is impossible to separate the spiritual being from the rest of oneself. It is true that the separation of church and state in schools has eliminated the domination of organized religion or dogma, but it has also cut off some of the rich inner life where our real wealth lies. Some of the most effective schools today are, surprisingly, the church schools. They don't have their vital forces sucked by a huge impersonal bureaucracy that severely restricts the teachers' creativity. We are not suggesting that we bring religion back into the public schools or that all church schools are positive, but that all schools would do well to look at what spiritual values public schools are missing. The spiritual and inner life can easily be integrated into teaching, without religious bias, through the Creative Conflict experience.

HOW TO START CREATIVE CONFLICT SESSIONS IN SCHOOL

In introducing Creative Conflict with children, teachers need to be clear about the rules, about setting limits and about the consequences of going beyond the limits. Within the set rules or parameters the children have freedom to express themselves. Right at the beginning the rules need to be presented along with reasons why each rule is necessary, and these should be discussed to make sure they are understood. In some areas the children might complain or resist and you can ask them to come up with an alternative rule or consequence that will achieve the same purpose. Setting clear boundaries that lead to definite consequences that are always carried out if the children overstep them is essential for harmony. This clarity and consistency on the part of adults gives children the chance to know their limits and to feel secure. What you want in these first sessions is to gain their agreement to work for the same purpose and to work together to achieve it. Small group discussions with older children on freedom and responsibility are very important to eliciting their cooperation.

Planned Creative Conflict sessions should take place at least once a week, preferably more. The afternoon is a good time. These are different from circle time, general sharing, or show-and-tell time. You begin by just teaching the basics of the process given in Part III, especially listening and mirroring, like becoming a blank photographic plate (see page 302). Children love it when you put colorful images with the exercises. You can help teach mirroring by having the children physically mirror each other in pairs with movement, similar to follow the leader, but facing each other. Next you move into the verbal sharing and mirroring. Then when two children are in a fight or ready to scream at each other or hurt each other, you apply what they have learned in the sessions. If one child hits another, have that child share how it feels to be hit and have the other mirror it back. Often the child who did the hitting will start crying because he is being confronted, and the separation which allows him to hit is dissolved very quickly as soon as he sees, "I've got to get into the other's world." You ask him to mirror and as soon as he opens his mouth to say what his mirror is, he is already in the heart and in the other child's world and his ego melts. Remorse flows in. It happens every time that way.

Being in the heart needs a lot of reinforcement to help see when the ego is operating and when it is not. And you help the child see by saying, "Feel the heart space you are in right now. In that space you have friendship and much love comes to you. The other space always creates pain." And you really get them to see the difference between the head and the heart and the cause and the effect. It becomes their own behavior modification program and they discover their own signals. One ego pattern you have to watch for is when kids start to abuse the process of Creative Conflict for attention: "We had a conflict on the playground, can we have a Creative Conflict?" It brings everybody's attention onto them, so you have to point out to them what their egos are doing and what the motivation is. If you learn the skill to get to the point where you can probe the motivation, the need for attention, then there can be an insight at a new level. Having the children who have already gained skill at Creative Conflict assist or even lead others through the process is an effective teaching device, provided that the other children can trust the leader. Older children coming into younger grades are often effective. It allows the older youngsters to feel that the tool is their own and gives them practice in initiating creative resolution of conflicts or probing problems. You will also need "action consequences" to discipline stubborn children who do not respond to the Creative Conflict methods because they see them as just words. Creative Conflict uses words, but it is rooted in action. When words don't achieve any results, action consequences that are directly related to the abuse of freedom are required, and this too is part of Creative Conflict.

In learning the Creative Conflict methods you may find your class spending weeks just on learning the basic mirroring skills, not only during the session but practicing them throughout the school day, and you can even use mirroring to help listening in academic lessons. Your ability to integrate the process into normal school activities will contribute to how fast your class will grow as a group. You will see the effects of the mirroring and listening not only in the individual relationships between children but also in their ability to receive instructions and be receptive to what they learn. It becomes a way of being that grows on everyone.

Sometimes children will develop standard defensive responses and seem completely unable and unwilling to take in what feedback is being given, as was the case with Tony. If a child responds, "I don't care," your skill in showing him what the effects of those words are will determine how much you can get through. When you are dealing with children you are dealing also with all their parents' patterns that they have acquired. The home life greatly conditions the children's school life and inevitably you will at times have to go into disturbing issues in the home with each child. But this is part of the learning process, part of what blocks creativity or suffocates potential. The role-playing or psychodrama technique can be excellent with children (see page 298) as it allows them to see themselves as others see them in action, and quickly puts them in touch with their real emotions. It can give them a clue as to how they might approach their parents or siblings or friends in a different way. But no technique is a substitute for your own integrity and consistency in discipline as a teacher.

Take the beginning sessions described for adults in Part III and introduce one point at a time with your group. Do not be afraid of repeating exercises or going slowly so everyone has a turn and can do it and feel successful. This process is very new to children and needs reinforcing even though a child may have a breakthrough on the first day. The next day could see a reversion because patterns are deeply rooted, or because there are more unresolved problems than just the one you dealt with. There is no rush. Proceed from the exercises to finding ways to apply them in real life. Awareness games help children also get in touch with the different parts of themselves and will supplement the Creative Conflict sessions.* These are explorations, while Creative Conflict is always trying to take issues back to the source, the cause, the ego, so that the real Self can look at it. Patching up squabbles so that we have

---

* See *Exploring Inner Space, Awareness Games for All Ages,* published by University of the Trees Press.

temporary peace is not Creative Conflict. Penetration to the real cause is the goal. Even if you don't get all the way to the cause, however far you can get to is *being real.*

It is not the purpose of Creative Conflict to act as only a mediator in conflict resolution. To resolve conflict for real there must be a breakthrough and not an appeasement. The group consensus is a natural mirror of what *is,* but this consensus must include both a reflection of what behavior infringes on others and what in the child is worthy, is loved, is beautiful, and reflective of his real being. The goal is to get him to identify with the latter so he can let go of the misbehavior which is a compensation for not being in touch with his real Self. Several exercises to take children as well as adults deeper in being real are the following. Share verbally in a circle or as a writing lesson. These are openers to the heart.

1. What was the time when you remember feeling hurt the most?
2. When was there a time that you felt you loved someone and they didn't love you?
3. When was there a time that you didn't love or respond to someone who was trying to love you?
4. When was a time that you felt the most loving, the most at one with others?

When one child opens up the other children usually become very attentive. If one or two children snicker or aren't with it, then the group goes into their need to divert energy by laughing at someone else so that they won't have to look at that part in themselves. Have other children share how the acting makes them feel. Then secure each disturbing child's agreement to be with the others again. If they continue to break agreements, then quickly confront their word and integrity. If they still won't cooperate remove them from the Creative Conflict group until they are willing to be there for others as well as for themselves and to honor their agreements. You must not force a child to be in Creative Conflict just because he has to come to school. It has to be responsibly chosen if it is to foster integrity. Children who whine or complain or become verbally abusive need to be confronted with their manifestation and have it mirrored by others who share how it makes them feel. Then ask them to re-express themselves from the heart. When they can re-express with a different vibe, it is time to give positive reinforcement and confirmation of the real being who is now sharing rather than relate to the former ego space.

As a child opens, it will often bring tears. This is not bad or negative but a release of emotion. After she or he is in touch, support the child for being open and willing to give emotionally to everyone in this important way. Ask the other children if they have any similar feelings or experiences. When kids see that they are not alone in their secret parts, so much more love and security comes to light for them. When their inner secret is out, as was the case with Tony, the trauma is over. They are freed up and can start creating a new life with more of their real self, more of their potential. As a teacher or parent you need to introduce the process naturally and just be yourself. Do your best. It is not psychotherapy where you have to have mastered the techniques before you can feel safe using them. It's just life, amplified. You will make "mistakes". But that is also part of life. As long as you use mirroring and share yourself you are being real and that will bring results.

HOW TO APPROACH YOUR ADMINISTRATION

One teacher expressed that she has difficulty with her administration letting her use anything like Creative Conflict or for that matter anything new or innovative in her class. She developed a creative communication program but as she said, "I know it threatens their structure and their sense of security. They like to think that they have got it together, but they haven't. Things are such a mess. Squabbles all the time. Bad vibes, bad feelings and now the teachers are divided about asking for more money. So I've presented how I feel about it all. I wrote my program all out, I spent days on it and reviewed it and felt, yes, that's exactly how I perceive this problem and here are some answers I feel will work. But there has been no response from the administrators. I call. No response. I get fobbed off. What do I do?"

Our response to her was that you first assert yourself—break down the door until you get an answer because you are in charge of your destiny, and if they say, "No, sorry, we don't like it," then you have a choice: you leave the situation, you try to storm the office until you find someone who will listen, or you end up trying to work within the system as best you can to keep your job. If this third option is a compromise and you still feel badly, then you have to work within yourself because it's your problem. Find other people you can work with to find another solution. You can never dictate another's reality. All you can do is present your own SO LOUD AND CLEAR THAT PEOPLE REACT AND CHANGE OR FIRE YOU OR WHATEVER THEY ARE GOING TO DO. Then she said, "They would be very threatened by having a confrontation like this; they are just used to having everybody accept what the administration says."

Isn't this just like our governmental system everywhere? You have to find ways to be at peace within yourself within the system and introduce vital change bit by bit or work in whatever way you can to alter the status quo. Or you have to look and see what your alternatives are, what you can create, and choose the one you can live with best. You can be at peace once you see and know your own integrity and that you've communicated and done your best. There is no more that any of us can do than this, but we have to find out what we must do daily to maintain our integrity. Then we will be admirable models for the next generation. The wayshowers know that the children of today are the controllers of human destiny in five or ten years time. We must teach them to show society, especially the government and politicians, that they will not stand for less than total integrity at every level of society.

11

CREATIVE CONFLICT IN THE FAMILY

As in the classroom, using the techniques of Creative Conflict in the family brings children up to feel responsible for themselves and to be integral. Integrity has always been touted as a social virtue to children in such heroic examples as Abraham Lincoln or George Washington, who chopped down the cherry tree and wouldn't lie about it. The Bible, too, is full of stories where the truth always wins out over falsity. But few children actually feel that telling the truth is worth the terrible consequences that might happen, especially if telling the truth may arouse the immediate wrath or disapproval of a parent or other adult in authority. The typical family adage is "peace at any price", and the cost of this peace often means lying and hanging on to repressed feelings. It is always difficult to measure the actual cost of lying. We don't know the cost to our psyches since we don't feel like a little lie is going to create any problems at the time that we tell it. In fact we believe that fibbing will prevent problems. Only by studying our wake, the track of troubled waters we leave behind us, can we see the mirror of our unfulfilled lives. Only by looking at the conflicts we have with life and within ourselves can we get in touch with the actual price of this superficial peace. Eventually the mask of peace crumbles as the deeper feelings erupt into conflict and manifest uncertainty and insecurity.

In the family, the most volatile relationships develop between adults and adolescents. But all the "petty" squabbles that go on between siblings and between parents and younger children— hurt feelings, put-downs, repressed anger and frustration, lashing out, etc.—are the substance that builds the foundation for trouble later on as teenagers and as adults. Bringing Creative Conflict into the family becomes more challenging than in any other situation because all the entwined ego relationships make our ability to see clearly very difficult. Some children are more open to Creative Conflict outside the family because they feel that people with whom they are less familiar may be more objective and thus less turmoil is at stake.

At times children can be more receptive to Creative Conflict than their parents, but the reverse may also be true, depending on the degree of trust and ego development. The main factor for readiness to begin the process is self-honesty. For teenagers some form of Creative Conflict is vital in order to cope creatively with all the moods, emotional storms, sensitivities and misperceptions— the rocky path that they travel over as they switch from childhood to adulthood. Creative Conflict is imperative for them to develop a truly healthy self-image and honest relationships. A lot of chaos that comes to households during adolescence will be eliminated when Creative Conflict becomes part of the way of life. The rebelliousness of adolescence blows up the ego patterns that have been building since early childhood. Several of our staff at University of the Trees who teach Creative Conflict to teenagers have remarked that some young people don't like the ego confrontations initially. The sessions are the first time anyone has demanded that they be real and look at themselves, which can be threatening to their carefully constructed ego positions and their sense of control.

One of the biggest problems in practicing family Creative Conflict is sorting out the traits we absorb or pick up from each other. Children take on their parents' ego patterns by a kind of osmosis as they grow up. Children are often like their parents are in the unconscious. Children are unconscious reflections of what goes on in the parent underneath. A man and a woman can seem to be nice, calm, sweet people and then they get married and have children who become monsters and you wonder, "How did they deserve that?" But if you probe very deep inside you'll find that the calm exterior is wrapped around a very deep problem of nonrecognition of self, and that deeper self gets mirrored in the child. At a certain stage children will test their parents to see how far they can go. If there is weakness in the parents then the children will use it absolutely. They are innocent reflections of your own being and they will test how far they can go with you to see what they can get away with. This is how they reveal your weakness to you. And if they get away with it, they'll go farther and farther until they find your limit of tolerance. It is false to think that you can give a child total freedom to run around and then expect some order, because he or she looks to you as a parent to show where the limits are, whether it's the social limits or the family limits or the financial limits or limits of power. The child's lack of order mirrors your own lack of order. Unconsciously the child tests your integrity. If your words are hollow and you don't follow through with actions, you are buying a problem because you will get no respect from the child. Sorting out this dynamic between parent and child is common in the practice of family Creative Conflict.

Most conflicts between parents and children are in relation to setting of boundaries. If you set common sense limits and stick to them in everything, children will not feel frustrated; they will breathe a sigh of relief at knowing where they stand because they will feel there is some stable order. They will feel some integrity and will respect that. If there isn't such solid reality, children will go on testing until they find something that feels real. They may look outside the family for that reality, that strength. Strength of character is not walking around barking orders at a child or saying, "No, no, no," but a question of setting things out clearly so the child can be free. "This is your freedom, between here and here, and if you step over this line the consequence will be this." The first thing that many children will try to do is step over the line because they want to test you to see if you're real or not. And if you fail to provide that consequence after you've said, "That will be the consequence," you have unconsciously moved the guideline out further. And your boundary is no longer real. Your words are not real to your children and they will not respect you because there is no integrity. Children are very literal in how they take what you say. And if they see your words mean nothing, if you are dithering and don't know where to go, or if you are uncertain of your previous decisions, children sense that uncertainty and will feel uncertain themselves. And that's where the big problems start. Our challenge in doing Creative Conflict with children is the same as our challenge in life with everything. Life is going to test us in our areas of weakness and that is why we are put here on earth. Cosmically speaking, we attract our particular children to us just as we attract all situations to us, according to the quality of our consciousness. We get just the challenge that we need, however full of peace and joy or full of pain and conflict it might be.

We have to be careful not to blame mothers and fathers. They are evolving through life too, and although they have attracted their children into their family the parents are not necessarily the cause of their children's hostilities and insecurities even though they may be the mirror for them. Children have deep-seated ego patterns of their own, due to their own true nature, which parents either amplify or abate. Which way ego evolves in the child depends upon the parent's understanding of his or her own ego as well as the child's ego. As children grow up they see more and more clearly the ego in the parent, and they may reject the parent or run the opposite way. As young adults we don't realize that we too have reacted from an ego position until later on when we can see the similarities between ourselves and our parents or wonder why we are so opposite. We find that we personally react to their traits and we don't quite know what to do with our feelings. Millions choose some form of therapy to deal with these frustrated feelings, but most suppress them out of family love for those who have nurtured them. We feel we cannot be open with our parents because they either won't understand or won't be willing to look at themselves honestly. So we carry our own negative feelings around until we are determined to create a new space for ourselves to let go of them.

Creative Conflict makes home life an evolutionary experience by using all the ego patterns as fuel for creative growth. If your family can work with other families or at least one adult, non-family member in the first few sessions you will get a lot farther. When husband and wife or parent and child mirror the same ego patterns, they react off each other or else they are so used to each other that they have a hard time seeing straight. A less involved person will often be a clearer mirror. Getting to truth makes life beautiful, even on its most earthly levels. Beauty without this penetrating truth is a delusion because it is short-lived and temporary. The beauty of a clean heart is worth the effort to achieve it.

Not all people can believe this process or can trust that being truthful is easier than being deceitful, especially since the skills of society often involve training in deceit and hypocrisy. Many family rules encourage behaving in stereotyped ways which forbid making waves or disturbing others by speaking out truthfully. The skill of when to speak or not to speak has nothing to do with blurting out the truth or with disguising the truth. There are many occasions when we know the truth but should remain silent because more harm may be done than good by speaking out in that situation. But we should never speak a lie to cover up truth; rather we need to learn how to be skillful at being integral with ourself and others. The practice of integrity begins in the family and without this, society rapidly accepts hypocrisy as the norm and deception and cunning as a virtue. Searching for truth should not be done at the expense of others but at our own expense. When we can speak truth and live truth without injuring others we learn to discriminate between ego hurt and real hurt. Many people don't speak truth for fear of hurting others, but they may only be protecting another's ego and thus they do the other a disservice. Real hurt is always inflicted with intent. The intention to hurt someone, even with truth, is not the way of integrity. But an ego reaction to innocently spoken truth is not to be pampered. The ability to discriminate real hurt from ego hurt is developed through Creative Conflict practice where you learn to see how your words and actions affect others. Love can only be built by speaking truthfully for the good of the whole, both in the family and in society at large.

We basically begin Creative Conflict in the family the same as in the school or in any group. We sit down together at a set time. We make our agreements and we agree to challenge any family member who breaks an agreement. Usually if a child elects not to be part of the Creative Conflict agreement at first, eventually he will want to be in because that's where the real dynamic family stuff is happening. Again, choice is integral to the process. But once an agreement is made everyone must stick to what was decided or alter it mutually together. Choice always bears consequences. Start with the same steps as adults use (see Part III), going point by point at your own speed, spending as long as necessary for everyone to have digested a point. Wait until everyone feels that it is time to move on to the next exercise. Where there is disagreement, you use that as the basis for Creative Conflict and use the process to reach the larger truth—the synthesis. Remember, synthesis is not compromise. Ban compromise from your agenda. It can never lead to fulfillment.

Once your family has integrated mirroring into interpersonal relating, you may find children from other families magnetically attracted to the openness and honesty they can feel in your family. You can extend simple Creative Conflict practices to neighborhood children to deal with the problems they create for each other from telling fibs, to tattling, to walking on the neighbor's newly planted grass after being told not to at least ten times. Don't try to force Creative Conflict onto the neighbor children's parents. Only use the techniques where the conflict concerns you or when help is requested. You can share your feelings about this new process, but the best way to convince others is to be integral in your own communication.

In our community, one of the fathers has frequently called together eight or nine of the neighborhood youngsters, ages four to nine, when there have been arguments and hurt feelings. The children sit down together and do Creative Conflict. The kids love it. The biggest problem the children seem to create for each other is when they pair off and get into small groups, excluding one child. Today Shauna and Tracy want to play and they say Ayesha can't play. "Don't want her around," they say heartlessly. In the middle of the game they run away from Ayesha and leave her feeling rejected and angry. The next day Ayesha and Shauna play and Tracy is out. They all know what it feels like to be odd person out, but they still keep inflicting rejection onto each other and then hate the experience when it happens to them. One comes home crying, complaining to an adult. Normally you just let them work their conflicts out amongst themselves. But you can help facilitate their communication with each other with Creative Conflict. And when the situation is there on top of you and you don't want the bickering in your house, or if you see a child really suffering, then for your own integrity you do something. You can sit them down, even on the street, or you can invite them indoors for a Creative Conflict session about the problem. You have Ayesha tell Shauna how she feels being left out. Then Shauna has to mirror, and almost immediately when she gets into Ayesha's world remorse comes, or another, more real conflict emerges. There is always remorse in the end for making another person feel sad. When the conflict is resolved, the children walk off happily together. But you are the agent and your skill will help each child become his own agent in initiating that kind of dialogue and ability to get into another's world on his own without you demanding it. That self-governing comes through repetition and learning to listen and to mirror, so the child gets used to making that transfer out of ego.

In our very first group Creative Conflict with children in our community there were three of our children, two sets of parents and one other adult, who described the session as follows:

"We had a tremendous experience. Shoki, age six, was very hurt because his sister, Ayesha, age eight and their friend Shauna, age seven, often rejected him and didn't want to play with him. Shoki, up to that time, was often labeled by his parents as a 'bad' boy. He was always getting in trouble, broke three windows in the first three months after he came to the community, and would laugh at other children when they fell and hurt themselves. He never said hello or even looked at you when he came into a room or when you talked to him. The only time he spoke to an adult was when he needed something and then he would ask with a whining voice. During this first Creative Conflict session we asked Shauna to sit in front of Shoki and share with him why she didn't like to play with him and why she rejected him. She said, with her usual difficulty in expressing herself and stumbling over her words, that it was because he wouldn't play fair. He'd break the rules or start teasing and disrupting the game. His father then came on with an accusing tone, 'Shoki, did you do that?' And Shoki cowered and shook his head no. I was the only adult there who wasn't a parent and I said to his father, 'You are jumping on him and not giving him a chance to mirror or do Creative Conflict and share his world.' 'Shoki,' I said, 'can you mirror back what Shauna said to you?' He shook his head no again. 'Shauna, would you please repeat what you said to Shoki?' Shauna did, again with ums and ahs between every word. 'Try mirroring that now Shoki.' He responded, 'You say you don't like to play with me,' looking at the floor. 'That's *not* what I said,' Shauna answered in a frustrated voice hands slapping her knees. 'Shoki, try again and look at Shauna.' Shoki looked at Shauna for one second and resumed looking at the floor. 'Look at Shauna,' his father ordered forcefully. Shoki looked. I winced at his father's unnecessary force. But this time Shoki was able to mirror the first part about breaking the rules. With further gentle reminding from Shauna's parents to look at Shauna, Shoki kept looking. Then they asked Shauna to repeat the part he missed about the teasing and disrupting.

"He was finally able to mirror the whole thing after about ten minutes, at which time he broke down and sobbed. No one said anything and he soon stopped. Shauna asked him, 'Why do you disrupt the games? It just makes us mad. You know people won't like you if you can't play with them nice, and you'll be lonely.' Shauna was now speaking clearly and without faltering, for the first time *ever* as far as I remember. Shoki looked at her straight, listening with a deeper part of his being. We asked him to mirror what she said and he did so, perfectly. There was more sharing and mirroring and sharing and mirroring. Shoki's eyes were glistening but he looked around at each person in the room, right in their eyes. His father and Shauna's father also shared some feelings that they too had. Both were speaking very sensitively now. Shoki mirrored them accurately but was unable to respond verbally. Nonverbally his being was responding. It was relaxed, not tense, and there was a definite feeling that he was here with us. Everyone gave him positive feedback on his wonderful mirroring and told him how glad they were that he was being himself and listening and being here with us, looking at us. It was as if he realized that his ego was cornered and he started to cry again, this time with deep sobs and tears, primal tears, as if they were between him and the universe. I went to hold him and so did his father. He nestled in his father's lap, quiet now, wide-eyed. Everyone came over to give him some loving touches and caresses. His mother came last and said to me, 'It was so hard for me not to rush up and comfort him from the first. But I knew he had to face reality himself.' A breakthrough had happened and everyone felt it. Shoki finally fell off to sleep in his father's lap. It was past 10:00 p.m.

"The next day Shoki came over to my house for something and when he walked in the door his face was filled with light. He looked up at me smiling, the first time ever, and said, 'Hi, Debbie, how are you?' Shoki was now part of life, ready to meet the world. For the next week Shoki's parents both commented that he was a changed person. He helped around the house and was expressing affection instead of demanding it and whining for it. The joy in this breakthrough, the first time we had really done Creative Conflict with children in depth, thrilled us with the possibilities. Since then we have been researching and practicing different ways to bring the process of Creative Conflict into family life with children as well as into the schools."

Getting to the deeper level of motivations with children takes time and is more possible with older children, ages ten and over, where the intellect can consciously probe the heart. The following is a consultation between several parents of teenagers, including a father of a nineteen-year-old, a mother with three teen-age children and a Creative Conflict consultant.

Father: The conflict is my relationship with my son. On the one hand I want to be a good father and give him the advice he is asking for. He is a junior in college, not sure where he wants to go, what he wants to do. But on the other hand, he reacts like crazy to me. I know that he needs to make his own choices about where he goes and what he does and so I am kind of torn between saying, "This is what *I* think you ought to do," and saying, "Stay with the moment and focus on each day and your studies and the next day will take care of itself."

Teacher: What is his resistance to that?

Father: His resistance, I think, is a need not to be dependent on me for *anything,* so he can make his own decisions.

Teacher: Remember, the conflict is in you. You have two motivations: one is to let him do his own thing and the other is feeling you won't be a "good father" unless you give him the wealth of your advice. And yet you meet with resistance when you give him the wealth of your experience, as he doesn't really want it and that creates a conflict in you because he's not receiving it and not hearing.

Father: Yeah.

Teacher: There are two ways you can go with this. One is you can probe yourself. Find out what your "good father" self-image is based on. Or you can talk with your son and share what you got in touch with and that you have these two different motivations happening in you. You can say to him direct, "Hey, I have these two things happening with me; I want to be the good father and give you the advice even though I know you don't like that part and I also want to let you do your thing yourself." This is heart to heart. If he's willing, start the process of active listening and mirroring with him. If he won't, then you do it without making anything of it. If you just start being this kind of friend to him you might find him becoming more receptive to your good advice because it won't be given in a know-it-all or preaching way. It will be given as a buddy, sharing. And that way you can fulfill your motivation to be a good father too.

Father: I just got in touch with something as you were talking. It may be my style of doing it rather than the words I use. I come on too weak with the message, and the message may need to be more potent.

Teacher: You could use the I-message,* and then you cover all

---

* See Part III for the I-message.

your bases. There may not be anything wrong with your motivation to be a good father, but if you practice this type of sharing *with* your son so that you get into his inner world and really feel how he feels through mirroring and confirming, you would see a new way to be with him. Then it would no longer feel right to share your ideas in the way you have been doing which you now realize is too weak. You are afraid. Your fear is, "If I come on any stronger he is going to reject me, so I'll just give a little peep so I still feel like I've said something."

Father: Yes, that's it.

Teacher: " . . . so I better stay weak and underplay even though I am churning inside to really let him know what I feel and why." He probably picks that up and can't respect that feeling in you. So there may be nothing wrong with the motivation, but the problem is that you're not being integral. To get back to your earlier question, "How do you get deeper into motivation?"—you've got to the part where you are now in touch. You've shared it with me, and from my experience I have shared back with you. But when you are on your own you need to learn to ask yourself, "Is there integrity in my motivation?"

Father: Well there is another part of this. I get caught up in my son's anxiety about where he is going, not knowing what's going to happen next year when he graduates, because that's very real.

Teacher: But in this process where we talk about integrity, if you can own that feeling you have and then share it with him—not lay a trip on him—but share just as you are doing now with us, being integral to say, "This is my experience; this is how I really feel," then he comes away seeing your truth just as it is. He doesn't feel you are judging him or dictating to him.

Father: Coming from the heart more instead of from my head, my ego?

Teacher: Right. Just your core being. It is what it is. And that is an awesome place to be. That's what integrity is. Anyone who is in that space—a baby, adult, cat, anybody—there is a vibration to integrity that the universe respects, and most people respond to. Again the vibration is not easy to be in all the time and we cannot achieve this state overnight. It takes practice with this process of Creative Conflict and self-confrontation but that is the answer to the question of what to do when you get in touch with your motivations and you want to go deeper. You ask yourself, "OK, what's my real feeling about these motivations; how do I really feel about the situation," and you start to work on your self-honesty, your integrity.

Another lady present, a mother, speaks up:

Mother: When you come to that integrity part, it seems that's where we all get stuck. (To the father) I'm hearing the same theme in your life as is in mine when you come across too weak. I have values but I'm afraid of putting them on my kids. What do I do about that?

Teacher: If you *own* your values, saying this is how *I* feel, then you are not laying a trip on anybody; you are being integral. And usually what happens is you begin to see your motivations, the real feelings behind your values. Then your values may start to shift.

Mother: I guess I'm afraid. As you spoke with him I was getting in touch with some of my fears and if I get to be real integral I'm really afraid that I'm a selfish person and not a good mother to my poor kids, and *then* what! So then I get scared that that's all I really am and what am I doing in this world.

Teacher: Stop right there. Integrity always leads you to see your real manifestation. You might even say, "I *am* really selfish and then you own *that.* "So, okay, I'm selfish." What does it feel like to be selfish? You get in touch with your selfishness, and then you can work on becoming *un*selfish if you don't like it. You can work on saying, "Okay, I'm a selfish person, that's a selfish act, I'm in touch with my selfishness, great! Do I want to be selfish right now? I have a choice." You can then make a choice from your real self, to be selfish or unselfish, not from, "Oh, I don't want to be seen to be selfish so I better not be," or "I can't face the idea of being selfish so I won't think about it. I will just keep on living my life as it is." You have the right to decide to be selfish. Everybody has the free will, but then you will see the consequences and that hits you in the heart.

In the practice of Creative Conflict we often get to the point where the person does own, "I'm selfish, I really don't care about you, I really haven't been caring about you." And that is hard. That is the hardest realization, to own that you are a lower being than you would like to be; to see yourself as God sees you, you see yourself as you are in reality. Some people are absolutely unwilling to look at that and face the hypocrisy of their self-image directly, so life has to show them over the long term. Such a self-image of self-importance which ignores reality slows down their evolution. But a beautiful moment dawns when you *can* see yourself as you are in the group because you have people around you who support you in your self-understanding. They can understand your conflict with yourself and have compassion because they are working on similar conflicts and patterns in themselves. Still some people say, "I prefer to stay selfish and try my luck at the consequences," or "I am happy with myself as I am right now." You will have this attitude crop up in every group. Such people will say, "I don't belong here, I really don't want to change or be unselfish. I want to fill out my selfish desires while I can. That's what I really want to do. I'm scared I won't get them if I don't stay selfish." Then you go into the fear behind that feeling of insecurity and see if you can get beneath it. Sometimes people are very stubborn and not open. So we say, "If that's what you really want, go do it." But we try to show them the consequences of what might happen from the direct experiences in our own lives and in the lives of others we know. If people haven't had enough pain in life they are often prepared to risk those consequences, but people who have had enough pain or who have some foresight or who really care, do have enough compassion to feel the pain of others, and dig deep in themselves for some unselfish altruism. They have made a spiritual decision from their heart that they don't want to be selfish. Their response will be, "I don't want to be a selfish person; I am that way; I own it; now what can I do to change that?"

Mother: And then I get scared of the consequences of changing that—these are the things I'm going to have to do not to be selfish. Maybe it means giving up wanting to do this or that, and being home more with my kids when I don't want to.

Teacher: That is when you work consciously with others to get a mirror of what you really can do, because the solution to the inner conflict is probably an area where you are spiritually blind. Your assumptions about what you would have to do in order to be unselfish may be totally incorrect. You may have only two ideas in your mind about your direction—"if I don't do what I want to do, then I'll be stuck with what I *don't* want to do"—it's an either/or. By getting feedback from others, you may find that your options are not really so limited. You may begin by saying, "Okay, I don't want to be selfish, I have to stay home with my kids but I don't really want to stay with them. They are brats. I hate them." Now I am not saying that your feelings are that you hate someone, but I am just using this as a possible example of self-honesty. If you share what is real to you, right or wrong, then you can get a mirror for a solution. Maybe you need to get some more help for you and your children so you can tolerate each other better or enjoy each other or give each other more space to grow without exploiting the situation at each other's expense. It would be a really selfless act for you to do what would be best for everyone and to find out that this doesn't mean sacrificing your own personal needs. Selflessness doesn't exclude you; it means acting for the good of the whole, making the whole more workable. Then you will have to say, "Gosh, I've got a huge self-image, but is it real? If I go to someone for help with my kids, it means that I have a problem and I'll have to own that I'm not the perfect parent I think I am. It means I need help, and I haven't been an all-knowing mother." Many people aren't prepared to accept that humiliation because it means the destruction of a false self-image.

Mother: You've got my number.

Teacher: There are layers. Once you own the first layer, the next one opens up. Once you own the next layer, another one opens up until you get right down to the quick. You penetrate what is going on in the depths of the ego. But you need to risk being open with your thoughts and feelings. This is your first task, to become totally open and defenseless. But you can only do this when you can trust the group to act in your best interests. You need the help of a mirror or some mirrors of the group members in order to peel the layers of the onion. We must not look at the group as a threat. We all have the same onion really. The mirror puts you in the heart, insists that you reason by the heart, and this gets you in touch with deep basic motivations, which in turn gets you in touch with your integrity or lack of it. This penetration of your ego defense mechanisms then gets you in touch with your self-image, which puts you right up against the universe, right to the source of your consciousness, the crux of how you are creating your reality. All this takes practice and a definite commitment to work through. How you or anyone will get to the source can only be accomplished in a setting where you are actually doing it, doing the process. No one can tell you what your breakthrough will be. You can start a group on your own and discover the ego penetration with others similarly committed. If you have no one to bounce your projections off just do the steps on your own. Use all of life—then everybody becomes your mirror.

Mother: What do I do when I can't get any response from my husband or daughter? They won't communicate.

Teacher: All you can do is to be integral and say, "Look, you don't care about me enough to respond," or communicate directly whatever you're feeling. You've got to say it, whatever it is. Then that person is free to respond or not respond, but you have become clear and open because you have spoken your feelings with integrity. That's not self-righteousness. It's just simple reality. Self-righteousness is when you speak for everybody.

Mother: The frustration lies in that nothing really changes.

Teacher: If you continue to be more and more real, your daughter or your husband will open up or break down or start to respond or react in a different way. It's inevitable. If you interact integrally with your husband and he still doesn't communicate, then at some point you have to count the consequences of living with someone with whom you have no relationship, no marriage really. You can't change the other. You can only be honest and change yourself and choose what to do with your own life. Your husband will choose to respond according to his real nature. But at least you are living in truth, in reality. That is where God or nature or life responds with great power.

12

CREATIVE CONFLICT
IN GOVERNMENT

Integrity training in government could have only one effect if practiced. It would transform the power trips and the whole rotting governmental system. Political systems run on deception, payoffs, favors and competing drives to get ahead at other people's expense. Service to the people is rarely a high priority. Our legal system has evolved so that lawyers defend criminals who are obviously dangerous and guilty, yet through legal twists, wheeling and dealing, fine words, and picayune definitions of legal jargon, the lawyers secure a release while the innocent citizen pays the bills for the dishonest. What is the motivation behind all this convoluted operating? To succeed at being a great lawyer, which to most attorneys means winning as many cases as possible or upholding the letter of the law, regardless of what the heart or spirit says. The victim of a crime is always the loser while the criminal always has many chances of winning.

The System runs on ego, on the cunning of one-up-manship to prove who is the best at getting ahead, whereas Creative Conflict runs on cooperation and finding the greatest truth presented from all the factors in any given situation. To change government around we have to first want the change. If we aren't prepared to become integral in our daily lives in the home and in our work situation, we can't really insist that our governmental representatives and bureaucrats be any different. If you attend the local council or board of supervisors meetings in your county, you would be shocked at the low level of communication. In our county, they are right now almost at the point of slugging each other. If you listen to most congressional or parliamentary debates, underneath the sophistry you find very little real communication. One, they don't listen to each other very well and they probably couldn't mirror accurately if they were asked to. Two, they have hidden agendas which conceal their real motivations to please vested interests or to keep themselves in power and to tout the party line, whether or not they personally agree with it, because they feel obligated, since it paid their way into office and because they want to continue to please their own pocketbooks with high salaries and fringe benefits. How can we get any honest governing with this self-perpetuating privileged class of political rulers and all these layers of garbage? We can't unless we begin to challenge the lack of integrity in our representatives and insist on having our own lives based on truth instead of falsity.

If we were to insist on Creative Conflict inside the newspaper office, the bureaucratic structure, in Congress and in the executive office, we would be able to feel good about our government and the policies that would then issue forth from it. Our democracy would be a natural, evolution-oriented government, a process wise to the ways of the ego, yet unafraid to confront when the need emerges. And no matter what happened, if we did our best in uncovering truth by fair means and dealing honestly in our affairs, we could feel good with ourselves. But most people do not realize they are being false with themselves. They think, in fact, that they are being upfront and true. They believe they are on the side of good while sanctioning harm and hurt to others. Or they feel it is somehow all right to use bribery or give payoffs because everyone else is doing it, especially competitors. They fear the consequences if they do not stoop to the same low actions. But just because the competition is prepared to use ruthless tactics to get what it wants does not mean we have to do the same. Being penniless with peace of mind is far better than material wealth and constant inner conflict. And the consequences that we may fear if we do not succumb to manipulative power plays generally are not what we imagine. We cannot know ourselves nor can we know if our self-images are valid unless we learn to question our thoughts and do this work on ourselves individually and collectively to probe reality.

Creative Conflict, introduced into our legal and governmental processes, would peel off the layers of self-deception and unfold a new system, a new example of integrity to the world. If we began using Creative Conflict in schools, businesses, families, small groups, eventually it would filter into our society and into government. How much more fulfilled we could be if that could happen Now! But how impossible when resistance among strong, entrenched egos abounds. Just as in totalitarian countries where the rulers cling to their power at any price, so do our politicians cling to their control to keep their egos intact. The ego works the same way in all. So what hope do we have? Hope will only become conviction if we can begin a grass–roots movement. Examples of integrity speak louder than any words or theories, and what the American populace seeks in leadership is someone who will risk being strong and integral and not wishy-washy and pushed hither and thither by publicity or the manipulation of special interests. If we think about the ideal person for president, we visualize someone who we can trust to be aware of many needs, yet strong and able to stand up to any threat to the national well-being with conviction and energy. We would love someone vitally in tune, and yet we seem to be at a loss to find anyone with that spiritual strength.

We want a hero. If we look in the tracks of our national wake, the founding fathers and the people who have since become our national heroes have all had that quality of integrity. How much more of a hero is one who will use Creative Conflict to strengthen his or her personal integrity and hold that achievement as the highest value! Sometimes conflicts will not always die down by passive acceptance of others but only by energetic confrontation. Remarkable examples do come to mind where confrontation brought common sense and understanding for years. At the height of the Cold War in the 1960s, President Kennedy risked a hot war confrontation with the Soviet Kremlin by turning back the Russian ships which were on their way to Cuba with rockets. The Russians were bent on testing the United States' weaknesses. To signal the limits of tolerance in any ultimatum is fatal if the ultimatum cannot be carried out, but proves salutary and integral if it is real and practical. The same situation is before us now again in dealing with Russian aggression in the world of 1980. Our future and our integrity depend on our response. People do not respect threats of a weakling. They respect statements of fact which can be tested in real life.

The situation in the 1980s has vastly changed since the 1960s as Russia has quietly armed herself to the teeth with every conceivable form of destruction, including poisonous gas and germ warfare. It is almost certain that any military ultimatum, however honest and truthful, cannot be carried out with any overwhelming success because Russia is now number one in military capability. Today the Soviets are destroying the fiercely independent tribesmen of Afghanistan, but the nonmilitary ultimatums of the United States to pull out of the Olympic games and to create economic sanctions seem weak and impotent to save the Afghan people. The United States is afraid to arm the rebels for self-defense, and this fear of the consequences dominates the present tension between the communist and capitalist worlds. The same fear of consequences straps the US President's actions against Iran, a country flagrantly flaunting international law in holding 50 American hostages. How can polarization be brought to creative resolution?

If your words and actions have no teeth and no real meaning because you are afraid of the possible consequences, then your adversary will think you are compromising and he will act accordingly. If the United States would be clear about its position instead of hiding behind a smokescreen of negotiations in the Iranian issue and weakly attempting to back up its position that Russia withdraw its troops in the Afghanistan issue, then there could be a change in the balance of power. The US must speak clearly and enunciate consequences clearly; otherwise there can be no real communication or results, even if that communication is to provide a deadlock which stops the onslaught of the opponent. There are many strong options that the United States could take. If Japan won't stop importing oil from Iran and thereby supporting the Khomeini regime, the US could refuse to import any more Japanese cars and instead convert the money saved from foreign exchange into designing Japanese-type cars to be built in the US. The US can refuse to do business with countries that do not ban attendance at the summer Olympics in the USSR. With stronger consequences the US could get Europe to agree to cooperate with its sanctions against both Iran and the USSR in five minutes flat. The US could threaten to withdraw from the UN or not pay the bill that keeps the UN alive, or it could withdraw troops from Germany to show it really means business. But the problem blocking strong action lies in the huge fear of the United States to be seen as a "bad guy". Worry about the national self-image foolishly dominates American foreign policy, even though the result is that the other countries of the world do not have one iota more respect for the US. On top of that, the politics of getting elected dominate the reality of both the allies and the US President, so that clear messages are not spoken for fear of not getting re-elected. The desire to preserve self-image at the expense of integrity at the national level is just a blown-up version of the same politics happening at the interpersonal level, and the solution therefore is the same.

Spiritual ardor, along with the ability to deal heroically and sensitively with the weighty problems of the world, is the only thing that is going to pull humanity out of the downward spiral of duplicity in which all world governments are now mired. If we knew how to listen to other countries' inner worlds, to mirror them, just like they were another human being, we could establish rapport with the soul of the country. We would know their motives very clearly and would be able to anticipate their integrity or lack of it and their moves. We don't need to conduct our foreign or national policy from a feeling of guilt or social propriety or ignorance, nor do we need to stoop to dominate by force, if we can learn to be real. And this policy of stating the stark reality is the opposite way the nations of the world have been going. Duplicity and clever propaganda for the purpose of power-seeking distorts all reality and has become the order of the day.

Each of us has a responsibility to reverse the present trend. Each of us has the social, personal and spiritual choice to make a change. A community of people doing this would be the new Peace Corps. But first we must gain the clarity to recognize the need and the consequences of not doing something. As long as we remain imprisoned in our narrow egocentric state of awareness, we will be swamped by the growing complexity and multiplicity of the world's problems. We must realize that all our present social methods of conflict-resolution do little more than compromise, adjudicate, depolarize sides, placate egos, or allow people to have a sounding board or pressure-relief valve. But they do not change the System which runs on *ego*. The wheels of the System turn on controversy, not on the resolution of differences or on the idea that harmony and unity between people is really possible. The principles of Creative Conflict tackle this problem at the root while the world only wallows in the effects.

Business and governmental "peace researchers" are more interested in national conflicts, in big labor-management bargaining, or in environmental disputes concerning rights and pollution. None of these socially-oriented, academic attempts to resolve conflict has really succeeded because they concentrate on mediation rather than on getting to the roots of the conflict, and consequently there are today just as many insoluble differences between nations as ever. Is it not strange that there are Institutes for the Study of Conflict, Federal Mediation and Conciliation Services, Labor and Industrial Relations Consultants, Journals of Conflict Resolution, Centers of Conflict Resolution, and none of them confesses to have any answers to curing the actual cause of conflict?

The answer which our living experiment at the University of the Trees has evolved is at the human level of people and not at the institutional level, because the human level is the only level where we can get to cause. Why are governments afraid of Creative Conflict? The obvious answer is that Creative Conflict goes deep into the ego structure, and we may find the very peace researcher himself exposed to searching his motives. Who will come willingly naked to learn of a totally original and deep way which first of all requires that we put away all the garbage that we know does not work? A method which brings only the bare consciousness to a meeting and insists on a willingness to explore the depths of being leaves all our egotistic self-important opinion-making behind and is not therefore to the liking of our academic experts or social theorists. The root of all conflict is within individuals who cause it and not in the external situations and scenarios at which the peace researchers look to compile their statistics.

No progress will be made until people all over the world understand that conflict-resolution begins with them, their philosophy of self, their images of themselves and not from the opinions of experts who may well be good at patching up, but not very effective at prevention at the source of conflict. Most psychologists understand that world problems are just a reflection of individual problems, but few psychologists even know their own egos well enough to be able to help others master their conflicts. Few people really appreciate that therein lies the answer to world peace. Because academicians have not investigated the structure of their own inner psychology, they are unable to see the real cause and effect operating either in their own lives or in the world. Our nation spends billions of dollars as a people academically tracing the world conflict to sociological, economic and political roots, but we never reach the causative factor that gives the answer to real change. This answer will not come until we understand what people do with their consciousness.

People visit our community at University of the Trees and marvel at how so many different individuals all get along so well with each other. Over and over, visitors and new community members tell us they have never seen a group of forty people who live and work so closely together and who all like each other and get along. Individuals join our business and our university from varied walks of life and from many educational backgrounds. We are each quite different personalities, but in the heart we are definitely all one, and this is visible to visitors. We solve our differences by considering the whole and not by aligning ourselves with two or three polarized positions. Governmental systems which depend either on State authority or on the polarizing of issues between two political parties, as in many democracies, would experience a difficulty in trying to do Creative Conflict since they are used to the opposing issues being reduced to verbal exchanges in debate which never probe the speaker's real motives.

This is why Creative Conflict must begin with individuals. And Creative Conflict only works from that level outward through our social structures. In time, the process you are reading about or similar natural processes will catch on like a brushfire and spread throughout communities and find their way onto national levels. But Creative Conflict cannot be legislated beyond giving everyone the opportunity to participate. If we continue to play games with ourself and refuse to look at our internal environment and its effect upon our external world, then we suffer both personally and collectively. Can we commit ourself to the nuclear bond of love and transcend our obsessions with our own person so preoccupied with self? Only when we can honestly share this commitment with others integrally without any external coercion can our tensions within be prevented from being vented in the social system without. The clinging to the self-sense (ego) is everyone's free choice and must be respected, but we must not waste time with people who do not have the will to learn or to listen. This attitude of noninterference is not a form of intolerance, but a cosmic principle. God, or nature, leaves us alone to our arrogance and does not waste time trying to maintain life in an inhospitable environment.

We need to bond closely with others who share the same desires and goals as we do. Most people are so busy earning some money and pursuing personal pleasures that they do not take time to stop and get to know their own psychological make-up nor to alter the ratio of selfishness/unselfishness. Most people are not even in touch with their selfishness or don't care if they are selfish, so their conflicts simmer under the surface and then burst forth in their ego drives. Only by working on the ego can we syphon away the frustrations of our civilization. We need to realize the mechanism of consciousness that enables us to escape from looking at ourselves by allowing us to project our own anger or feelings of inferiority onto society, onto government, onto certain leaders.

Creative Conflict works in ways that religion or politics have never worked because its method is an exact replica of the way nature communicates with itself. It can work for anyone who has the simple wish to communicate more deeply. But you have to *want* it. Whether you are an industrial union leader, a capitalist, or a communist with different ideas of truth in your head, will make no difference once you begin to communicate from your heart. Whatever your religion, bigotry cannot exist because in skillful Creative Conflict there is this heart fusion. Belief systems, politics, ideals, concepts do not bring such love, whatever they may claim, but creative communication does. Creative Conflict brings a synthesis irrespective of all religious or political labels because it does not seek uniformity of agreement in ideals or ideas, but penetrates to the reality of being, which we call in Creative Conflict the realm of the heart.

Groups of individuals tuned to nature's ways, tuned to seeing in the material universe the laws of consciousness working in oneness, can through the sheer force of their love, raise the potential of the entire human race, because if any part of the whole has been raised, the whole has been raised by that much. When this change appears in daily life, in work, home and school, it will penetrate our governmental process and lift it up to conform to nature's laws. When the laws of consciousness are understood within, then they will manifest in our social institutions without.

How can you as an individual be an instrument of this change? Bring Creative Conflict to your local political meetings, to your church, your school, your work, your home. Organize groups to use the process and become an example of it in your own life so that you gain the humility that comes from living in truth and you take it wherever you go. When you have peeled off more of your own layers of the onion than those around you have experienced, your presence is felt by others and you will make a mark in their world. You serve evolution. In our life today the deeper question is no longer a matter of ideologies, of splits between spirit and matter, between Democrat and Republican, communism and capitalism, libertarianism or totalitarianism, religious people or heathens. It is solely a matter of discovering that reality is whole, and then applying ourselves to manifesting that wholeness.

Every founder of every religion, in essence has said the same simple fact—that the universe is one whole, integrated, interactive system, but mankind uses its emotions to find differences and to create dogmas which destroy unity at the level of our true being.

PART III

13

THE CREATIVE CONFLICT PROCESS— HOW TO DO IT

Moving from the general social strata to the particular personality is a matter of getting down to work with each individual's own unique ego structure. The difference between Creative Conflict theory and fact is the same difference as between the imaginative architectural schemer of a new building complex and the carpenter who rolls up his sleeves and dips his hands in the mud to mix the cement for laying the foundation. Creative Conflict will never be practiced by egotistical people who glibly spout off solutions to the world's problems, whether amidst the banter at the local bars or among ivory tower elitists at the universities. Only the individual who can see that something is missing from his life and who yearns to fill that gap will be prepared to start shoveling the encrustations of his own unconscious mind.

For most of us the ego subtly prevents us from seeing any situation clearly as it really is and therefore it blocks our real listening to life. As a consequence, even though we may think that we are perceptive, intelligent and aware beings talking with each other, there generally is very little communication taking place, very little transfer of meaning and perception from one person's mindstuff to another's, so that what lies in one mind becomes replicated in another's mind. We hear words, but not the layers of meaning and the inner being behind them. We see flowers, people, animals, etc., but not the light of consciousness within them. Only by accepting the most enormous challenge to expand our personal egocentric view of the world can we succeed in raising our consciousness to a higher level. In order to do this work on ourselves, together with others or alone, we must balance its depth and intensity with a light heart, humor and joy in relations. By making this work light we make *light* work. When light works for us we are in tune with nature and we can tackle anything, even transforming the manure of our own negativity into rich compost to assist nature in growing beautiful flowers in us.

To begin transformation of the human animal, we start from scratch, not assuming we know already where we are going. Such an attitude of openness forms the basis of learning something new, entirely beyond our present perspective. Practicing Creative Conflict begins with a number of simple but specific keys to real

Creative Conflict

WHO ARE YOU LISTENING TO?

All the inner tapes filter the real communication.

listening. As we utilize these keys we must also be on the watch for the subtle blocks to real listening, rising in consciousness, which we explored in chapter two. All the time when we listen, our goal is to hear the real motive behind the words and to tune into the integrity or the lack of it coming from the being. Without this awareness of the human ego at work in our perceptions, it is impossible to get beyond the superficialities in our relating.

KEYS TO REAL LISTENING

1. Centering: The first key is the centering meditation, some form of relaxing the body, feelings and thoughts so you can get in touch with your inner being and listen to yourself. You cannot really listen to anyone else fully until you can listen to yourself. When you listen to your inner being, your intuition speaks and your perceptions of life and your real situation are much more accurate. Some type of daily practice of relaxing your body and getting in touch with your feelings and mind will quieten your ego reactions and help you become gradually more open and clear.

2. Receptivity: Receptivity is the second key to real listening, where you consciously put aside all thoughts going on in your mind while another person communicates with you. If you are playing mental tapes about *your* feelings, *your* needs, *your* expectations, *your* analysis of the situation, circulating these tapes in your mindstuff while the other is speaking to you, you will be blocking your receptivity to the other person. Receptivity should not be confused with a passive state. It is a dynamic, conscious, willful act of opening your heart and mind to focus on the other, to let the other in, to merge the consciousness of each together, and to do this you have to clear your mind of what is going through it so that the mind is not racing ahead of the heart. Being receptive to another is like meditating on the other person with your full attention while he or she communicates.

3. Active Listening: Active listening is the third key, but it only works if you are in a receptive state, that is, if you are really *being with* the other person, receptively caring about him or her. In active listening you repeat back what the other has said to you as clearly as you can but you use your own words. Replay helps the other to feel that you are in rapport and are understanding. Most of us depend, much more than we realize, on other people intuiting what we really mean, or knowing exactly what is in our mind or heart, and we even feel hurt if loved ones do not do this mind-reading. We yearn for someone who can effortlessly understand us just as we are, without our having to exert any effort. Yet we believe we are good communicators and that we are clear in what we are talking about. We don't see that we are communicating just from our own egocentric perspective and expecting the other to have the same inner picture as we have. If we ever had to be a silent watcher, listening to ourselves communicate a message in a discussion with someone else, most of us would be shocked to find that not only do we have a difficult time listening to others in depth, but we are also incapable of listening to ourselves speaking with any depth or any guarantee that we would understand if we were the other person. We project our need to be understood onto others, looking for someone who can confirm our heart because we are not fully in touch with the heart ourself.

4. Mirroring: The fourth key, the technique of mirroring, reveals almost immediately how well our communication came across, how much miscommunication was the fault of the listener, how much was our own fault, and how much miscommunicating was due to just sheer laziness and sloppiness of the speaker of the communication. Mirroring trains the intuitive listening both to yourself and to others. Mirroring means to feed back what has been shared, not just in words but in vibration. As an extension of active listening, mirroring goes deeper into the nonverbal levels of relating. When you mirror, you are trying to reflect back what the other person's being is saying to you behind the words, which may be something totally different to what is said to you in words. You develop a skill to mirror back the feelings you pick up from other people as well as their words, so they feel that you are at one with them and can feel their hearts. You might begin to mirror by saying, for example, "Let me see if I understand you. What you're really saying is . . . " In active listening you must say back to the other what has just been said, which makes the other feel heard correctly and encourages him or her to continue speaking; but in mirroring you are actually trying to experience others as they inwardly experience themselves, becoming one, and taking the communication to a deeper vibrational level of being and then expressing from there. The other person must confirm or deny whether he feels you heard rightly before you may respond to what he initially said.

So if husband says to wife, "You don't care about what I want to do, you only care about what you want," the normal ego reaction is for wife to retort, "I feel the same about you; you don't want me around. You always go off by yourself." Then they go their separate ways in a huff and two hours later come together in cold silence until wife mentions, "Did you see the letter that came from Jan . . . , " and life goes on with the earlier resentful feelings repressed. They both try to smooth over problems and end up being silently angry. A zoom lens journey into their inner worlds reveals that the basic problem is that wife has certain expectations of what a relationship should be and husband wants things to be on his terms, so he disregards her expectations. She enjoys small talk and idle time together, and he doesn't usually have much to say and gets bored sitting around. Because neither understands the dynamic, they each question how much the other really cares and they develop a contagious insecurity. Instead, if wife decided to make this conflict creative and take their normal dead way of relating to a new level, she would begin to use the keys. She would first take a deep breath and relax. Then she would remind herself to put her own resentment and churning thoughts aside, just for the moment, to get in touch with *her* inner being beyond mental words and to listen fully to what *his* being is really saying. Then she would use active listening and mirroring: "I hear you saying to me that you are really frustrated because you feel that I only care about my interests and I don't care about you or what you want to do. It really bothers you." As soon as he feels received, as soon as he feels heard, the mirroring touches him and there comes a heart contact—being to being communication. You can feel the contact when it happens. The other person will soften and respond with a different energy, and that energy, too, is the heart.

Wife might still differ in the head. Her perceptions might still be telling her, "You never suggest things we can do together that I

like. You plan all your time and only fit me in when it's convenient. You want me to go along with the things you like which I
don't enjoy." But with mirroring first, she makes that being-to-
being contact which establishes a respect for one another and a
rapport. Then she can share her different view, and husband takes
his turn at active listening and mirroring. In mirroring you touch
each other at a deeper level so that you *can* listen, where communication can have meaning. That's why listening is the door to
the heart. So it is very important to remember to mirror, to insist
on mirroring, especially in the heat of an emotional interaction.
You are doing a dance in Creative Conflict, moving and responding in a pattern to enable you to be in harmony together. Like
Aikido or Kung Fu, Creative Conflict could be seen as a martial
art, but of the unconscious and the mindstuff where the only
winner is when everyone wins, when everyone comes away with a
broadened realization of themselves.

With practice, letting go of ego becomes natural. You are then
able to listen to life all the time. Mirroring becomes woven into the
fabric of your relating until you don't think of the steps as an
obvious exercise. Sometimes when you first begin to mirror, you
feel like you are practicing a technique, and the words may sound
stilted, even artificial, because you are unaccustomed to sharing
this way. Your children might react to the mirror saying, "You're
just a parrot, you're just doing your psychological thing on me.
Don't give me that psychology." This reaction can only come if
you mouth the words but leave the heart contact out. If you make
the desire for heart contact the most important thing, then mirroring comes across as genuine caring.

Normally the other person's defenses begin to melt as soon as
you mirror his real being back to him. He listens more. But if the
block lies very deep, mirroring may not penetrate the heart. To
reach the deep parts may take yet another of the methods of
Creative Conflict described later, or penetration may involve the
pain of life's trials to give some kind of jolt before there can be an
opening to a greater reality. Communing on the being level rarely
happens overnight, and to shove the ego aside is not going to be
easy in the moment, especially with someone whose egocentricity

makes you hot under the collar. Judgements and misperceptions are usually what stand in the way of hearing. If the other person is not able to hear you, you can make a point of hearing him. Then perhaps he will follow your example. If not, if he is so stubborn and selfish that he will not meet you half-way even after you have extended yourself, then do not give him the satisfaction of inter-acting with you further. Your silence will be a good mirror of his noncooperation. Eventually he may approach you in a more humble state. On the other hand, you yourself must be prepared to not only be a giver of feedback but also a receiver. One of the typical occurrences in Creative Conflict is to bring up an issue, certain that the problem is 99 percent the other person's, and then be shocked to have the entire criticism land right back in your own lap as your projection. You must always be ready for that to happen and ready to open to the possibility of its being true when it does. Establishing being-to-being communication takes time and practice. Seek out those who are ready to make self-honesty part of their lives to practice with you. If your closest friends or mate is unwilling to embark on this quest for truth with you or tries to impede your progress, you may have to consider the possibility of changing your environment and seeking out new friends, a spiritual family who, like yourself, are committed to truth. Find or form a group who will practice the methods and who will agree to support each other openly and patiently through the first steps at real communication.

Through practice your intuition becomes finely tuned, like a sensitive antenna that you use both to listen while receiving feedback and to tune into the worlds of others when you give feedback. You may find that you are tuning into the other person even beyond the point where he is in touch with himself. Some-times people who have difficulty expressing themselves (especially children) will come out with a statement and when you mirror it back, they say, "No, that is not what I said." You may have mir-rored what is really bothering them deeper down, but they are not yet aware of that part. So a good practice is to repeat what they verbally said before you mirror the real thing that you sense is bothering them. That will help them get in touch. Some people are threatened by having their real motives and inner being seen and mirrored by others because of inner difficulties with their own sense of worth. They are threatened at being open in the heart and making themselves vulnerable. They fear that nothing will be left of them. But in real surrender to truth, that sense of nothingness expands to a dynamic awareness of all-inclusive being. Instead of bringing them rejection, as they fear, this new state of humility brings greater acceptance from others.

As you practice, you develop a sensitivity to better ways to mirror because you are into others' worlds, in touch with their beings beyond their egos. At times you may get a feeling that what you are about to say will be too threatening for them. Then you have to draw their feelings out more first, to establish some trust between you. Draw out their judgements, their fears, their blocks that are twisting up their perceptions. Your caring will work right away, like magic, to take the communication to a level where true communion can be experienced. Communication implies two separate identities sharing information, whereas in communion, you experience two as one. Only when people stubbornly cling to their separate ego positions and refuse to see does Creative Conflict fail. But with such people even life will fail them again and again until eventually they must listen. If they do not have the will to communicate, there is nothing anyone can do. Coercive communication at the physical or mental level can force compliance, but communion can only come from freedom of the spirit.

When you really listen you will find that you can talk with strangers or with even the most defensive people and almost all the time you can get them to open up to you to some degree. You're not consciously trying to do a technique on them; the key is that they feel you're into their world. And that sums up the essence of successful mirroring—concentrating more on the other person's world than on your techniques. But you've got to have the technique memorized enough to have the know-how to get *into* their world. "Mirroring" is a term used by many groups to mean different things. Some people use it to mean nonverbal communicating, where a person stands opposite another and mirrors them physically, like "follow the leader". Physical mirroring can be a good first step, especially in teaching children how to mirror. But in Creative Conflict, mirroring is the way to become one with the psychic body of the other rather than the physical body, so that you feel it in yourself, and your goal is to mirror back that psychic body in the inner depth of being. Mirroring is the most important key in the whole universe of relationships because it establishes unity in relating. Even with stubborn egocentric people who do not wish to change or make any concessions or respect the world of another, correct mirroring will establish a clear view of their ego structures and they will see themselves as they are—stubbornly clinging to their ego positions—making absolute statements of opinion, unsupported by facts. Nevertheless, they are the only ones who can choose by their own free will to change, or not to change.

5. Confirmation: After you mirror you look for *confirmation,* the fifth key. The other person may confirm your mirror by saying, "Yeah, that's how I feel," or he may just relax and nod his head and go on to say more now that you have given him an opener to go ahead. By mirroring you create the space for sharing to take place. You are in essence saying, "It's okay to be feeling what you are feeling, sharing what you are sharing. I accept your being and your right to say whatever you want to say even though I may disagree with it." Then the person can share more openly and the communication can become more real. Sometimes your mirror will be off and the other person will say, "No, that's not what I mean." You begin to train yourself in mirroring by first active listening (repeating back the other's words) until you can do that easily. When you gain some confidence, then you add to your feedback what you *infer* or *intuit* is underneath the words and vibration. This is much riskier because there is a greater margin for error. If the other person replies, "No, I didn't say that," or "I don't feel that," don't panic. Relax, become receptive again, let go and listen more deeply and feed back again until your mirror is confirmed. Remember, you may be picking up something in the unconscious that the other person is not yet in touch with, in which case it may take him awhile to confirm. Because a person may feel threatened, he or she may be unable to confirm. This is not the time to push but to back up and give them space until you get some confirmation that you are mirroring correctly.

6. Response: When the other person has confirmed your mirror or asks you to explain further, then you may respond to the communication, but not before. Remaining open, with ego aside until the other has finished expressing or until the other confirms, takes self-discipline, but this is the only way to insure communication. If you are with someone who is receptive but inexperienced in these methods, go ahead and ask him to mirror your response as well, to help the communication to be deep on both sides. If you are with someone who reacts and doesn't hear you, you can say, "I don't feel heard. I don't feel you are really listening to what I'm trying to say." You cannot require people to listen, but you can share how you feel about their not listening and not hearing you. You can do this with anyone—friend or stranger—and it will be integral and leave the door open for them in turn to open up to you.

These keys to achieving in-depth communication are basically simple. They may even seem too simple to be able to bring the powerful results promised. But if you try them out you will certainly have a completely new experience in communication. Creative Conflict offers a way that you can give and receive feedback without fear of criticism or the separating, destructive effects which criticism can have. This communication process may at first glance seem laborious and initially it can be, but soon the interaction becomes quite fulfilling as you develop the skill to penetrate to deeper layers of sharing. The fact that 99 percent of all people cannot do this process of speaking, active listening and mirroring properly without practice is proof enough that we *think* we understand but do not. The saying, "Hearing, they hear not" becomes vividly illustrated. So it is wise to request and to use mirroring even when you *think* the other is listening to you because he probably is not.

7. I-Messages: One purpose for I-messages is to keep the finger of blame from pointing too severely outwards at the other person. The first impulse of the ego, when it thinks it has been hurt and that its case against another person is solid, is to indulge in justified anger or criticism or to sum the person up in a label and to write them off. "You're a dummy," is a typical retort. The

I-message makes sure that you do not make statements about others whom you may or may not be seeing purely, but confine yourself to saying your own feelings. As long as you are expressing what you feel, no one can contradict you, for you are the world's greatest authority on your own feelings. The moment you accuse the other person, even with comments like, "You make me mad," you have left the level of sharing and have left the possibility of touching the other person's heart, because in blaming him for your feelings, you have put him on the defensive. If instead you had used an I-message, you would have said, "I feel angry when you doubt me or don't believe me," and if you then said why, "because I am afraid I will lose you," then you pave the way for a communication rather than a fight. The four parts which express deep feelings are:

1) "I feel", owning your own feeling. When you accuse others, it relieves you from taking responsibility for your own feelings. It may *not* be his fault that you are disturbed, even though it was his remark that triggered off a disturbing pattern in yourself.
2) "angry" tells *how* or *what* you feel and describes your inner space.
3) "when you don't believe me" tells what triggered the angry feeling, and in this case the trigger was something done by another which then triggered your thoughts of fear.
4) "because I am afraid I will lose you" is the deepest and most important part because it gets to the fear. You usually need the first three parts of the I-message to set the groundwork and to get you in touch with this fourth part. It is only here that you reach the basic motivation, where you contact the thoughts that were triggered by the other person's actions. These thoughts that he might leave you may be pure projection, or they may be based on some prior action on his part when he did leave. When you get to this fourth part through practicing the four-part I-message, you also take yourself deeper into your own motivations. Ordinarily you are not often in touch with this feeling behind the feeling, that your anger is really caused by your fear.

I-messages take you closer to total honesty with yourself, the domain of the heart. When you are relating heart to heart you can become very vulnerable because you are being so open. With the ego defenses down you are in touch with your humble inner self. You don't have to make excuses; that is just how you are. You don't have to fear someone taking advantage of this vulnerability because when you are being that real, when you are that in touch with deeper motives, you are strong. You are speaking truth, and there is strength that emanates in that truth. It is real for you, truth from the heart, which is clear truth uncolored by ego filters, and that integrity is always supported by the cosmos. In being integral, you are acknowledging your *connectedness* with the cosmos; and because you are trusting your integrity, the universe will honor that trust.

Because this fourth part *is* vulnerable it does take time to learn to be in that deep place of honesty. When you mirror the four-part I-message from another or when someone mirrors your own, you get in touch with each other's threatened feelings. And you can, if you will, go deeper and deeper together. You can get very real, probing deep patterns together almost impersonally, because you can look at yourselves without getting all caught up in your ego. When done in a group, the four-part I-message takes the whole group consciousness deeper as a collective entity in probing real motivations. It leads to the nitty-gritty questions of life where there is a tremendous energy locked up that can be released for maximum spiritual growth. Confusion clears up. You are able to ask and answer questions that you were never able to penetrate when you were in a more superficial state of consciousness, questions like· "Why *am* I here?" "Why *are* we together if this is how I *really* feel?" "What *am* I trying to get out of this job or this relationship?" "Is that what the other person really wants to give?" The method leads to a deep self-probing and probing with each other. In a group you have many mirrors at this level of openness, many soul mirrors who can take you deeper in your confrontation with self. They will help you ask the nitty-gritty questions and give I-messages to get to your deepest truth. The group learns to flow and to bring in the right questions at the right time.

Here is an example of probing the heart through mirroring in a real live Creative Conflict:

Joan: (Teary-eyed) I found myself extremely and embarrassingly touched by Richard's statement about his commitment and I guess by the look in his eyes, and it kind of tunes into how I was feeling when I came in, which was that I'm afraid of tears. It seems to me that everything I do around here ends up with me blubbering. And I'm not real used to that, you know. I cry on occasion and I've never been real terrified by tears but it seems like it just keeps coming up here. I guess that's the part of me that is really afraid. It shows in little actions. Like somehow I set my alarm wrong and didn't wake up in time for coming to class, and then I couldn't find the place. You see, I'm excited about being here, but also I'm really afraid, and one of the things I'm afraid of is that I have a close relationship with my husband and I'm wondering if this course and being with the university is going to put me in a space which he isn't quite ready to enter yet, because although we can talk to each other, I don't know if he could open up to a large group of strangers to the degree that he would need to if he were to enter a course like this. And I don't want to be in that separate space from him.

Nat: (a new person to Creative Conflict attempts to mirror) Joan feels that she wouldn't be able to talk with her husband being here.

Joan: Being here, coming here regularly, I would be coming from a different space from where he was. Which is a little bit different from what you said. *(Note she is not giving complete confirmation to his partial mirror.)* We are very open with each other and can say almost anything to each other at any time. But I don't know if he could open up in groups like this. In fact he hasn't said that he's ready to do that. So we would be living in two different worlds and that might mean somehow that we wouldn't communicate as well. *(She clarifies)* As I am saying this I can see that that shouldn't really happen, because if through this class I gain some skill in communication then I will use it with him *(here she rationalizes her feelings.)*

Nat: (again mirrors, this time more fully)

Joan: (nods in confirmation but does not respond; Ann responds instead)

Ann: I picked up a lot from your vibration as you spoke and had some very strong feelings about it, so maybe everybody can double-check me to see if I'm off the wall. When you first began to talk, I got the feeling of somebody who was trying to walk across this frozen pond to get to the other side, but the ice was cracking underfoot—I felt thin ice. *(Ann is using her intuition, tuning into the being's message behind her words, which is hard to convey in print.)*

Joan: (exclaiming) I dreamed about that just the other night!

Ann: I bet! I felt there were two important parts of your communication. The first was when you said, "I'm not used to crying." It said so much about your inner world from the standpoint of . . . well, you've been in Creative Conflict ever since you've been here and your ego structure is cracking up . . and you can feel it. A little at a time every week. You're starting to get in touch with these deep problems for the first time since you were a child, maybe, and the tears are coming now. Your old self is cracking and saying, "This doesn't fit with the old self-image! Tears is not me."

The second thing is that part where you switched from your feelings to your head when you were responding to Nat's mirror. The fear you have with your husband is that some unknown thing will happen in the relationship. I felt that the first time you communicated it to Nat before you changed it, was ambiguous. When you said about your husband not being able to speak in a large group, that was a different point, a different feeling from your first expression of the fear. And then after Nat mirrored, you changed it again and you said, "But, of course, if I have more skill then I *will* be able to communicate with him." So that was three different things, each with a different feeling happening, and what I picked up was that at a deep level you must know that you're going to be a different person after you get across to the other side of the pond. And you're not quite sure that that person will be able to live with your husband in the same way that you have been, unless he also can come and do the same trip.

But then when you switched it on Nat, it was back up to the shallower level of yourself saying, "Oh, it's going to be alright because I'll just be able to communicate better," but there's a deeper feeling down there where the tears are coming, which has a feeling of the handwriting on the wall, and that's what we need to get to. But I *did* feel your willingness to go through with it, to get to truth.

Stephanie: Could you mirror the essence of what Ann said?

Joan: (slowly) There were three or four different things happening . . .

Ann: Mirror what you got out of it first so you can stay in touch, and then mirror back the details.

Joan: . . . that my switch to saying, "Oh, my communication skills will actually help me," was an intellectual reaction, whereas I was feeling something deeper and clear when I made that statement about not wanting to end up in a different space from where my husband was, so that we would be farther apart than where we had been before. And you felt that the head reaction of saying, "Okay, I can use these communication skills," wasn't as real. (Ann nods) But at the moment I said it, I felt it was an insight to me. And you felt that it was not as valid a reaction or as deep as the first point.

Ann: Let's say, "not as deeply felt". The head reaction is valid to a point, but your deep feelings are something else.

Joan: You're saying that my deep feelings are the fear of creating a rift between us and that my head reaction is that, "I can do something with that and use it to help my communication skills and therefore mend whatever rifts might happen."

Ann: Right. And there was something else said about *you* after you had come to the University of the Trees.

Joan: That I've already been through a great deal of actual

Creative Conflict in my role of teacher at the children's school. So I'm determined to go through with it even though my ego's cracking up around me and I am going to end up in a different space because of this class.

Sue: Yes. Do you know what Ann is sensing . . . and what it makes you feel like?

Joan: About the fears? Gee. I can't remember the fears now. I'm blanking out.

Stephanie: Just to give the new members here an overview about Creative Conflict, if Joan cannot mirror that part, it means that it might be very close to the truth. When something is really close to the truth in us we tend to forget or fog it out and we don't see it. It might be something . . .

Ann: Nitty-gritty . . . close to the bone.

Joan: It really is close to the bone.

(Editor's Note: Although this Creative Conflict did not delve too much deeper into Joan's fears of what might happen in the future, just getting her to recognize her unconscious feelings and opening that level was an important release. Stephanie shared that the next day at school Joan was singing and laughing, lighter and spriter than she had ever seen her.)

Once you are at that depth of feeling, the whole group tries to help everybody stay at that depth, to keep that intuitive contact going. The group force becomes an agent for the deepest truth to emerge that the collective group members can perceive, having done their best to use the keys to open to a greater intelligence than any one person's perspective. Of course you or even the whole group can be *off.* And it is very important to maintain the humility that is open to correction or to another's more intuitive perception at any moment that may change your perception around 180 degrees. But through this Creative Conflict process you learn to go to your own inner authority for truth, not to accept another perception as truth if it doesn't feel resonant or in tune with that deep space inside you.

When you speak with others who are also accustomed to being very real you have an ideal situation, and usually you can get to the place of oneness and true understanding very quickly. Most people, whether they know about these steps or not, will respect your interest and desire to have the communication clear. With a little guidance they will also respond well to your request that they should mirror back what you have said, because your interest shows you really do care that they hear you. But you have to ask them to mirror in a way that doesn't make them feel that you doubt their hearing, but that you doubt whether your own communication was clear. Just watching someone else use these skills evokes a feeling of dynamic concern and puts people in touch with a deeper part of themselves which makes them want to gain the skills too. Find others to work with you who really want that integrity. Many may say they want that depth, but you will find that in the acid test of the Creative Conflict group they are not really prepared to do the self-confrontation needed to get there. Don't worry about this. Just go as far as you can. Remember in humility that this work to conquer our own self is the most difficult work on the planet and the most selfless work you can do. You can't force a horse to drink, and the human animal is just as stubborn if it does not want to see its own egotism. This truism applies to the whole species from top to bottom, from the most gifted to the most stupid person who thinks he has all the answers. Egotism is the worldwide human problem which Creative Conflict squarely confronts.

14

IDENTIFICATION

Every action that a being takes involves the mysterious process of identification. A cauliflower has the identity of its own cosmic image patterned into its cell life. The imprint in its being includes all the qualities of cauliflower. A cauliflower could never be a radish, nor a radish a cauliflower unless the DNA was somehow modified. In human beings, the secret of how we create our reality lies in this process of identification. Our self-image as a human being that says to itself, "I have two eyes, two ears, a nose, mouth, certain thoughts, certain color hair and eyes, etc.," is the cosmic patterning of human being in our DNA that programs our initial identification as a body. As our thoughts and feelings develop, we make choices which affect our concept of who we are. We evolve negative or positive self-images according to which thoughts or feelings we identify with in our minds.

Our skill in mastering consciousness and re-creating anew the reality we experience, lies in acknowledging how the identification process works in us. A seven-year old girl who comes to our children's school each day is extremely cooperative for weeks at a time. She acts like a leader to the entire class. Then one day she comes to school and balks at following directions or being told what to do. No matter how you try to reason with her, she goes on a rebellion streak, often for a week or two, until something shakes her out of it. Over a period of two months her behavior vacillates between the two extremes of positive leadership and stubborn resistance. What causes the switching? Upon questioning each time, she shares that her mother or father became upset with her and she fears they don't love her. Each time her behavior becomes a problem, invariably the cause turns out to be a feeling of not being loved. She identifies herself then as unlovable, and this identification in her mind permeates all her actions, which alienate other children and adults from her, and confirms her feelings of being unlovable. When she finally feels loved again, usually through sharing in Creative Conflict or through strong parental discipline where she is sent home from school to do schoolwork alone or be put to bed until she can be civil, she transforms herself again into a loving and lovable child. Her identity changes. What causes the chameleon-like change? She either learns that the disobedient behavior will not be tolerated, and the pain of the consequence of going to bed motivates her to change her actions, or she becomes convinced in her mind again that she is loved.

For all of us, the attitudes that we hold, the positions we take, the feelings and thought trains that flow through our minds that we latch onto and give energy to, are what determine our reality. Identification entraps our pure consciousness into a mold. When we identify with a feeling or thought we feed that impression; we own it as our own and become one with that experience. We color our reality with its quality, just as the quality of cauliflowerness forms that plant's experience of reality. Pure consciousness is made impure and sullied by the images, thoughts, feelings and concepts that lie deep in the unconscious and by those impressions that flow through the mind. When we identify with these expressions of human consciousness, we bind our pure consciousness in self-limitation.

Mastering the vagaries of the human mind is the function of all spiritual paths and disciplines. If we can understand and conquer the identification process we attain self-mastery. Biological conditioning, personal conditioning and cultural conditioning all operate through the process of identification. Because the structure of Creative Conflict penetrates to the root of identity, Creative Conflict embraces and amplifies all true spiritual paths and evolutionary growth processes. We learn to see that human understanding of identification is essential not only for individual evolution but for world transformation. The identification process explains why millions of people worship and identify with power seekers— Hitlers, Mussolinis, Mao Tse-tungs, Khomeinis and other world dictators. In Creative Conflict we transfer our identity from various impure expressions of consciousness to the One, the pure being in all. We do this not just in theory or just in imagination and in ideas, but in reality. And the only proof is our fulfillment in life. Life confirms our achievement by mirroring a change back to us in the form of greater harmony, peace, joy and heightened awareness. When we are involved in ego transforming *for real,* the personality undergoes many changes. But we have to be prepared to look at ourselves, to hear the feedback clearly. Many people are not ready to listen to other people and feel attacked at even the gentlest feedback. They cling for dear life to the identity they have built up, threatened to look at any part lest they see something they do not want to admit. The basic change demanded by Creative Conflict requires us to identify with the One, the pure being whose doorway is the heart, and from that new center of identification to work on the ego. Only at this deep level of identification can love smooth the process of growth.

Gradually we learn to tell what to allow into our mindstuff and what thoughts not to entertain. One woman expressed her insight: "I can't believe this is happening to me. It seems too good to be true. If I go with my doubts and worries then the road invariably leads to pain and misery. If I stay with my attunement to God, to feeling that joy, then it's magic that happens. I swear it's magic. Everything turns out. I've read that this is what is supposed to happen, but it is so different to experience it and see that it really works."

People come to Creative Conflict looking for the heart, the love, something that will fill them. Intellectual working on the ego from the head is not fulfilling, nor can such attempts work for long, because identification with headstuff causes a separative energy that breaks down trust and butts ego against ego. The result is more negativity. Working on the ego from the heart, from that center where we feel our being, leads to cooperation and trust. We not only trust others, but trust in that evolutionary thrust which is taking us toward our higher potential, towards oneness. Positive identification with pure consciousness awakens the hero in a human being.

The goal and the vision of Creative Conflict is to re-enact the ancient role of the mythical hero who dedicates all to conquer the limitations of self. The ancient idea was that the gods helped those who stretched themselves to their ultimate potential. In your group, if you keep tuning to love, you change your identification and your thoughts automatically. In an early Creative Conflict group, one of the facilitators kept feeling that something was not going quite right. He said, "The energy in our group is scattered, and the facilitators are not together. Everybody throws in their opinion and people interrupt each other and the energy is really intense, but no one gets to that depth that unifies or penetrates. It's making me full of doubt. I feel like I may be in my head, and I'm not sure whether what I'm going to say will be right or not." A more experienced facilitator responded, "I can see you identifying with a lot of self-doubt now, and I am sure that your vibration communicates to these new people. It may be helping to create the problem in your class. If you identify with your love, instead of with your unsureness, you will stop worrying so much about penetrating and will begin to draw people out and give them space to share instead of coming at them head-on. Share your perceptions in a spirit of searching, of humility and openness. As long as you maintain that identity with love, you're on safe ground, even when you don't have all the answers. From that center you can still be real and fiery if need be, and confront directly, but you won't be coming from your head as you have done. There will be a different vibration then, and everyone else will catch the same vibrations. Vibrations are contagious."

GROUP IDENTIFICATION

In the same way that we identify with our families and culture from childhood, we also identify with groups and adopt the standards of the groups we are connected with. Usually we adopt a group's favorite forms of rationalizing and characteristic modes of communicating, without realizing we are doing that. Many German prisoners in concentration camps during the war imitated the brutality of the guards by unleashing violence on their fellow inmates. Unconsciously people tend to take on the psychic shading of those around them. Truly our minds are not separate. Our mindstuff permeates space and influences the mindstuff of others in our environment and vice versa. A very important responsibility for all individuals is to be on the look-out for collective group identification which may blind us and block a greater truth.

To strongly identify with a particular profession or persuasion or person in authority, be they revolutionary leaders, gurus, rock and film stars, a beloved teacher, religion, or way of life, can be positive for a period of our life if it expands our boundaries of self, but becomes dangerous if we lose our own center. You can use identification with others to awaken the hero in you to excell, but too frequently identification with someone else acts as a compensation for unconscious feelings of anger and insecurity that have been repressed throughout life. An identification with another can be a creative stepping-stone to higher consciousness, but even that identification brings self-concepts and roles which are self-limiting.

The danger in identifying with a group is that we think we have expanded our boundaries of self, but we have also taken on a new ego-identity called "the group". Because of its numbers, identifying with the group collective ego often feels more secure than building up our own identity. In the Creative Conflict group situation we are aware of the potential danger of group identity and constantly challenge each other to think for ourselves. Compliance is the block that betrays ego identification with the group. We can't just live out the movie of our personal or group identity in true Creative Conflict without receiving a mirror back, either from within the group or from without, that we are limiting ourselves. Any group identity will be vulnerable to challenge from outsiders because they look at the group as separate from them. The more we practice Creative Conflict, the more we learn to test the mirror to see if the messages are truth or are projections. Within the mirror of the group also are too many eyes looking for the tell-tale signs of defensive behavior and irrational gaps in our listening, reacting and manifesting that reveal any false identity. The aware group consciousness constantly watches, awake to the identification patterns, helping each other to not limit ourselves. Through tuning to pure consciousness, group consciousness becomes the omnipresent consciousness in the Garden of Eden allegory.

THE GROUP AS OUR REAL SELF

As the group identification becomes more and more pure, the mirror for each member becomes clearer and more intense. As sun reflecting off of a mirror intensifies its fire, so does pure group consciousness intensify penetration into people's souls.

"And Adam and his wife hid themselves from the presence of the Lord God amongst the trees in the garden. And the Lord God called unto Adam (through Adam's inner voice) and said unto him, 'Where art thou?' "

"And Adam said, 'I heard your voice in the garden and I was afraid because I was naked; and I hid myself.' And God said, 'Who told thee thou wast naked? Has thou eaten of the tree?' "

Genesis 3: 9, 10, 11

Our psychic nakedness or embarrassment before the gaze of the Lord, incarnate in so many mirrors in the eyes of a loving group of people, comes from the question that we inevitably face: "Where art thou?" "Who are you really?" which forces us to expose ourself and to ask the naked question, "Who am I, beyond any identity?" for if "I" was truly one with everything and everyone, how could "I" ever feel naked? Only by identifying with our sensory skin and the ego that develops from that identification do we ever feel psychologically naked. Group consciousness becomes the eye of God, God incarnate in many mirrors, so you cannot hide your naked self among the trees of knowledge—of comparison, of judgements, rationalizations, projections, identification, basic assumptions, all the ego patterns—because your mirrors are asking, "Who are you, Where art thou? Have you become identified not with your whole self, the Tree of Life, but with your drives, your sensations, with your crystallizing images, with the ego?" Then, through love, we have a chance to let go and hear the inner voice speaking again. We can feel the presence again. There is no other alternative in a Creative Conflict session but to let go, come clean and bare our soul or to run away and leave the group, because we cannot hide from our own conflict and frustration if the group is determined to search to the depths of consciousness until the causes of our problems and self-limitations are found. How willing we are to cooperate in this search will be reflected back to us in the group's supporting, loving, patient assistance or in a more aggressive, penetrating kind of mirror.

Like Adam, we will probably have to go through a whole gamut of trips, including the idea of leaving the group heart before we can begin to understand the difference between identifying with what is pure and identifying with ego thoughts. This is called spiritual discrimination, or the ability to sift the false from the true, which is the sign of self-mastery. You know when you are gaining this mastery by what happens in your life outside the group throughout your daily experience, as well as within the group.

You can't really know what takes place deep in the being of a person in Creative Conflict until it happens to you. You can be giving clear feedback to others and you can read all about the changes other people experience, but when you are the one who has to come up against your own ego, then you have a whole different ball game.

To love more deeply means to care more deeply, and this quality is developed by constant practice of identification with the selflessness of pure consciousness in the center of every being. Such selflessness taken to its fullest expression saturates us with the bliss and love of a heart overflowing. The waters of clear love well up from the soul and overflow the heart in radiant joy. Each step in the process of Creative Conflict, once we make the choiceless choice to dissolve our ego, sparks off the next step. Discovering and facing up to what we are creating or identifying with will be the trigger to set off the unfoldment of limitless love.

Identification is the important process that determines the whole of our reality as humans. To understand how identification works in fact and not just in theory is to understand the cause of your own ego. Identification with "Self" is a big subject and I have developed a whole system of yoga* on its many ramifications for human consciousness. As we identify with the total environment and do not separate from anything around us, our personality undergoes a change at the nuclear center of being, the most fundamental part of our self, and we are no longer orientated only to the human race but to the whole of existence. The mandala of life is all around us; we are not limited to any one part but are in the center, and therefore one with the whole. In the ultimate manifestation of this state we are either looked at by other humans as mad or as gods (the divine fool). Examples of identification with pure consciousness can be seen in all great religions and in the words of Christ and of Krishna, who both see a greater reality than the egotistic human one.

I pray that they all may be one; as thou, Father, art in me, and I in thee, that they also may be one in us.
(St. John 17:21)

The yogi sees me in all things, and all things within me. He never loses sight of me, nor I of him. He is established in union with me, and worships me devoutly in all beings.
(Bhagavad Gita)

I am come in my Father's name, and ye receive me not: if another shall come in his own name, him ye will receive.
(St. John 5:43)

This entire universe is pervaded by me in that eternal form of mine which is not manifest to the senses.

* See *Rumf Roomph Yoga* tape course—24 sessions available from University of the Trees Press.

> Although I am not exclusively within any creature, all creatures exist within me. I do not mean that they exist within me physically. That is my divine mystery.
>
> *(Bhagavad Gita)*

Whatever we identify with, that is who we are. The mystical teachings of all great religions point the way to identification with the entire universe in order to discover our ultimate self. The ultimate self referred to in all our most profound scriptures is pure consciousness itself. Everything takes place in consciousness, and without it nothing can be experienced or exist. Consciousness has no limits unless they are self-imposed through identification. These are the limits that Creative Conflict seeks to remove from our consciousness.

CAN WE DO IT?

Any deep and lasting commitment to ego penetration and realization of self must always come from what one sincerely *wants* to do, not from what we think we should do. Most people are not in touch with their heart's desire to be selfless and united with the whole. Apart from the example of a few saints, ordinary religion fails to build the kind of bond that can stand through heavy testing. Only when a religious person breaks through to a level beyond doctrine and concepts can he be tested in the fires of life and come through to a new understanding. The spiritual forces needed for the building of lasting bonds between people cannot come from within the framework of institutional religion or politics, but can only spring from the living truth which embodies the original spiritual essence of all religions. Ordinary religion tends to be highly conceptual, masking the original pure essence vibration. For Christians, God is the Father, Christ is the Son; Christ was a godlike being who told us that we must die before we could have eternal life. He obviously meant dying to our *little* self rather than a physical death. But in spite of these many explanations and ministerial interpretations, people don't really know what these concepts mean. They have no direct experiential knowledge of the wisdom that founded the religion.

The direct experience, if not of God, at least of one's own

states of relative light and darkness, becomes the first step toward a truth that lives and which therefore has the power to transform us. By practicing spiritual principles, we discover for ourselves how our senses create an illusory world and that, in reality, all of this world is made up of impressions in consciousness. We then begin to experience other states than the normal one and we taste the ever-increasing joy of God's presence, the closer we tune ourselves to that space. We become motivated from within our hearts, not just from some ideal in our heads, to constantly seek the One and to remove all the obstacles that keep us from that feeling of sweetness inside. Do you feel sweet inside right now? Are you disturbed, worried, or in pain? Do you feel unloved? Do you doubt yourself? Can you get in touch with what you are identifying with right now? The spiritual forces which are necessary before there can be a real gathering together of people on this planet must be able to produce a real bonding among people so that they no longer feel separate from each other but are secure in each other's understanding. These forces are none other than our own will to live truth, to search truth out, to practice truth and to face how we create our reality.

The following deep spiritual principles are used in the practice of Creative Conflict to help bring that force to life, and are given for those who really want to go beyond the ego into the cosmic self. Meditation upon them and identification with them helps you make the quantum leap to cosmic consciousness. See if you can use them during Creative Conflict.

FIVE PRINCIPLES OF CREATIVE CONFLICT

To understand fully each of the following five essence principles, you will need to take time to meditate on each one. These are very profound spiritual truths that need to be experienced, not just understood intellectually. The aim of all of these principles, these aphorisms, is to master obsession with our egos which the yogis call self-intoxication and replace it with the self-saturation of love and bliss.

PRINCIPLE #1

**WHATEVER YOU CAN SEE
WHATEVER YOU EXPERIENCE
WHATEVER DISTURBS YOU
WHATEVER IS NOT MASTERED—
THAT IS THE TRUE QUALITY
OF THE MANIFESTED SELF.**

This first principle is based on the reality that life is our mirror. Whatever you are manifesting from yourself gets reflected in what you think, see and experience. It is also reflected in whatever bothers you. Who is being disturbed? You—your consciousness! Something in you needs mastering or changing to deal with the situation and regain equilibrium. Then the mirror will reflect a different picture back to you and you will feel and think differently. The self which you are aware of now, both what you see clearly and what you have yet to fully understand, that is the true quality of your manifested self. That self is what is manifest in you now, in whatever situation you are in, in the body that you are in and in the self-limitations that you have not mastered. The self that is your cosmic self is quite different from this manifested self. The cosmic self is what you have not yet manifested in human awareness. This unmanifested self lies even beyond the unfolding glimpses of higher consciousness which increasingly come into your awareness as you practice Creative Conflict and true meditation. The deeper, unmanifest self cannot be experienced with the normal conscious mind because in that state there is no experiencer. You can only experience that One superconsciously, where the experience and the experiencer become one.

To have a personal realization of what I am saying requires reflecting upon your manifest self. One way you can approach experiencing these concepts as reality is to take one at a time, meditate on it quietly, then apply it to your own thought life. Eventually you will have an insight on how these patterns of consciousness work in you. All is one in reality and to reach the unmanifest we have to recognize that what is happening out there in the world is not separated from what is happening in here, inside our consciousness. The true self cannot be disturbed by anything because everything is itself. Any turmoil, any problem in consciousness is created by a self and being self-created, can be stopped by the same self. So as long as you are seeing something separate from yourself, that is the true quality of your *manifested* self and that is what you have to master. But it is not your true self. The only feedback you have on your manifested self is the quality of your everyday living on this earth as reflected in the quality of your thoughts, feelings and actions.

So, whatever you are seeing, that's IT, whatever you are experiencing, that's IT, whatever disturbs you, that's IT, that is the universe that you are manifesting through your consciousness at every moment—NOW. If you see the world as full of troubles and strife created by other selves and you separate yourself from all that mess, saying "I'm not like that," you are cutting off a part of your consciousness. The true self is whole, encompassing all. In your reactions to how others use or misuse their consciousness you discover the projections of your own unconscious and the quality of your own consciousness.

PRINCIPLE #2

- **WHAT WE DO NOT SEE AND KNOW AS MANIFESTED AROUND US IS WHAT WE REALLY ARE.**

- **WHAT WE APPEAR TO BE IN OUR MANIFESTED SELF IS ONLY APPARENT IN WHAT WE ARE SEEING AND THINKING.**

- **ONLY CONSCIOUSNESS ITSELF IS REAL. ALL ELSE IS AN APPEARANCE CREATED BY THOUGHT.**

What we are seeing and thinking are only effects, appearances caused by something much deeper in us. What is that something and where do we find it? That is who and what we really are—the cause of our own consciousness. We are too caught up in the machinations of our own mindstuff, sensations and feelings to be able to perceive the cause of our very own self. Too much is vibrating, whirling, ruffling within to clearly see through it all.

Only consciousness is real. And the state of pure consciousness is where we go beyond personality identification, where we have the penetrating insight into our own soul. We do not yet see pure consciousness or know pure consciousness, yet it is the ground of our being. All that we are seeing and thinking is merely a *reflection* of our manifested self, only what we appear to ourself to be in any moment in time. That is ego. But that is not the impenetrable essence. Ego is the grand appearance, the *accretion* of many moments in time. When you feel your "isness", you are not thinking, you are being, and then soul is reflected in the clear, calm waters of your consciousness, like the mirrored surface of a still lake. Oneness is beyond the personality and its reflection in life's mirror. So whatever you experience as separate is a reflection of your ego, an appearance created by your thoughts. An enlightened person sees nothing separate from him or her self because there is no ego self to know any difference. Even the soul mirror disappears and there is no experiencer, no I, no mirror—just pure experience, just *that.*

PRINCIPLE #3

THE EASIEST AND QUICKEST WAY TO DISCOVER OUR TRUE NATURE IS THROUGH LEARNING THE CESSATION OF IDENTITY WITH OUR EGOS.

The object of Creative Conflict is to transcend ego reactions. Working with others is the fastest way to do this. These reactions come from identifying ourselves with our self-limitations built up over a long period of time. Through the group mirror we discover what the one consciousness is doing differently through each of us, which enables us to discover the quality of our own consciousness and the nature of our identifications. Through working together in this way we release our egos into the One Self.

How do we do this? We watch our reactions in thoughts and feelings and share them to see what they are creating in others' minds and what they are manifesting in our lives. All mindstuff which is disturbed by what it experiences is being ruffled by the thoughts which flow through it. That ruffling can become our mirror, our teacher, even when we are alone. The teacher becomes the situation we are in, because however we experience the situation we are in has a direct cause in ourself. How are you experiencing what you are reading now? What does your experience tell you about yourself?

Positive feedback in the Creative Conflict group is necessary to keep the motivation to work on ourself alive and growing. It builds trust and strength. But we don't have that much spiritual need for the positive interaction because it does not disturb us. It is the things that are disturbing that make valuable teachers, because whatever disturbs you is what you have to work on. You sharpen your critical faculties when you can evaluate clearly without getting disturbed. A mutual backslapping society is not the place to be if you want to perfect your being. You can take a Dale Carnegie course for that. Some spiritual and psychological growth centers are just that, and they are completely unable to handle the real world with its fear, jealousy, doubt, etc. Most spiritual teachings in themselves are not enough to handle the situations that emerge because people are unwilling and unable to look squarely at and challenge the knee-high negativity in which they walk. They prefer to avoid negative identification by running away from it, rather than mastering it.

In the process of life the farmer has only to remove the weeds, dig a channel for the water to flow, remove the obstructions and hey presto!—irrigation and growth, nature runs to the right levels and does everything. Nature does everything if we move the obstructions in consciousness. Dig a place for the water to flow and it will go. The same with these methods of Creative Conflict.

We dig pits for ourselves in life so that we can fall into them and learn what we did wrong. When we know what errors we made, we know how to get out of the pit we've dug so we can get up and go dig another pit. Gradually we learn to avoid digging new pits. In Creative Conflict we learn discrimination. To a discriminating one there is a complete cessation of identity of mindstuff, senses and body as the self. Then you can enjoy the senses more purely. There is no limiting identification with this body and the senses it is using any more than we would think of ourself as a telescope. When we use a telescope to look at the stars or when we use a microscope, we don't think we are the microscope or the telescope. These instruments that we are using—the eyes, the ears, the taste—they are just instruments, they are no more intelligent than the user. So to a discriminating one there is a complete cessation of identification with all this stuff you are experiencing. We learn not to evaluate this universe through these instruments of the senses, because there is nothing true about our sensory knowledge, absolutely nothing. The stars only appear as they do because they are limited by the limitations of your physical eyes. But the stars are much more than what the eyes convey about them. Can you tell with your senses what the atoms are saying in the wall? Can you hear them speaking with your ears? Yet we know they are singing their own song, vibrating there beyond the sensory limits, and they can be experienced when we go beyond the separate self-sense, the idea of being separate. Take any situation . . . if we look deep enough there is something about it we don't know. If we look at its interconnectedness with the entire universe, there's some reason why we are in that situation even if we can't think of a reason. And the more we probe into any action or any disturbance or any situation we happen to be in, the more expanded a view we will gain, and the more we will know what we don't know.

Pure consciousness is cosmic "I", the "I" that is in all of us thinking it is itself. Whatever conscious thoughts you put into that pure consciousness are powerfully manifested by the creative force of nature. The creative force that flows through us, whatever we put into it—there it is, creating our reality. So the primordial creative force of the universe manifests whatever you have in your head, whether it is nonsense or beauty. The only way to master your reality is to go beyond even the positive identity with beauty, goodness, etc., to identify with pure consciousness. Without such identity, duality and problems will remain in one form or another. The task may seem Herculean and terribly idealistic, but have we as a human species really any choice if we are to survive? To establish this supreme identity requires practice. It is the purpose of all worship, prayer, concentration, contemplation, meditation, samadhi—the destiny of human evolution.

PRINCIPLE #4

THE CESSATION OF IDENTITY WITH WHAT YOU FEEL YOU NEED IS NECESSARY FOR CONFLICT TO BECOME CREATIVE.

What we are looking at in our thoughts always is the effect, not the cause. So how do you trace your thoughts back to the source and get to the cause of your being?

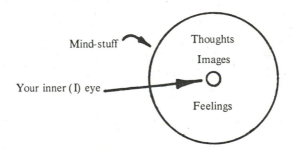

Thoughts and feelings bounce off the screen of your mind for the real you to see, choose or let be. We must always realize how conflict arises in thought and whether we need to have it at all. An alcoholic cannot control his habit because he feels he needs liquor. "I need a drink," he says. And behind all our words and at the back of all our desires and drives there is a feeling which says, "I need it." Sex, food, romance, excitement, thrills, love, husband, wife, baby, ice cream, whatever . . . "I need it, I must have that to be happy. Unless I have it I won't feel happy. I must yearn for it and wish for it to happen in order to live intensely and happily." Such identity with some object that will make us happy is the cause of all our suffering and conflict because we create pain for ourself when we do not have that object. Happiness comes from a state of being.

Within the life situations in which we find ourselves, conflict arises. Therefore, we have to learn how to identify with the center, the peaceful pure consciousness, and to cease identifying with other people and their needs, with our own felt needs and wishes, and with our concepts or images of reality. This does not mean we do not have compassion for others or that we cannot have personal needs or desires or have them filled. It means we put them aside for awhile so they don't color our perception of others and of truth.

When people have value differences, especially husband and wife or parents and children, they often want to change each other. And both parties usually feel they *need* to hold onto their viewpoints for autonomy, which means that the other is the one who is supposed to do the changing. With Creative Conflict both parties agree to release their need to hold onto their viewpoint temporarily in order to discover the ego drive and motive behind their own differences. They do this to gain direct perception, a clear view.

PRINCIPLE #5

ONE REMAINS SERENE AND CALM WHILE LISTENING TO ALL THE PROBLEMS OR WHILE CONFLICT IS RAGING INSIDE AN- OTHER PERSON.

Let us meditate positively on this thought for it is how we test ourselves. The world's negativity is seen with equal clarity as the positivity; we can see it all around us, hang-ups, conflicts, contra- dictions, violence . . . . Creative Conflict is like a garden. Can we look around the huge cosmic garden and say, "Why do I have to relate to all these people?" What kind of palette is the Universal Intelligence painting the cosmic scene with? All these different colors. And did you decide what colors were going to be put on the palette? No. Life just says, "Here's a great big brush, and you go and paint a new world, a new scene," and you've got to use the colors that life gave you, which are the people in your life, or the people in your group.

Contemplate this idea: Have you gone around and looked at all the weeds? The weeds in the garden can be likened to all the blocks and especially the doubts and fears in the mind. Do you accept that they are there whether you like it or not? This involves knowing the difference between that sublime state of acceptance (in which you are humbly in touch with yourself and therefore can begin to truly grow) and the state where you identify with distorting tapes that have been going on in the mind and buried in the unconscious.

Even listening to the tapes that others play and identifying with them spoils the garden. The tapes are grinding away like too much loud music so that we can't have peace. We must know, clearly know, that the mind habitually identifies itself with the body and senses and false perceptions, and that only through developing a certain power of discrimination do we realize the difference between the weeds and the flowers that we want to grow in life's garden. We then perceive what they both truly are—creations of consciousness. Through seeing this difference between what our mind does when it is identified with the body and the senses—and when it is identified with the heart and sees clearly, we don't have any more problems. Then what is a weed to one person may be a wildflower to another, because it depends on what we identify with. Then the true self floats peacefully in the purified garden where there is no weed to be seen. Even if we identify with pure consciousness with one degree of vision out of the 360 degree vision, we will be motivated towards investigating the deeper nature of that expanded state, eventually becoming the 360 degree vision of consciousness which is looking everywhere at once, out of the back of the head as well as the front. Our desire and curiosity for freedom are awakened in such a way that we can't go back. We feel like we are trapped into the spiritual trip, because it's a trip of no return once you get on it. We always think we can go back because we believe we have unlimited free will, but once we go so far, all the bridges have been burned.

THE SHOCK POINT OF REST

At some point in Creative Conflict if you are totally open you will experience the nakedness of the ego as it fights to stay afloat on the sea of vanity which we have cultivated. From birth we have been exhorted, cajoled or driven by ambition to perform, compete, become someone as a personality or to shine like a superstar. The whole culture worships the superstar, from Jesus Christ to rock musicians. We all want to become super personalities, and then we are confronted with the real message of all sages: become nothing, surrender ego to the One, go through the Dark Night of the Soul, persist to the end however difficult; the way is not wide and easy but narrow and difficult, like walking along the edge of a razor, say the Hindu Vedas. At this point in life the ego is faced with a decision—either to escape and stay limited or go deeper and accept the feedback of the group teacher to re-evaluate itself. It does one of two things: it writes off the group as a bunch of unseeing, hurtful, misunderstanding and blind people or it takes a look at its track record of pains, hurts, mistakes and missed opportunities. It will either re-evaluate the group or itself. This is the point when people often blank out, and the self-sense feels lost without the familiar egocentric scenery to relate itself to. We can call it the Dark Night of the Soul because when the ego is threatened and has no longer any defenses, it must get off the throne or be cornered in the tremendous black uncertainty, the pain of loss and annihilation. Rather than face this fear and pain, some people choose to repress it or go into a dark night of deep confusion or depression for months while they are resisting life's message.

Most people are in awe when they see another reach this point and believe Creative Conflict is great, until their own turn comes to look into that gaping dark hole and then the entire scene changes. But if we want growth, if our soul is ready, it will meet this shock point as a turning point in our evolution and this moment of truth becomes our most productive experience leading to self-mastery. Such challenge is how life teaches us. Creative Conflict is an intensification and amplification of life.

DARK NIGHT OF THE SOUL

Why should we have to have a Dark Night of the Soul? There are so many people telling us we can avoid the Dark Night and have growth all easy. You can just take a drug or meditate or do Sufi dancing or be tapped on the head and have Shaktipat or the guru looks you in the eyes and you're instantly away without any dark night at all, just bliss and ecstacy. Is this a self-delusion leading to smugness and blindness? There seems to be this division between what we consciously experience as ourself and that tremendous storage of old tapes, many of which have been re-pressed so that they are very hard to get out into the open because the mind has these tremendous bolts and locks on it. Under those locks is the unknown self, the thing which we bring with us into life, and very few people ever get in touch with what is down there in that dark deep pit with all those strong battens on it. The Dark Night of the Soul means walking through the valley of the shadow of death, as David puts it in the Psalms: "I shall fear no evil, for Thou art with me." The evil is nothing external but those ghosts waiting to jump out of our own minds at the slightest opportunity— self-doubt, negation, guilt and a whole host of demons waiting to suck our vital force and keep us from radiating. So the Dark Night of the Soul merely means how do we get through that fear of losing our life, losing what we have, losing our idea of ourself, losing all those memories? Some people think that without those they wouldn't be anybody. That's the only treasure they have and they feel if they didn't have all that, they'd be all empty, they'd have nothing to live for, because they really can't trust that state of being empty. So the dark night requires a dying to oneself, a dying to the idea of being a separate individual. The separation is not real. It's only in our mind, creating a wall between our personality and the unknown self which is the rest of the total environment around us which we don't know about. You can't really know what the dark night feels like until it happens to you. This confrontation with your soul will most certainly come at some point in Creative Conflict when you have to decide whether you are going to surrender and let a bit more ego entrenchment go.

With a supportive group the Dark night doesn't look so dark because you can explore other options and ways to be or to approach life. When it comes to letting go of a pattern, the fear is that there will be a vacuum, a void left, when actually there is a richer world ahead if we can only see it. That is where a supportive group can help. Others who can be with us in our inner world can help us to see the many wonderful possibilities that are before us. Some questions to ask ourself when we feel that darkness are, "If I let go of _____ that I am holding on to (whether a person, a career, a self-image, a way of relating, etc.) let me list on paper ten new things that I can do with my time/energy/love/interest. What options do I really have? Let me list them. How would I really feel without that baggage that I am holding onto? How would I relate to others?" These questions help us both to prepare for the dark night where our deepest unconscious attachments are threatened and to go through darkness to a greater, brighter light when we find ourselves in the position of having to confront our fears.

We can go through life fearing and avoiding the confrontation with our unknown self because we can't really know beforehand what it will be, or we can face the dark night. This is the meaning of the saying, "We have to lose our life in order to find it," which doesn't mean we have to die in the body. It is a terrifying experience to feel that we are going to be annihilated, to face that big black hole, the unknown self out there and we don't know what it is like. Can we really trust it? Our mental stability seems to depend on having all those battens and padlocks on the mind. But what lies under those locks is the soul, the true self. All you need is to touch that place—your inner sanctum—just once, and the memory of something positive and releasing will take you through the ego confrontations to come.

When the soul begins to listen to its real self, all pretense disappears and we become defenseless since there is nothing to defend, nothing to lose but ego, nothing to gain by filtering all the feedback to make it acceptable to our ego self. The blocks and blindnesses on the way to this state are many, but the main ones which the ego uses to prevent complete listening to feedback have been given so that when the moment of the dark night comes to us, we are not left hanging but put into a sublime state of choosing the ultimate, or choosing to continue our own petty lives on a tiny planet floating amongst billions of other planets, suns and stars. To recognize that choice of a lifetime when it is given is rare on the face of the planet. Is it not worth penetrating the ego traps strewn like mines upon the field of human consciousness?

15

CREATIVE CONFLICT AND THE SEVEN LEVELS

Very few people ever ask themselves just where their consciousness or awareness comes from or how this marvelous stuff functions inside the brain. Most material scientists think that consciousness is a product of brain matter which is capable of storing impressions from the senses. But the author's own scientific research into the structure of consciousness over the past twenty-five years clearly demonstrates that *human consciousness is an effect of light.* In the cosmic sense, light and consciousness are one and the same—a profound realization to meditate upon. How is this so? Just as white light refracts into the spectrum of seven rainbow colors, so do we absorb light from cosmic rays bombarding us at every moment and refract that light into seven major energy levels which correspond to our *chakras,** those vortices of energy in the human etheric body which are whirlpools of invisible light. They absorb the radiant energy from cosmic rays and translate this light into what we call awareness. Each of the seven centers directly influences our different glands and our different areas of specialization in the brain. Our state of evolution and the levels of consciousness we function on are a reflection of the amount of activity in each *chakra.* Going in-depth into the nature of light, color and levels of consciousness is not for this book, since it is covered thoroughly in my books *Supersensonics, Nuclear*

---

* *Chakras* in Sanskrit, means a wheel or revolving center of mental or bioelectrical currents.

Evolution, Rise of the Phoenix and *Exploring Inner Space.* Nevertheless, Creative Conflict is an outgrowth of this investigation into nature's process and laws. Its techniques are based on the way humans process radiant invisible light into drives, instincts, personality and consciousness. Creative Conflict is the active process by

Lux or light is the experience of the spectrum of the universe within our own awareness.

which we get in touch with the natural operation of the nuclear evolution within each person, and realize both physically and spiritually that the stars *are* within us. This may sound absurd to those imprisoned in the concept that our beings are limited to our physical bodies, but even they will admit that wherever the stars are situated in space they are ultimately experienced in the vibrations and electrical impulses of our consciousness. That is what I mean when I say the stars are physically experienced within us.

To understand this deeper nature of Creative Conflict, we need to look briefly at the seven different interdependent levels of awareness, each having its own time world, its own method of perception and its own experience of the universe, and how these levels affect day-to-day communication. Because people tend to identify with one or more of these chakra levels at the expense of other levels, communication problems become amplified, and communication across the levels becomes difficult, not only from person to person, but even within *oneself.*

The assumption of most humans is that in one-to-one relationships we can talk with each other in-depth. But one of the first things that the mirroring exercise shows us is the difference between our own dominant level of consciousness and another's. For example, one person may be dominant on the physical level, living in a world of action, food, wine and sex. The negative aspect of this level is severely limiting in that the consciousness dwells on sensory stimulation and pleasures, craving them all the time, and is unable to see the vaster vistas of life. The positive side of the physical level translates into dynamic action that gets things manifested, enjoys the senses wholesomely, and is well grounded.

A physical level fellow fancies a genteel, idealistic lady who has certain qualities he would like to have but doesn't. She feels attracted to his sexual "roomphiness" because his dynamism gives her energy and triggers a joy of life that is dormant in her. They get married. After awhile they have problems. He wants excitement, stimulation, sex every day, and she only enjoys this physical intensity about once every week and prefers to stay at home quietly reading and contemplating. She wants to be able to share sensitive feelings with him and he laughs at her, telling her to stop thinking about all that nonsense. He gets angry and she gets depressed. Big gaps in communication bring unfulfillment to each of them. These people are living in two totally different time worlds and perceptual worlds. Until each knows how to enter into the inner world of the other and feel what drives and motivates the other, acknowledging that they are different, their marriage will never be fulfilling. Once they are able to enter each other's inner reality, they will be able to learn a great deal from each other and the new view from a different level will be an incredible revelation to both of them. We are normally so stuck in our own tunnel vision, so obsessed with our own thoughts, that we do not have 360 degree vision that can look through everyone else from behind their eyes. When we lose that tunnel vision, we experience an initial shock at how differently we see people and how differently others think and respond to life.

In Beginning Creative Conflict we are so concerned about just mirroring the vibration and words of the communication that we don't often look for the different levels of awareness in different people. Discovering the levels requires more detachment from our own subjective reality. But in Advanced Creative Conflict, we begin to penetrate the self-image at subtler and subtler levels and to see which levels of consciousness the self-image has emerged from.

The following chart shows the seven levels and the personality types with their typical behavior in a group situation. Learn to look for the level operating within people as they speak and within yourself as you speak. Each level is labeled with a color which most closely approximates the color of the aura which can be seen around the face and head when a person is functioning in that energy level. By watching for these levels of awareness, we gain insight into the thresholds of the ego. Through the acquisition of experiences, whether touching or seeing something, or loving someone and getting hurt, we get entrenched in our usual reactions to that experience and build up our identity, believing that is who we are. Suppose you lived a very hurtful life, always getting rejected. As a result, you built up psychic scars and insecurity. Now you yearn for ego food so much you even do disrupting things to gain negative attention, rather than feel you get no attention at all. Your aura flashes green from insecurity and yellow in your drives to use your intellect to get security. The ego builds up all sorts of explanations and opinions from its experiences. How do we deal with this natural process? We understand and then gain mastery over this process by becoming aware of our own private world and how it is uniquely different from the worlds of those who are close to us or with whom we relate on a daily basis. Developing such awareness requires much receptivity and application of Creative Conflict.

THE SEVEN LEVELS OF CONSCIOUSNESS

The following list is nonlinear in the sense that no one level is more important than another, and the order in which we discover these characteristics in ourself varies from person to person, depending upon which chakra dominates in our life. We learn to discover where our consciousness is at in evolution in our present circumstances.

Aura Color: Red *Level Dominating:* Sensory Awareness
Personality: Reacts quickly to stimulus, sensations, words, actions. Physical consciousness which is aware of separate bodies because it sees itself mainly as a physical body. Identifies with the physical. Seeks stimulation, quick to anger. Reactiveness is out of control because it bounces off a stimulus unconsciously like a reflex. NEED is to control reactions internally and stay receptive to discriminate real existence from one's reactions to it.

Aura Color: Orange *Level Dominating:* Social Awareness
Personality: Wants to say the right thing in order to be accepted. Is concerned with and identifies with how others see us. Enjoys social activities. May get caught up in social chit-chat and superficial relating, finding it difficult to be real about deeper feelings. NEED is to risk one's image and get beyond feelings of personal prestige and self-importance, to transcend the milieu in which we are born which gave us our cultural brainwashing. Then the social drive becomes a desire to expand and share new awareness with others. We achieve this social transcendence by meetings with

others who are similarly committed to discovering otherness. If we can discover what otherness is, then we can get beyond the feeling of being "other", allowing real union to take place.

Aura Color: Yellow   *Level Dominating:* Intellectual Awareness *Personality:* Verbal, intellectual agility, analytical, may deflect feedback with lots of words and rationalizations. Can get caught up with the head and lose contact with the heart, feeling separate or cut off from others as a result. May be sharply penetrating in giving feedback and able to really dig out the conflict in another. NEED is to slow down, stop rationalizing or expecting people to be a certain way without questioning our own basic assumptions and perceptions, to get in touch and stay with feelings and to tune into the inner worlds of others to feel what they are feeling. If we don't understand how our intellect works when it sees another, we won't understand our blocks to pure perception. Only self-analysis will tranform this level. This means probing the heart with the intellect. We cannot do this alone, analyzing ourself in our room, but analyzing ourself in a group as we are experiencing others. The best method is to watch our judgements and point the finger at ourself at the same time as we are pointing the finger at another.

Aura Color: Green   *Level Dominating:* Security Awareness *Personality:* Insecure and untrusting of the group. May be very warm and loving as well. Fearful of rejection or of losing something. Jealousy and possessiveness are problems. Identifies with desires and gets attached to desires or possessions. NEED is to work on opening up and sharing love, risking feelings and trusting the cosmos to bring us what we need for fulfillment. NEED is also to gain control over our desires for other people, money or objects and control over the body's cravings. We do this by letting go and letting be.

Aura Color: Blue   *Level Dominating:* Conceptual Awareness *Personality:* Idealistic, may often refer to situations from the past. Often the hurts or slights we have experienced were not intentional and yet we have a psychic memory of them stuck in our mind. We conceptualize them and those memories influence our communications with others and filter our perceptions. People on this level frequently get stuck in concepts of how things should or ought to be and therefore are unable to experience how things really are. Can be very good at positive identification and also prone to negatively identifying with another's reality and getting pulled off center, because on this level we are so prone to identifying with our own moods and concepts as reality. May take time to process feedback. This level always remembers afterwards what it should have said during the Creative Conflict. NEED is to work on listening more deeply without playing tapes in our own minds; to look for the real, not just the ideal. NEED is also to learn to live without expectations and concepts of how things ought to be, thus creating stubborn basic assumptions. This will bring mastery over our own thoughts and emotions and the way they program our memories with morals, ethics, concepts, and help us to stay in touch with the real message of the here and now. This gets rid of self-programing.

Aura Color: Indigo   *Level Dominating:* Intuitive Awareness
Personality: Able to see the future potential. May be so much in the expectations of the future that we are out of touch with the present, and always feel the grass is greener somewhere else. May be very sensitive and perceptive in tuning into another's reality. Identifies with the future and with abstract thinking, and may seem far away to people not dominant on this level. NEED is to work on being more grounded and responsible in the now. We develop intuition by discriminating between knowledge we have acquired second-hand from others and knowledge we acquire from our own subjective hunches and impressions. Then we need to discriminate which of our subjective impressions are true intuitions. By getting inside the other, or inside nature, we bring subject and object together and then we reach the intuitional faculties which only work when subject and object are one. Then we just know. We may not know how we know, we just feel at-one. By learning to listen from a nonverbal, nonconceptual, nonsensory angle beyond people's worlds, ideas and body language, we develop this intuition or direct perception. This brings extra-sensory perception, which can be trained by proper mirroring and identification (See advanced mirroring exercise on page 301).

Aura Color: Violet *Level Dominating:* Imaginative Awareness
Personality: Lives in a world of images. Can be spaced-out or

dreamy, cloaking feedback in vivid, descriptive images. Can be caught in fantasy and cut off from the heart. When the heart is one with the imagination, then the images are true. Our emotions, thoughts and feelings are often dictated by the images we hide in our imaginations about others and about ourself, which may be false pictures. Many of our self-images are not in tune with our capacities. They are either too little or too grandiose. Yet we identify with our images and believe they are real. This may make us proud and arrogant or small and belittling of ourself. Someone on the blue level may not believe in their images, but identify with their emotions and the concepts they have worked out by putting two and two together, except that they may get five instead of four. Someone on the yellow level identifies not with their concepts or images, but with their rationalizations, expectations and deductions. On the imagination level the NEED is to discover how we create false pictures and to not believe all our images. We need to master the jumping of our imaginations that sets up the false pictures which block communication with others and which make reality seem very harsh when it conflicts with the imagination. We can get through this barrier by checking our self-image with our actual manifestation, comparing our manifestation with others who do the same task, so that we can gain an accurate perception of where we are at. At the same time, we have to free ourself from acting according to the images that others have of us. In its highest use, the imagination is a creative energy that can be used to take the communication to deeper, primal levels of being and powerfully re-create our reality.

In looking for all these aspects of consciousness in the make-up of our group, we set a challenge for ourself which guarantees expansion of consciousness and communication. Only through commitment to discriminate our perceptions can we achieve the super-penetration of our egos that will bring us the vaster reality of cosmic consciousness. That will, in turn, bring the cosmic communication skills that people and the world so desperately need. There is an elaborate balance between all the seven levels, in fact these levels frequently overlap in each individual. Nevertheless each person has one or possibly two dominant levels that shine through as he or she communicates. We are all rainbows, but our personality has developed and crystallized along the path of least resistance for us, one of the spectrum of colors which becomes our resting level. Each person sits inside his uniquely combined time-space bubble and experiences a different kaleidoscope of reality.

In Advanced Creative Conflict you get first-hand knowledge of these facts of personality. You learn to see others not just through the filter of your own predominant level but through all the seven levels that compose the white light of pure consciousness. Any *one* level or threshold of energy taken alone is a distortion of the wider reality that synthesizes all seven into one encompassing consciousness. You discover the seven levels in the Creative Conflict group by learning to see the individuals as many TV cameras all seeing the same objective situation, but from different angles. *When you see from the level of consciousness of others at the same time as you see from your own you are learning to see from a wider reality.* The picture of another from inside-out is far different than what we imagine when we look at them through our own perceptual mode from outside-in. The normal human outside-in tunnel vision is so strongly colored by our identification with our way of looking and by our own filters, that other people appear pretty much all the same. When we can really experience the gestalt of others' inner worlds we perceive an incredible collage of color and energies, different motives, different views, different chakras vibrating. Yet true perception of the universe merges all in one, because you and the others become one. This is the "nuclear" way of viewing things, thoughts, people and their words as we go beyond our obsession with ourself and move toward synthesis and oneness. We are compelled to get beyond our own egocentric way of viewing. We discover what we do not know, and we gain humility and awe at the vastness of this inner space.

When you see out of the sluice valve of just your predominant *chakra* you are motivated only by the drives of that *chakra.* Multiply the red levels of those who crave stimulation and action to the point of fighting, and the blue levels who crave peace to the point of appeasing the fighters, and you can see why there is the polarization of energies that we have in society. Multiply these conflicting qualities by the other five unique levels of consciousness coming from the other five chakras and you can see the world scene and why communication in the world is at such a primitive stage. Only when you can penetrate your own drives and motives can you choose to control the forces moving you, not by manipulating them outwardly in your words and actions but by understanding them from within. Then the *chakra* energies change and so does your personality.

To work for the evolution of humanity through Creative Conflict means to experience both the pains of self-growth and the joys of selfless work. You can serve humanity through working on the structure of consciousness, though you must begin with your own blindnesses for any transformation to occur. The idea that you *are* society, you *are* the whole, you *are* what you see, you *are* what you hear, you *are* what disturbs you, means that you can no longer look to some analytical observer to scientifically define a situation for you and be satisfied with that as your reality. In evolving to the nuclear center—the essence center of your being—you are responsible for everything in your reality. The validator and what is being validated are one, subject and object are one, the individual and society are all one—all mirror reflections of the other. Creative Conflict methods reveal that all the facets are part of the one diamond of consciousness. When we look from the center we are in harmony with the whole although our individuality remains unique. We experience this ultimate reality for ourself only by contacting that essence being. By planting the seed-vision into the earthy group consciousness of our own immediate group we awaken the planetary awareness of a world brain, a union, of one-planet-one-people. We can together then awaken to the nonseparateness and union of cosmic consciousness.

THE CALL TO SAINTHOOD

If you read the mystical literature of the world and especially of India, you would read about a force called *kundalini* which rises upward from the base of the spine to the top *chakra* in the brain which is located in the area of the pineal gland. You would read how the powerful *kundalini* rises upward in any person who has purified the seven levels of his consciousness of hang-ups, blocks, limits, negative thinking, and ego identity—in other words, those limiting self-images which make each of us think we are separate from the whole. Memories, mind-tapes, dreams, hopes, desires, ambitions, resentments, regrets, possessions, roles, thoughts and feelings define the sense of the separateness of "me" which keeps the *kundalini* from rising and keeps us from the state called enlightenment, Christ-consciousness, cosmic consciousness or Buddhahood.

If you read enough about the bliss of the saints and buddhas, you will begin to want to purify the seven levels yourself and to make a passageway by which the *kundalini* can rise upward, lifting your consciousness into those selfless states of ecstacy, but automatically there will be reluctance to let go of the self-sense. You may dream a lot about being one with the whole, yet even so simple a step as developing a social consciousness and a caring for "others", you may find exceedingly difficult or be unwilling to take when you confront what that really means.

We can talk about the physiological structure of the brain and the coronas of fire which are illumined by the rising life current of *kundalini* into a halo of radiance but very few people actually experience the awakening. Anyone can experience the rise of *kundalini* to the first of the seven levels in the sexual orgasm as it rises to a climax and then subsides. In various kinds of therapy, such as the massage techniques of Wilhelm Reich, we can actually feel our life force flowing differently in our body and our mind, once a "block" has been removed. We can imagine how enlightenment must feel, like a sexual climax that never ends or a never-ending radiance, like that first wonderful moment when we fall in love, except that the enlightened being has fallen in love with everything and with everybody. While it is nice to think about this ideal state like a fairy tale, we are very reluctant to let go of the binding self-sense which stands at the threshold of each of the seven levels and bars the way. We feel we are unable, unready to leave behind our familiar self-sense which we have created and grown so accustomed to over the years.

The final challenge of Creative Conflict is asking nothing less than for you to become a saint. Whatever your life situation, you can make some move toward selflessness which may feel insecure but which is actually more secure. Saints do not have to live in monasteries or meditate in caves. They may be your next door neighbors. They are people who are secure and certain that what they do is not for self alone but for the whole, and therefore in tune with the highest state of consciousness.

You may respond to this call with your self-image. "I'm just an ordinary person," you may say. "All I want is a good job and a mate and some kids, and a little growth." These are the limits that keep the *kundalini* from moving up the spine to the Cave of Brahma in the center of the brain. Perhaps you have never even heard of *kundalini* before. It is hard for you to care about something you are not even aware that you have. If I say to you that *kundalini* is your consciousness, that, too, is something you are not terribly aware of. Most people are quite content with the uses they make of the consciousness, the places they let it wander, the desires they let it become attached to, the programs they imprint upon it. They do not wonder whether all these aspects of "me" are leaking away the power of some very intense and wonderful gift that they spend upon worthless baubles. It might be worth our while to speculate upon the structure of this marvelous consciousness within each of us which works through the seven levels of self-limiting awareness, and then ask ourselves, what are we missing?

16

STARTING YOUR OWN CREATIVE CONFLICT GROUP

Once you have tested out the keys to real listening, examined the blocks, and have decided you want to get together with a group of people to practice Creative Conflict, it is time to form your group. Gather the people together and begin your first session with a discussion of the central purpose of the group so that all group members are in agreement with how the group mind is formed. It is important to remind each other that everyone is responsible for organizing the sessions and doing their own work. What they are embarking on is an exciting adventure in growth. *Heart power* is the motto of Creative Conflict. Gandhi called it "soul force" and said it was the most potent force in the world.

There are a minimum number of rules and guidelines necessary for Creative Conflict which help to put the keys into practice and minimize the blocks, so that deep communication can develop. We wish there did not have to be rules at all, but we find that these few rules are necessary guides to the experience of loving others as ourself. The rules of Creative Conflict are the real leaders of the group. The leadership is then based on truth, not on a personality. The only authority is the group consensus of what that truth really is, and even then you may want to question the group's conclusion. It is possible, but not *necessary*, to have a trained facilitator or leader present. But even when a leader is present, his or her role is to facilitate the use of the guidelines and keys for Creative Conflict which people do tend to forget in the beginning. Most people have ingrained habits of communication which make them forget.

It is very important not to deviate from the rules, since they are based on natural models and have proven effective over and over again. Of course, you are always free to learn on your own, but the temptation to change the rules, thinking your case is exceptional, will slow your progress. Our experience has been that every time we felt we had an exceptional situation and let the rule in question go, we wasted a lot of time and ended up going back to the rule with greater understanding of why it was instituted in the first place.

THE RULES

After agreeing that *you are responsible for cleaning up your own mess,* implementing the keys to real listening is the next most important rule of the Creative Conflict process (see pgs. 199-208.)

Size

If you are beginning with a new group, it is best to limit the size to eight to ten members at first. Of course, in some classrooms and businesses, you will have to work with more people unless you can break up into smaller groups within the large group.

Setting a definite time period

It is very important that you agree upon a time period wherein everyone commits themselves to practicing the process and to attending the group sessions. We suggest ten sessions, meeting once a week for two and one half to three hours.* In this way we can see whether our words really match our commitment. In one group that we facilitated the commitment was made by each member to attend each session, but when a musician came to town to give a concert on one of the dates, the priority changed for one couple. There is a need for continuity in these sessions because you are really getting nitty-gritty with people. Drifters and people who idly come in and out are not sensitive to the depths that you are trying to seek. They spoil the whole group trust and vibration. They put their own preferences first and not the souls of others.

---

* In business or with children you will need shorter but more frequent sessions.

Actions speak louder than words, and whatever we choose to do shows where our real commitment is. By setting a definite time period we commit ourselves to looking at our integrity and working on our egos for that period even if it gets rough or feels distasteful. At the end of the period we can review whether or not we want to continue. This choice, at periodic intervals, allows us to have the fulfillment of completing a commitment we have set for ourselves, and gives us the freedom to choose a different direction at the end of the period with integrity.

Admitting new members

We suggest that when you begin your group with a ten-week commitment, you open the group to new members only at the beginning of the next ten-week period. If you have an ongoing group that is committed beyond a ten-week period, we have found it essential to institute a two-week period of silence for admitting new members, as well as a one-week probation after that to make sure all feel in tune with that person. It also gives that person a chance to become familiar with the rules and keys and be able to apply them in an experienced group. Often it will take the new person longer. If the group is very experienced a four-week silence period is needed. Since there are subtle energies for the newcomer to learn to tune into, this long time of learning how to listen and be receptive should be welcomed. At the end of each session the new member can share his or her feelings and the group should make every effort to draw them out. Some people are very reactive and cannot sit still for the entire period. They feel they just have to contribute their ideas and insist on speaking. Even though they might have a valid point, a test of willingness to discipline the ego is in being able to hold comments until the designated period of silence is completed. Some people are only too eager to put in their two cents worth regardless of what is happening, or to take over and dominate. They are so much in their ego they cannot believe it will take them four weeks to learn how to listen correctly. They will find out later it takes a lifetime to listen with a pure heart.

Some people want attention for themselves and some feel they are so knowledgeable about others that they do not need the humbling experience of keeping silent. Again, if a person cannot comply with this necessary rule, he is not really ready for your in-depth group.

Centering meditation

In order to loosen everyone up and get the heart energy flowing, it is a good idea to begin the first few sessions with trust exercises from the book *Exploring Inner Space*, page 62*. After the exercise everyone should sit comfortably in a circle and center for a few minutes to tune the group mind to higher consciousness. You can meditate silently or do one of the guided meditations from *Exploring Inner Space* or the centering meditation given here on page 288-291.

Every Creative Conflict session should begin with a group centering meditation to tune all the separate energies within each individual and blend them into a united group vibration. This is the first of the keys to real listening. It helps develop the art of being centered while you interact in daily life. After you feel tuned in meditation, look into the major conflict in your life at the moment or to a conflict you feel with someone in the group or elsewhere (it may be minor). Remember, the purpose for looking into the conflict is not to give it energy, but to get to the cause of how you are creating it in your consciousness. You may feel you have no conflicts, but everyone has some challenge to face. Until we are perfect, we have conflicts facing us and work to do on our egos, because that is nature's way. Try to get in touch with the part of yourself that you need to work on. What is the one thing you don't want anyone to know about you or see in you? The meditation helps you to release the ego-mind and identify with the oneness and the pure consciousness in which you can see clearly what you need to develop. It opens the intuition to work for you. Meditating together provides group heart power and keener insight. After a few more moments for getting in touch, one person reads aloud one of the guidelines of Creative Conflict as part of the meditation, and everyone contemplates that principle in relation to the conflict they have brought. In each session a new principle, guideline, rule, key

---

* *Exploring Inner Space*, by Christopher Hills and Deborah Rozman, University of the Trees Press.

or block is read and contemplated until all the teachings of Creative Conflict have been considered. Confine yourselves to contemplating only one new teaching at a time so you can consider it in its depth. At some point someone spontaneously ends the meditation with an affirmation such as, "Let us keep this vibration throughout the evening," or "Thank you for sharing in this silence."

During the session, try to really apply the keys and guidelines, especially the one chosen for the meditation. If there is anyone who is confused as to its application, discuss it as a group, bringing in examples from personal experience. Over the weeks the group will cumulatively study the entire Creative Conflict process. Refer to the list of the rules, guidelines, keys and blocks on pages 252-253 and put them up on a large piece of paper on the wall in clear view, or xerox them so everyone has a copy. Each person should read and review them all before each session, or the group can read them quickly aloud at the beginning of each session after the meditation. It is essential to memorize the entire process so that it becomes part of your way of relating. The quicker the entire group can make the process part of their being, the deeper and more effective the group experience will be.

Some people rebel at the idea of a set of rules or techniques as the authority, even though the rules are not arbitrary but have been tested and found to be necessary for many reasons. To become a craftsman at any skill, we have first to follow the directions of the teacher and be a receptive apprentice. If we feel we have failed without having followed the guidance given, then we have no one to blame but our own egos. This entire process is very subtle, yet it works swiftly to enable us to be able to deal with conflicts on many different levels. Master it first before you modify it.

In a leaderless group or a group in which the guidelines are the leader, it is only a matter of time before natural leaders evolve. These are people who can tune into and grasp the essence of the guidelines and work with the spirit of truth more readily. The function of such natural leaders is to make sure that the spirit of the teachings is carried through. Everybody needs to become a

The Creative Conflict Process—
A Reference List

GUIDELINES
1. You are whatever disturbs you.
2. I agree to disagree.
3 I agree to work for synthesis.
4. I agree that each person has truth from the point of view from which it is seen.
5. I will examine my own motives for disagreeing before doubting the statements of another. I will look for the basic assumptions and needs behind what is said.
6. Red Herring.
7. Quibbling.
8. I will seek out the conflict in the heart of each person and not the conflict in their words and ideas. I will not engage in their internal controversy. I will not challenge what I don't understand. Instead I will sit back and listen.
9. Making a speech.

PRINCIPLES
1. Whatever we see, whatever we experience, whatever disturbs us, whatever is not mastered, that is the true quality of the manifested self.

2. What we do not see and know as manifested around us is what we really are.

— What we appear to be in our manifested self is only apparent in what we are seeing and thinking.

— Only consciousness itself is real. All else is an appearance created by thought.

3. The easiest and quickest way to discover our true nature is through the cessation of identity with our egos.

4. The cessation of identity with what we feel we need is necessary for conflict to become creative.

5. We remain serene and calm while listening to all the problems or while conflict is raging inside another person.

KEYS TO REAL LISTENING
1. Centering Meditation
2. Receptivity
3. Active Listening
4. Mirroring
5. Confirmation
6. Response
7. Four-part I-messages

BLOCKS TO LISTENING
basic assumptions
projections
negative identification
rationalizations
expectations
judgements/wrong perceptions
internalization
emotionalism

Yes, but . . .
playing tapes/self-obsession
stereotyping
compliance

TOOLS/TECHNIQUES
Use the tools for order:
   Rod of Power
   Red Bat of Reaction
Trust-building exercises
Mirroring exercise
Love seat
Beginning centering meditatior
Psychodrama
Creative Conflict meditation
Taking stock
Soul mirror
Advanced mirroring exercise

RULES
1. Implement the keys to real listening.
2. Limit the size of your group to eight to ten members maximum, or break up into small groups.
3. Set a definite time period, e.g., ten weeks, every Monday for two and one-half to three hours, to which everyone agrees and commits themselves to honoring.
4. Admit new members at the start of a new commitment period. Institute a period of silence, say two weeks.
5. Test out and master the rules before you modify them.
6. Come to decisions with a silent vote showing consensus.
7. Tape record each session and agree that the subject of the Creative Conflict listen to the tape before the next session.
8. Meditate at the beginning of each session and choose one key, block, rule, technique, guideline or principle as the subject of the meditation.
9. Simplify the terms but use the same process when using Creative Conflict with children. Modify the times for the sessions when applying Creative Conflict to children, business or other special groups.
10. Keep a spiral notebook as a personal journal to review your progress and the group progress.

leader in the Creative Conflict group and be integral and responsible. The true leader makes sure that everyone expands his or her consciousness so that deeper insights can be expressed through the group awareness. The group awareness in the Creative Conflict process is special only because it becomes tuned to going beyond the individual ego to the ability to realize and express oneness and pure perception. The group must always make room for the *deus ex machina*, the spirit of truth that may come through any one of the members at any time. Through constantly listening for an intuition we are always ready for it to appear. In an advanced group, the direct perception that cuts through to truth rings from one person to the next, and maintains a very high, pure energy level of wisdom throughout the group session. This type of Creative Conflict is reached through dedication and commitment and becomes a dynamic learning situation for all.

The silent vote

All decisions, such as agreement as to whose situation should be mirrored first, or whether we should admit a new member, should be unanimous. By taking a silent vote in meditation on the proposal or issue presented, the group can use intuition or higher consciousness in coming to any decision. The silent vote works in the following way: one person puts a proposal to the group. If there are immediate objections, the group discusses them and applies the keys to real listening to the discussion as needed until they come up with a unanimous proposal. Then they take a silent vote on the final proposal. If anyone feels a doubt or a funny feeling concerning the proposal, they may break the silence and speak out. Then the group reconsiders in the light of their input. The process is repeated until the silent vote goes through without objections. When nobody speaks during the short silence the vote has passed.

Tape recording

It is essential to tape record every group session. So much is missed in conversation. Even when we are trying our best to listen, our blind spots often prevent us from hearing. We must remember that it is not ordinary conversation we are looking for, but in-depth hearing. The group mirror may seem like too much to handle while we are present with our own ego defenses, holding onto our positions, not able to change, but it may sound very reasonable when we play the tape back in a day or two. Some people play their feedback sessions again and again and gain new insights each time. Each person can take turns supplying tapes and recording the sessions, or the person wanting to listen to the tape can purchase it from the common group stock invested in by everybody at the beginning. You can be economical by re-using old tapes. Most people like to save them as a record of growth and in case any dispute about who said what comes up at a later date. There is no greater authority on your ego than a tape of yourself saying something you would never dream of saying!

Sharing Needs

The initial meditation and contemplation of the guideline, rule, key or block need not last longer than five to ten minutes. After the meditation each person goes around the circle and shares the priority of his or her need briefly, or an expression of what he or she got in touch with during the meditation. After the first few sessions there will not be time each session to have everyone share their need, especially in a large group where just the sharing time could take over an hour. Develop a policy to share the most urgent needs first but be watchful of those who never feel they have a chance to share or those who don't speak up. Often you will find that the personal needs also relate to some larger group need and, as the group consciousness gets stronger, many people's needs will coincide. This is especially true in a business, family, community or group that lives or works together. The group then decides which personal need to work with first. The decision should be unanimous. If there are differences of opinion at this point, discuss them so you can come to a unanimous agreement. Meditate a few minutes more, silently tuning into the being of the person, clearing your own filters out of the way as much as possible and focussing the group mind energy for greater perception. When the person whose need is to be dealt with first is ready, he or she shares feelings on it as deeply as possible. Another person mirrors the problem to make sure it has been heard correctly and to bring rapport. If the conflict is with someone in the group, that person should be the mirror. When confirmation is received, the other party can share his or her feelings. The group must watch to make certain that all the communication steps in the keys to real listening are completed, especially in the early sessions. When the mirroring is completed on both sides, the group mind brings deeper penetration by the different members sharing their feelings and insights.

Usually penetration, understanding and release will come in one session, but sometimes it takes a long time if the ego is stubborn or unwilling, or if the block to clear seeing is deep. The group must gently, constantly bring each other back to real listening by all giving I-messages, all saying how they actually experience the other person, mirroring their beings, and guiding them to mirror and share their own I-messages.

For beginners in Creative Conflict the temptation is to go into the most emotional needs first, but this is a trap and not necessarily the wisest decision. To always gravitate to the most emotional issue only leads to group therapy and feeds emotionalism. The purpose of Creative Conflict is not for the group to play rescuer to a victim of a problem. Group consciousness comes from the group mind meditating upon all presented needs and tuning together to intuition for the real priority. Usually there will be a very clear feeling as to which situation is most ready for the group feedback. If you focus on just the outer issues, like specific marital disputes, you will find yourself enmeshed and will go around in circles within the group trying to find out who did what. The best way to deal with relationship problems of any kind is to use them to get each person in touch with his own reality, his own unconscious fears or doubts, not to try to solve the problem first. The problem is only an external effect, a doorway into the real issue. You want to get to cause.

During each session, bring in the guidelines, point out the blocks and apply the keys and rules wherever you can. Soon they will become part of you and you will experience how these teachings tune you to nature. They are the lever that will help lift you and the group consciousness into full awareness for penetrating and transcending the ego. There is no faster way for transforming the ego, especially when coupled with selfless service and meditation. To understand that Creative Conflict teaches you more about yourself and the way you react and think than you can find in any ashram or with any psychologist, you must practice it properly. Without practice all your thoughts about it are merely assumptions and speculations. This statement applies even more so to that group of spiritual athletes who go deeply into the workings of the mindstuff in the eastern religions, where the danger is in developing a narcissism that enhances egotism.

Children

When working with children you will have to simplify the terms of the process with words they can understand and with examples they can relate to, according to the age. Nevertheless, the keys to real listening can be taught to any age and they are the core of the Creative Conflict process. (See chapters ten and eleven.)

Time limit

If you have time you can go into more than one member's need, again deciding unanimously which need is to be next. Some sessions you will be able to go around the whole group, and the other times one or two people's needs will occupy the entire group time. Decide on a time limit for your sessions or you could be there all day and night. Sometimes you may not be able to resolve an issue during the set time. If you cannot extend the time, then be sure to arrange a follow-up, perhaps with just a few of the group members if the matter cannot wait until the next scheduled session. Remember, you are learning to love and care about each other and if you *can* do more there is no need to leave a person hanging. If it is not possible to arrange more time, then give the person love and support before they leave and ask them to listen to the tape to take the issues further and to share the next time.

Review

Keep a spiral notebook as a personal journal and at the end of each session write your after-thoughts and feelings. Also allow time to evaluate the session at the end and give a short summary so as to give yourselves feedback on how the whole session went. This is an important time to also confront those who did not speak up or participate. Find out why. At the end of your ten-week periods review your individual commitments and share what you have learned. What have you been able to carry over into your daily encounters with other people? In what aspect of Creative Conflict are you still weak? These review periods are very important to help you see where you have been and where you need to go. Review at these times of summary what each person's role in the group has been and give feedback. Successful Creative Conflict creates a dynamic energy which leaves everyone feeling energized. It feels electrical, as hidden creative energies are released and a particular direct perception is experienced. Many people come to a Creative Conflict session tired from work, and leave feeling rejuvenated and high. If the energy is flagging, you must own responsibility for it and contribute the missing electricity yourself. A dull meeting results because you are not prepared to lift it up and risk your own ego.

Remind each other of your vision and goal together. Creative Conflict makes you a participator in life, a co-creator, rather than a passive observer. People's inner worlds are fascinating and Creative Conflict can be more interesting and more stimulating than any movie. Right before your eyes the drama of life unfolds with intrigues, soap operas and revelations that surpass any theater. You see that each person is the actor, the playwright, the audience and the director in charge of their own scene. Discovering that each one is a co-creator in life keeps the process always unfolding.

17

TECHNIQUES AND TOOLS FOR GROWTH

Once you finally sit down together for Creative Conflict as a group, anything can happen. The process, the techniques and tools are all provided to help you stay on course, but people are unpredictable. You have to be prepared for any unexpected turns of events, especially when you are dealing with people's egos, which can become very tricky, even to them. All of the following special techniques take study, contemplation and practice time to understand. You don't have to worry about digesting them all at once. Take one at a time and get familiar with them so you can use what is applicable at any point in your daily relating. Nor do you have to worry about being inexperienced or harming anyone. As long as you keep mirroring and caring you will keep the heart connection and everyone will feel safe even when you think you are risking. Establishing this heart link is the focus of the process and once the link happens, then everything else follows like a smooth flow and feels very in tune. We have provided the process and the techniques for various challenging situations, but only you can work the process and provide the patience and caring in your own unique group experience. Always remember—the first reaction of any ego is to reject any statement that implies criticism which undermines the self-image. The skill is to get beneath this reaction.

The most important technique, as we keep saying, is *mirroring*. When someone is not listening to a point being made, especially a delicate or sensitive issue, be sure to remind him to mirror what has been said. When you meet with someone who is very much in the head and finding it difficult to get in touch with feelings of the heart, *psychodrama** is a very useful type of mirror to put them in touch with emotions. You have to keep pulling the Creative Conflict back to the feelings, back to the real I-messages and not let it go off into a bunch of heads tossing in their opinions. Watch out for head questions like, "What do you think?" because they will never bring heart answers, even if they are intelligent questions. If people are stuck in their heads, getting frustrated with them will not help. It will only result in their feeling more threatened and hanging on stronger to the head. The head and heart are very different levels of consciousness and we slip out of one into the other so fast without knowing how it happened because it's all "I" to the beginner. But from the point of view of the group, the change is a dramatic switch and easy to recognize. Psychodrama helps the person feel the difference and learn to identify with the heart rather than the head. A person can know all the scriptures and wise quotes and yet still be very much a big head.

Only from learning this tuning to heart can the group function as one whole, as an organism. The pace is important. You need to *give the person who is in conflict time* to feel heard in addition to giving him feedback, and give him time to digest the feedback. Otherwise he will feel that every time he shares his feelings he gets clobbered with a different person's viewpoint. If someone does get told by everyone in the group that his point is "off", or is a "red herring", explain to him why you are responding to him in that way. You also have to watch the head responses rising up in yourself and in everyone. Stay in the space of wanting to serve. Do not allow the ego to rule with thoughts like, "I'm the one who has to make this point" or "I'm the one who needs to shine" or "I'm the only one who knows how to do this right." When words or ideas pop into your mind, pause, tune in to see where they are really coming from in you—head or heart—and *tune to the gestalt of the group before you speak.* If you stay in touch with everyone, as well as with the person experiencing the conflict, there will be a

---

* See psychodrama exercise in Chapter Eighteen, pages 298-301.

feeling of togetherness in the group as a whole, and whatever you say will be in tune because you will be speaking from the heart.

BEGINNING A SESSION

Be very careful at the beginning of each session when you are deciding where to focus the group energy. Some groups will go around an entire circle of people and each will share where he or she is at or what is happening in their lives at the moment. The danger in this technique is that half the meeting time can be taken up by a long sharing, and when you do begin a Creative Conflict, you may not have time to do it justice. Beginning a serious Creative Conflict at 9:30 or 10:00 at night is foolish if you have to stop at 10:30, because you will get the person deep enough to be disturbed yet not deep enough to break through.

Another way to begin the session if you have a large group, rather than having everyone share, is to ask if there are any pressing needs. Then someone who really needs the different angles of the group's mirror can speak up, and if there are several needs, the group can decide which one has priority. Take some time to make this decision; do not just go with the most demanding person. An example of what can happen if you do not consider the priority carefully happened one evening in a beginning Creative Conflict group. One group member stated very clearly that she did not want to go into Paul who was demanding some help; she felt he was not yet ready to take feedback, that he asked for feedback every week but was unable to listen when any was given. Another member contradicted her, saying, "Maybe he has to go through the experience and blow it before he will learn how to be receptive." The woman who spoke first was unable to clarify her feelings further, so the group went back and forth trying to decide what to do, waffling the time away, and finally did drift into a session with Paul who, in fact, turned out to be unready. He parried people's points with "yes, but's" and rationalizations and a whole sampling of other defenses. This was only their third Creative Conflict experience, but turned out to be a hard-learned lesson. Paul was unable to mirror any of the feedback for three hours. Several members became frustrated with him but did not speak up. Others identified negatively with Paul and felt that the group was being unduly heavy with him, but they also did not speak up. So the conflict took a different course than would have occurred if people had not complied but instead had expressed what they were really experiencing. The group learned painfully an important technique—to stop when the process is obviously not working correctly. They also learned that they must communicate openly when their "still, small voice" prompts them.

Expecially in the first few classes of a new Creative Conflict group, make time to *stop at convenient moments to ask quiet people what they are feeling* and to draw them into the process, because their insights may shift the whole direction. If their input is "off," you may find it in tune to just stop right there and take five or ten minutes in a mini-Creative Conflict to set their misperceptions straight. Then you have their energy involved again in the group. In the above example, where the group learned how *not* to do Creative Conflict, the members all talked *at* Paul and did not communicate with *each other*. The beginning facilitators forgot to refer back to the rules, and they also forgot to insist on two very important tools for order—the "rod of power" and the "bat of reaction."* They lost eye contact with each other as well as with the newcomers in the group in the heat of reacting to Paul. Thus the group failed to reach a consensus of agreement and, because they were not doing Creative Conflict when they thought they were, the energy became scattered in all directions, first trying one thing and then another, with people interrupting each other right and left and, of course, the feedback did not penetrate Paul's ego at all. In reviewing the disappointing evening, the group at first felt that Paul was to blame for the unfulfilling experience, but in fact the responsibility belonged to everyone and they all finally saw that. This fiasco was actually a good teaching because the members were forced to re-think how they could pull the group together, how to build a group consensus, and how to do the Creative Conflict process properly.

---

*See page 263.

TECHNIQUES TO HANDLE
THE UNEXPECTED

If the energy in the group gets wildly scattered or sluggishly low, every single member of the group is responsible for the group dynamic and for focussing and raising the energy level. You have to act as though the responsibility is entirely yours, otherwise you will be tempted to think or hope that others will handle it. How do you do this? *You tune into the whole as best you can and you risk sharing your gut level feelings.* Energies get low if someone or several people are stuck in their heads or if they are afraid to risk.

The biggest danger with a beginning group is that the pace will be much too fast, that people will forget to mirror and will begin to interrupt each other and speak out of turn as insights start flashing into their minds. The entire communication can then easily gravitate to the head where the thoughts are coming so fast that the heart is left behind completely. Several techniques can be used to slow the tempo down, and you have to be disciplined in applying them. The use of the automatic chairman, or "rod of power" as we sometimes call it, and the "bat of reaction" creates order and discipline in the matter of who speaks next. Often there will be a procedural problem of who gets to talk, who is monopolizing the conversation and how to avoid interrupting each other, which greatly confuse or scatter the deeper issues. In our group at the University of the Trees we bought a child's baton for our "rod of power", and whoever holds this magic wand has the floor until he or she is finished and cannot be interrupted while speaking. For the "bat of reaction" we took an old baseball bat which we painted red for reactiveness. The bat lies in the middle of the circle until someone picks it up when he is reacting and feels he just has to speak next; he cannot wait. Whoever is holding the bat is saying without words, "I'm reacting." As soon as the person with the rod is finished talking, the bat holder has the floor next. But the group needs to be alert to the fact that he is reacting and that he may have been playing tapes and not listening to the interchange that has just taken place. Each group member must ask himself what this person's motivation for reacting is. The group still needs to insist on the use of the keys to real listening and proper mirroring, but these physical tools, the rod and bat, allow for channels of expression that might otherwise result in "confusion of tongues" with everyone trying to talk at once. They are especially effective in families and with children, and are generally essential for the beginning group for quite awhile.

Another technique to slow down the process so that everyone stays in tune with the communication is to refuse to let any new point be pursued until the last point is really finished. Some undisciplined minds might inject a new thought into the conflict that will lead the conversation off onto an unimportant track. If the momentum moves too fast, you can always risk saying, "I feel we are moving too fast; could we take a few minutes to tune in and get back in a centered space again?"

Of course the opposite problem, low energy, needs other solutions. You might turn to the psychodrama exercise to activate expression of feelings, but if no one is even willing to share something to dramatize, you need to throw something into the middle. A good facilitator will be able to draw a real feeling out of someone. He may "play the devil" or dramatize with something positive or negative that people can identify with. When reactions are spoken, then you have energy to work with. Usually reactions are occurring silently in a group; the challenge is to get them voiced. But *you* are the one who must initiate the sharing. Then the group mind can work with what is shared. You have to get people to the point where they won't sit passive. You have to risk being different. Confront nonparticipants for not giving of themselves.

With very stubborn people who refuse to respond with any energy or refuse to communicate and get in touch with their feelings, share how their nonaction makes you feel, and leave them be for awhile. Move on to someone else. Often stubbornness emerges as an unconscious device for attention-getting. In that case, especially if one person is sucking a lot of group time and energy and getting nowhere, the best course is to let him stew and cut off the source of the ego food which is attention, albeit negative attention. Only through your ever-increasing intuitive discrimination will you know when you are letting someone's ego off the hook by moving on to someone else, or when moving on is the perfect response needed to create a real reaction in the other to which you can then respond. People are just like boxes, closed boxes, and you have to find out how to open them. Be interested in extending your antennae out to those boxes. The process needs a willingness to risk being very honest. Using these direct techniques, plus your commitment to stick through the entire ten-week period, will take your group through most reefs. Everyone, including you, is the navigator and you cannot blame others if the session is not on course.

Older people often have more difficulty with Creative Conflict because they are more entrenched in their egos. They may be quite unprepared to rock their ego structures and upset what they have taken so many years to build up. Much of their ego positions consist of opinions which they now hold dear as the basis of their security. On the other hand, some older people have a desperate desire for spiritual purification and truth before they die. Try to find out what older people are prepared to commit themselves to before you spend a great deal of energy trying to probe their ego positions.

One pitfall we have to be aware of with people we highly respect is that we will water down the true expression of our feelings out of fear of losing their love. By dealing with their manifestation, the issues that have generated the conflict, and by tuning into their inner conflict more, you can transfer out of your identification with your fear, into the direct perception needed to put truth and integrity first. Anything less is a form of hypocrisy which eventually leads to a shallow and empty life. Risk the truth and you will feel free. Normally you will be able to get the energy in your group moving freely with just a few simple questions. You *tune into the relationships within the group and usually you can key into some area to work on.* You can ask someone, "How are you and so-and-so getting along? I heard you and she had such-and-such going on . . . " You may find that she will try to brush your question off or say that old situation is all cleared up. This may or may not be true. Your job is to listen with your heart to see if you can tune into any feeling behind the words that betrays what is coming out of the mouth. If this questioning does not yield any deep sharing, *draw on other people's experience.* You can ask, "Steve, you had a similar experience with Jan a few weeks ago, didn't you? Can you share what happened there and help Jan get in touch?" Get the examples real and specific. Then you will get somewhere. Abstractions never get deep into the heart at all. Pull in someone from the group who has had a conflict with the person who is not in touch and put that person on the spot. Take the issue to the end until all feelings have been expressed and everyone feels *clear.*

In our group, Al was having a problem feeling cut off and no matter what anyone would say he fended it off. He said he didn't really care and didn't know why he didn't care. After a stalemate, for awhile the group finally turned to Amy who had been in a relationship with Al three years before and had been very hurt when he cut off the relationship. We asked her to share what she had felt and if she had any residue feelings. That was the key to put Al in touch. His cut-off feeling now was a replay of the same pattern as when he cut off from Amy three years before. His separating was now happening on another level, but the resemblance was clear. The opportunity for Al to clear up some old buried feelings with Amy was presented and the group was finally able to help him see his long-standing pattern with new light.

The important thing to realize with all these techniques is that they are only tools to help the other person get in touch. You are not telling the other anything. "Telling" does not have a transforming effect. What you are doing is to create the situation in which the other person has the opportunity to reveal himself to himself. This self-realization is the ongoing focus of Creative Conflict. For this reason you need to be creative in helping people work through long pauses, or ego reactions, or "the fog" when the ego is blocking and nothing is forthcoming. It is better they be in the fog, a space caught between the head and the real heart, than to be rationalizing in the head. So skill is necessary in order not to be satisfied with a head response.

People are not going to reveal the deeper parts of themselves to those whom they do not trust. And if you are insensitive or probing out of curiosity instead of from a heartfelt feeling of caring, you will find people unable to open up, especially if they feel they understand their own nature better than you do. They will feel that you are intruding into areas that are none of your business, into areas that you are not prepared to look at in yourself, or into areas that neither you nor they may be able to handle if they do open up. These are normal developments in a group of people and the only way through them is to build trust, work with the areas you can work with and deepen your own sensitivity. Most of all, the techniques of Creative Conflict require practice, practice, practice and that you put yourself out there and do your best. If you fall on your face it will only be a mirror for your own next step. If the group overall has a real problem in trusting one another, a very important step will be to *spend some time doing trust-building exercises.* The book *Exploring Inner Space* has an abundance of trust explorations that will build a deep bond between people before jumping off into the more threatening territory of ego refinement.

FOCUSSING ON POSITIVES OR NEGATIVES

After a few sessions the question will probably arise, "Why are we focussing so much on conflict?" One lady in a beginning group spoke up and said, "I'd rather be sharing positives, music and dance and good feelings, not looking for or dwelling on the negative. Let's focus on the positive, and the negative will take care of itself." Another beginner responded lucidly, "But Patty, it's the conflicts that block us from celebrating. No one is saying let's not have music or dance, but this is your opportunity to understand your conflicts and get free of them. I feel like you cover over real feelings of pain and confusion that you told me have been bothering you. You know you are going to have to face these pains anywhere you go. Here or anywhere, the conflicts will go with you and come up for you. Do you *want* to penetrate them?"

That question you will always come to with people who prefer to avoid the negative or are stubbornly resistant to dealing with their own blindnesses. Do they really *want* to master them? A lot of precious time can go down the drain with people who live in their ideals or dreams and narcissistic worlds who do not really want to change, which is why probing motivations becomes such an important issue. Some Creative Conflict groups may attract people who have a tendency to identify with the negatives. Identifying with negatives rather than *probing* negatives will scatter the energy and is the surest way to take the creativity out of Creative Conflict. Constantly reminding ourselves to identify with the positive, with oneness, with the One, which is pure consciousness and love, keeps us on the evolutionary path. Positive identification whilst using our sharpened intellects to probe our negatives with the heart provides creativity to the conflict and reveals the true spiritual path which encompasses all paths.

The direct path to the heart vibration is found by taking the Creative Conflict from the most vulnerable point. If you see people reacting, follow along what is making them react. Look at the expressions on their faces and in their bodies for your clues. Direct your comments and questions from the heart as the surest way of helping another to slip into their heart. This is the opposite of accusing, which can come across very cutting and will destroy any fragile heart contact and trust which you've built. By far the most useful and easiest technique will be simply to ask the other person, "How are you feeling?" or "What are you feeling now?" Allow the person to help guide you to the nitty-gritty; no one knows the way better than he. Ninety percent of the time these questions will be enough to take you to the real level where the conflict lies and keep the Creative Conflict moving.

If you remember that Creative Conflict is a natural process that develops along certain lines, that the map from head to heart is the same course for everyone, you will not be afraid of exploring together. Keep in mind the progression from the head—discovering projections, basic assumptions, rationalizations and other usual ego blocks, to probing motivations, to integrity, to self-image, to the vulnerable heart underneath. Under all the ego defenses lives the child at heart who just wants to be loved and to love and not be rejected. Self-image, along with fear of being unloved or unwanted or being rejected are the root causes at the base of ego defenses, and realizing how these work in each of us opens the door to the cave of the pure heart. Be aware and on the watch for what comes next in the process of ego-unveiling. You can help this progression by occasionally *taking stock,* which means to stop the discussion and ask the group as a whole, "What is happening now, where is the group at?" Everybody steps back when someone says, "Let's take stock," (provided of course the timing is in tune and not a diversion) and gets an overall view of the group dynamic and group gestalt. Often out of this pause a new inspiration will come to the intuition, a new truth will reveal itself, which will take the group to the next level.

BREAKING THROUGH

Often when a person receives heavy feedback or occasionally even gentle feedback on a pattern that he finds particularly difficult, he will go into the head automatically so he will not have to feel the humiliation of looking at what he fears is ugliness in himself. This can be frustrating for everybody else because the group knows that he cannot really change the pattern until he feels a true remorse, and he cannot feel remorse until he really sees himself, and he cannot see himself until he is willing to let go and look. But he fears the vulnerable humility of the heart space, expecting that to be devastating. At times a Creative Conflict session may end on this note with someone stuck in his head, consciously trying to get in touch with feelings but unconsciously determined *not* to feel because he does not feel enough self-worth to look at anything that might be humiliating or need changing inside himself. The group has no choice at this point but to give up trying to reach him or make the feedback more forceful, which is what life will eventually do. But getting heavier often only drives the person farther and farther into the head.

What can we do in such situations? The only way that the person caught in his head can dare to feel what he is being asked to feel is if he identifies with the positive part of himself at the same time as he gets in touch with the negative part. So one way is to begin by expressing how we experience him when he manifests his higher self. If he tends to be a habitual self-doubter, it will be hard

THE SEQUENTIAL STEPS OF CREATIVE CONFLICT and QUESTIONS TO ASK

The Sequential Steps

Those individuals who have practiced Creative Conflict for some time have realized that a natural process occurs as a person or group moves from relating to life from the head to living in the center of being deep in the heart. In every Creative Conflict session we want to look for this process in action and guide it to the deep well of oneness. We use "The Sequential Steps" as our guide, asking of ourself or the group the following questions in order. We may want to photocopy this page for use in many sessions and for everyone to be able to write down their answers.

1. Background, Facts of the Situation
   a. Why is _____ in conflict? What is the problem?
   b. Do I have a clear picture of _____'s situation? What really happened?

2. Feelings
   a. How does _____ feel *really*, from inside his/her world?
   b. How would I feel in that same situation?

3. Ego Block (Assumptions, Projections, Rationalizations, etc.)
   a. What is blocking _____ from fulfillment?
   b. What is the limiting attitude?
   c. What is it, if only he/she could put it aside, all would be okay?
   d. How would I describe _____'s fundamental ego position?

4. Motive
   a. What is _____'s motive for doing this?
   b. What is the reason behind the limiting attitude?

5. Integrity
   a. Is _____ ready to be honest with him/herself?

6. Self-Image/Need Identification
   a. Who would _____ be without that?
   b. Can _____ explore another way to be?
   c. What's the worst that could happen? Can he/she live with it?

7. Vulnerable Heart–The Moment of Truth, The Choiceless Choice
   a. What does _____ really want in his/her heart of hearts?
   b. Does _____ have the will to change?

to get him to believe in this highest part of himself, so you will need to mention concrete instances that he can remember. Instead of allowing frustration to make you get heavier with him, let him know that you understand his mind space, that he is avoiding humiliation like the plague and so does everybody when their ego first gets confronted. Then he can trust you more. Always mirror what you feel he is feeling so that he feels understood and heard. He can correct you if you are wrong. He may then venture forth with you into the new territory in himself. Let him know that even though he has parts of himself that need changing, you are not judging but are supporting him and will love him even if he admits to himself that what you are saying is true. He doesn't really realize that you already know it is true; he thinks that so long as he doesn't fully admit what you are saying and feel it, that somehow he is controlling the reality. The ego wants to stave off the dreadful moment when everyone will see him as he is, without anything to cover and hide that dark part of himself, because the ego fears it might be rejected or lose some self-worth. Hedging is a very self-deluding ego mechanism but very normal and real. We actually believe that others will see us as we see ourselves, and we cannot realize that they are not also blinded when we are blind to ourselves.

Often in Creative Conflict, the very people who are most frustrated with a person who remains stuck in the head are themselves stuck in the exact same space when their own turn to be confronted comes up. So it is always good to have compassion. Sometimes a person is prevented from getting in touch because of something as simple as a fear that he may cry in front of the group or appear as a little child. Many men find this kind of surrender to truth particularly hard. Sometimes a group will keep giving more and more feedback even though it is clear that nothing is getting through, and no one stops to think of simply asking that person what is keeping the feedback from getting through. With one woman, the reason was that her sweetheart was present and she was afraid to be really open with him sitting there. But no one asked her and she was too scared to say, for fear he might reject her. So for a long time she attended Creative Conflict without being open or telling anyone the reason why she wasn't open. Another technique to ask the person who is stuck and not able to receive the feedback is, "Which way do *you* think we should go?" This makes the person identify not with his own threatened ego but with the group who is trying to help. If he doesn't know which way to go, ask him what are the strongest feelings in him just now. Simple questioning may lead him into a feeling that is deeper and more real. Perhaps he will say, "I'm feeling that everyone is mad at me," and his expression will open the channels of communication so the group can say, "No one is mad at all; we're only trying to help," and this will allow him to trust a little more and open to the love that is there but is so difficult to accept at this sensitive level.

On the other hand, there are times when a person willfully stays in the head because he has no real wish to change and is not really in harmony with the Creative Conflict process at all. His motives for being there are to get ego assurance or attention, not to transform himself. And in these cases, continuing this kind of compassion would be the worst approach possible. For someone who is really dug into an ego position and bent on making the rest of the world dance to his tune, being ruthless with truth is the only integral thing to do. It is a greater love and compassion to be ruthless about truth as long as the expression does not come from a disturbed or self-righteous space but from a genuine selfless desire to help the person break through to reality, knowing that so long as he stays stubbornly stuck in the ego, he will be in pain and much in his life will go awry for him. If he is still unwilling to hear feedback and does not want to change, don't send your love down the bath hole by trying to persuade him or trying to discover some magic technique that might work. Let him go.

When the group gets stuck and you are unsure what to do, try to direct the group to more of an intuitive focus. One way to take the group deeper is to directly say, "I would like to take the group process deeper. Let's go around and offer what is most vulnerable, most nitty-gritty in each of our lives now." The honest sharings that come will give you much more to work with. And if people have trouble expressing, you can re-phrase the question to, "What is the one thing you don't want anyone to ask you?" How much everyone is able to share depends on your particular group. In each session you will go as deep as you know how to go. Patience and understanding are very important to group consciousness. Over a period of time, and with commitment to practice in truth and love, all will come out and stand in the light of truth.

STAYING IN TUNE

An excellent technique to use at any time is to choose someone who has proven to be especially skilled and willing to risk saying what he feels to serve as *soul mirror.* You may want to choose two or three people to work together as soul mirror. A soul mirror stays silent during the first part of the session and makes notes on what occurs. He looks to see how well the process is being used, how well people are mirroring and how the entire flow is going. At various intervals, either every half-hour or you can leave the timing up to his intuition, he breaks in and shares his perception on what has happened and what he feels needs to be done to take the dynamic deeper. He may remind the group of one of the guidelines or principles, or he may suggest a technique to use. Whatever the soul mirror's intuition suggests to take the entire group to a more aware space, the group follows unless someone else has a strong feeling that the soul mirror himself is off. The group as a whole should experiment with testing out the soul mirror's suggestions unless someone has a better suggestion. Again, we are all exploring together to sharpen our intuitions and it is important to remember that no one is right or wrong; everyone is seeing from their own perspective. The question is only, what essence truth emerges amid all the viewpoints?

Another indispensable tool to aid the opening of the intuition in Creative Conflict when the group reaches an impasse is to do a centering meditation to review the situation at hand. In the heat of family troubles, business conflicts, group uncertainty and people losing their cool and not using the keys to real listening, we can cut through quickly with everyone by calling for a centering meditation. People must agree that to stop at this moment and tune in will not be a diversion of energy. The following Creative Conflict meditation enables us to become more aware of the whole. One person leads the others, reading slowly.

CREATIVE CONFLICT MEDITATION

Close your eyes and relax. Concentrate all the energy at the point between the eyebrows. Draw the energy up from the base of your spine into the heart, then from the heart to the point between the eyebrows. Now concentrate at a point in the center of the group. Expand your awareness from the center to the whole group and let go of any feeling of separation. Put your mind and heart in the center of the group and expand into the whole to include the whole inside your being. Experience the Oneness. Experience the One Self in all as clear consciousness, the penetrator of truth. See truth manifested as love, clarity and wisdom applied to any situation.

(The person who called for the meditation then must choose one or two of the following questions that he feels are appropriate and ask them aloud. Each person meditates on how that question applies to himself or herself.)

1. "You are whatever disturbs you." What is disturbing me?
2. What am I identifying with?
3. Am I identifying with the conflict or the being of the persons involved?
4. Am I identifying with what I feel I need?
5. Am I separating myself from the group or judging others?
6. Has my participation been helpful to the group consciousness, or have I been playing it safe?   ʼ
7. Am I really listening?
8. Am I really understanding the other's being?
9. Are my emotions or reactions preventing my seeing the situation clearly?
10. Have I been examining my own motives?
11. Have I been rationalizing my own thoughts and feelings?
12. Have I been perceiving the basic assumptions in what has been said?
13. Have I been challenging what I don't understand?

14. What am I expecting?
15. Am I remaining sensitive and loving to the group members?
16. Is what I have been feeling and thinking due to an image that I have of myself or of others in the group?
17. Does my manifestation in the group now fit my self-image?
18. Do my actions stem from what I believe others expect of me?
19. How much am I referring back to I, I, I, all the time?
20. What is the need now?

YOU ARE THE GROUP

The above questions for meditation all relate to one of the sixteen principles or guidelines of Creative Conflict to help you get in touch with yourself at a deeper level. Everyone in the group is really yourself, so if anyone gets in touch and shares it, the whole group gets in touch on that level. This is the real secret of Creative Conflict and of the group dynamic. Everyone else is yourself. When the psychic energy in one person changes and deepens, it deepens for the whole. Since Creative Conflict works on the psychic body of the group as a whole, each person is responsible for going deeper themselves; then the whole can go deeper. YOU ARE THE GROUP. Realizing that fact is the purpose of the Creative Conflict meditation and the objective of Creative Conflict itself. So if there is a lack in the group, if you do not feel enough heart in it, the answer is very simple. You open the group heart by opening your own heart. You don't have to worry about opening the group heart. The minute you open your own heart, that opens the group heart. There shouldn't be any preoccupation with the group heart really. The group heart is automatic once you begin to open yourself. When you are the group, your consciousness is going to supply the lack in the group that you see. Even if no one else sees the lack, you're the one who sees the lack and if you sit back and say, "The group lacks this," then you are separating yourself from the group heart. When you are the group, then you supply whatever lack you see. If there is a lack of heart, of love, and you supply it, the whole group starts radiating that same vibration.

It is quite like magic, and this is what we see happen in every

Creative Conflict group. If you go all out to open up your heart, to be totally open, to say what you are feeling and risk, to let it hang out and be spontaneous, then you forget your obsession with yourself. That obsession is the only thing that closes people's hearts off. Obsession is worrying all the time about yourself, or about how you will come across or whether people will see you in the right way—meaning the way you want them to see you. You have to become as spontaneous as a little child to enter the heart. This is what Christ said, you cannot enter the kingdom of heaven except you become as a little child. That innocence of the child-like quality doesn't worry about what others are thinking about you. As you grow older you lose that heart of the child and that is what you must bring back in order to see nature or life pure, as it is.

Can you really think of how you were before you lost the purity of your own child-like mind, when you weren't thinking about yourself all day long, when the universe and you were just to-gether? You ran in the fields with joy and you asked lots of stupid questions and accepted the answers and didn't care much what the answers were anyway. Can you remember those days? You didn't think so much about what you were going to say. There was a sort of new joy to life. Then the prison-house of self-consciousness built up around you and hardened in adult life. And that is what stops the group heart.

Everyone has that inhibition to some extent as long as they are adults, and the extent to which you can forget that self-conscious self and get to the real you, the real vulnerable you, the you that's afraid to be open, the you that feels it's going to be rejected if people know what you are really thinking or feeling, then you will get to your heart. And that fear of rejection is in fact a subtle mirage. Nobody is going to reject you for truth except those that don't want truth. If you get inside their world and just be yourself they will accept you as you. If they do not accept you when you open yourself to truth, you are better off without their company and you do not need them as part of your world. Leave them free to live with their own untruth. No one committed to knowing themselves stops loving you when you truly express from the heart, even if they disagree with you. They warm to you, even if you are a fool. Because if you are a fool then they can be foolish with you too, and not have to feel self-conscious either. When people open their hearts, you feel safe and you can trust people more. You can then open up with safety. Do not expose yourself before a wolf in sheeps clothing but test the spirit of openness. If you can be open with others, generally they feel they can be open with you. Then you don't have to fear that your heart is going to get wounded or stepped on.

People only feel wounded in the supportive situation of Creative Conflict when they are resisting feedback or not expressing themselves. Resistance only comes when there is pressure and this pressure comes from being closed-in. You can't have any pressure in the universe without some containment. There's no natural vacuum in the universe. And that's the secret of the heart too. There's no container to it. The container we put around it is what hurts. You feel the heart expanding and trying to reach out, and the pressure is only the ego binding it. True love is expansive and doesn't feel that pressure. It just releases and radiates, and people feel it. It's infectious. Real love makes you fall in love with the whole world, with everybody. You're always shining and radiating and that's because your love is not dependent on something or someone that is outside you. It is the love of an open heart. And that only comes from risking our heart, getting beyond our ego attachments, giving our love. If people then take your truth and twist it for some purpose of their own, they cannot hurt you because there is no place for hurt to lodge. When you are that love then there is no other to hurt you, for you see all as yourself.

Love Seat Grid

Vertical column is group's feedback to name at top of column.
Horizontal band is feedback from name at left to rest of group.

Name of person in the Love Seat

	What person says about him/her self (Diagonal)	1	2	3	4	5	Themes in Feedback Given
1							
2							
3							
4							
5							
Themes in Feedback Received							

Name of person giving feedback

See instructions on page 293

18

MORE TOOLS FOR
WORKING ON THE EGO

The exercises and guidelines in this chapter are your file cabinet to draw from in the Creative Conflict sessions. Use them in conjunction with the course outlines in Chapter Nineteen and as a resource when you want to inject a new energy into the group. Read the guidelines and exercises thoroughly before you introduce them into your practice so that they may be smoothly integrated with the other techniques.

INDEX

GUIDELINES FOR WORKING ON THE EGO

Guideline #1
YOU ARE WHATEVER DISTURBS YOU

If someone is disturbing you, it is *your* mind and emotions that are being disturbed, not the other's. You are identifying with your thoughts about what you see or hear and are letting those thoughts bother you. It is entirely your problem. The other might not be having a problem at all. So own the disturbance as your own. Then you can free yourself. Realize that if you hold the attitude of identifying with your pure self and not with the ego that gets disturbed, you can gain insight into why you allow yourself to be disturbed. So when someone bothers you, point the finger first at yourself to see what part of you is reacting. What is the mirror of life, reflected from that person, trying to show *you*? This does not mean you may not have a valid perception of the other person, but if you are letting it disturb you, then you have a problem.

One major problem with conflicts and a reason why they can be so destructive is that we often refuse to own our disturbances. We lash back or say, "That's his fault. I'm all right." In Creative Conflict we cannot do that because it does not matter whose fault it is. What matters is how we are handling our reactions. Often we find that when we judge others, the next minute we are being judged. Life's mirror works very quickly at times. For example, Dave gets disturbed by Sue's authoritative manner. Sue says, "You left your milk on the table again, please clean it up," and "When are you going to take out the garbage?" Dave riles inside. Why? Does he want to be the authority? This he has to look at first. Then, instead of retorting, "Do it yourself!" and creating bad vibes between them, he can say, "You know, I have a problem with authority myself. I'd like to be aware enough to be the boss. But I do feel that you spoil your communication in the way you lay down the law and come across so strongly. I would find it much easier to accept what you say if it were expressed with a more humble, more caring vibe. Maybe others experience you the way I do."

In order to do this kind of communicating we have to be able to allow everyone the right to be whatever they are. Agree now that you are different from everybody, and everybody is unique and entitled to use the *One* consciousness in any way they choose in absolute freedom.

Guideline #2
I AGREE TO DISAGREE

This is the essence of Creative Conflict. In other words, you are so kind as to give others absolute freedom, when of course they already have it. We pride ourselves in giving others the freedom to be themselves, but life has given them that freedom whether we like it or not. You also have that freedom to be yourself every day. It is the only real freedom you have. So just as you demand that freedom for yourself, you give it to others. They have a divine right to say and do what disturbs you, providing they do not enforce it upon you harmfully and take away your freedom to do likewise. Pulling up the weeds of each other's hidden delusions is done first by acknowledging and accepting differences, then by confronting the motivation and truth behind each viewpont. Only in this way can we begin the creative process. This is especially true between people or over issues in which we have a lot of emotional investment. A mother does not want to know her teenage daughter is having sex. A father does not want his son to drop out of school, as he feels it will ruin his life. One government does not like to see another government selling arms to a third country. Real peace can only come from having the self-honesty to probe the motives and causes of disagreements together, after respecting each other's right to be different.

Guideline #3
I AGREE TO WORK FOR SYNTHESIS
    The disagreement which does not take into account all the areas that *you do agree upon* is not creative. If the areas of *agreement* exceed the areas of *disagreement* you can have a conflict which leads to synthesis. As long as there is a fundamental unity which is stronger than the disagreements, you can work it out if you are willing. For example, you might be arguing about one particular point and getting worked up and passionately feeling your mind spinning and your emotions rushing. But there may be fifty other things you can agree on. But do you think of those fifty things at the time you are disagreeing? Creative Conflict always has this in mind, that there may be all these areas of agreement and there is just one little area of disagreement which needs to be worked out to a synthesis with the rest. Therefore, at times when we feel ourselves having negative thoughts about someone, or feel poles apart on an issue, we remember this guideline and remind ourselves of some of our common areas of agreement. We reaffirm, "I agree to work for synthesis." This re-establishes the feeling of unity in the heart, the positive energy that can resolve any differences in the head.

Guideline #4
I AGREE THAT EACH PERSON HAS TRUTH FROM THE POINT OF VIEW FROM WHICH IT IS SEEN
    Everything is true from the level of consciousness from which it is seen. Everyone sees true from their own level of consciousness, even if it differs from another's truth. So we say to ourselves, "I agree to be the same consciousness, even when we are talking about the same object in different terms." That same consciousness is making all things seem different. In other words, the guideline "I agree to disagree" becomes agreeing to be the same in being, even though we are disagreeing mentally,

because we may be talking about the same thing in different ways. One of the problems with human beings is that we never want to be the same as anybody else. The minute you share something you think others will relate to they say, "Ah, but my thing is different." They just want to be different, so they argue. Creative Conflict involves seeing that we may be egocentric in talking about picky differences when the differences may be just a product of the ego separating itself from the experience and thoughts of others. That is why so many couples can fight one minute and make love the next. So many children can be tearing each other's hair out one minute and playing the next. People fall in love, react to praise or criticism the same, whether they are priests, hoodlums, communists or capitalists. The situation is different, but the underlying emotion is the same. So even though what is true for one person may not be true for another in the head, together we can probe our beliefs and motives and expand to a greater truth from the heart.

We can challenge another's truth, but we have to be able to see that what John says is true for him and what Mary says is true for her, even though they may be totally different truths, and from another view they may both be limiting. To get to the greater, synthesizing truth, both parties must be willing to examine themselves and be willing to change. An example of this guideline might be, "I need two women," says John. Mary replies, "I need a man who wants only me." A friend, Bill, says, "You are both identifying with your needs, but Mary's need is based on her insecurity and fear of rejection which makes her cling. John's need is based on Mary's clinging, which he cannot cope with, yet he loves her and does not want to leave her." The other woman has beautiful qualities that Mary does not have, but Mary also has beautiful qualities that the other woman does not have, so John feels he needs them both and is unfulfilled with only one. In Creative Conflict, John's and Mary's views are both true, but the underlying needs are the forces that are causing the views. These needs are what we must probe, share feelings about, mirror and penetrate in order to find a synthesis, a greater truth than either is seeing.

Guideline #5
I WILL EXAMINE MY OWN MOTIVES FOR DISAGREEING BEFORE DOUBTING THE STATEMENTS OF ANOTHER. I WILL LOOK FOR THE BASIC ASSUMPTIONS AND THE NEEDS BEHIND WHAT IS SAID.
It is difficult to stop ourselves from reacting and ask, "What is my motive for disagreeing?" But we have to learn to get to the cause of our disturbance for conflict to be transformed. We have to continually ask ourself, "What is the basic assumption in what he or she is saying? What is my basic assumption in my position?" For example, "He always thinks his way is the only right way. He assumes he's always right. What arrogance! What real feeling of inadequacy must be under all that! The

need to be confirmed must be there." The underlying, unspoken assumptions form our view of truth and we base our opinions of others and of our own egos on them. The quicker we can uncover and check out the basic assumptions in any point of view, the sooner the penetration to greater truth will take place. For example, "I'm upset, Jeff, because you didn't call me," says Laura. But Laura must examine her own motives for being upset before doubting Jeff's motives for not calling. She is upset because she is jealous and lonely. So she goes on a big trip in her mind about that, worrying for hours. Jeff finally tells her that he lost her new phone number and the operator did not have it listed. What a lot of time she has wasted worrying.

Another example, "Mary, you shouldn't handle the money anymore," says John. Mary reacts and walks out in a huff. John is astonished. Does Mary ask what John's basic assumption is? Or check out her own? No! Perhaps John feels she mismanages money. That is Mary's fear. But John really feels that it is for his own growth that he wants the change, not for hers. He feels he needs to master handling money and Mary does it for him, so he is always feeling there is not enough because he doesn't know where it is going. We can only get to the causes of conflict when we constantly look behind the surface, behind the apparent situation, to the basic assumptions. The seven steps, especially the mirroring step, allow us to experience directly our own and the other person's basic assumptions that we cannot normally see in conversation. We must learn to probe together and share the basic assumptions we see operating, as we are mostly blind to them.

Guideline #6
RED HERRING*
One of the greatest blocks to communication is going off on a tangent, away from the center of concentration. Someone may think he has an insight and offer it, but really it is way off the point. The group mind has to be aware of this and gently but firmly say, "That is off the point, a red herring!" Then the group must lead the energy back to the real point. Sometimes the person being confronted will bring in a red herring. Just as you are about to share a deep feeling you haven't been able to express to that person before, the other will say, "I need a glass of water," or "Isn't it time for tea?" "Oh, I must put the baby to bed," or "The dinner's got to be made," or any number of things that short circuit the energy and deny the communication. You usually then shut up like a clam and the conflict is pushed down inside and repressed. The group intuition must become

---

* Origin of the term: In hunting, a red herring was dragged across the path of the quarry to distract the dogs away from the scent of the animal so they wouldn't chase after it.

finely tuned to one-pointedness and the energies that accompany deep soul-searching must be kept concentrated and directed. Otherwise depth will not be reached. Children are famous for bringing in red herrings to avoid facing themselves. We even go off on red herrings when we are alone in thought to avoid looking at ourselves. How many times have you been in a nitty-gritty situation and somebody pulls in a completely irrelevant statement which sends you off chasing that one track and you end up spinning wheels? So then you get a wheel spinning, or what we sometimes call a "waffling" situation. The group must be able to spot this instantly and call out "red herring!" whenever it occurs, otherwise the session goes nowhere and is a waste of time. The red herring guideline is likely to be used more than any other guideline. It will train the group intuition and make the difference between a low energy session and a concentrated, electrifying and deep experience, bringing growth.

Guideline #7
QUIBBLING

To define a definition of a word and then challenge the definition of the definition is to get stuck completely in the trap of quibbling. "What do you mean when you say so-and-so?" We hear this all the time. It is usually a way of diverting, of not listening to the being of the person. Some people love to get caught up in semantics and avoid the real being. When we communicate effectively we are listening to the being of a person, not the words! The words are merely second-hand symbols invented by others. They are not the most important part of the communication. To use double meanings, words which are ambiguous, is another quibble. An example is, "You're too clever!" We do not mean he is clever at all. Or, "You're a wise guy." Are we really thinking he is wise? A wise guy is somebody who is too clever and therefore looks stupid. This is how we speak in words that have no integrity and so we keep communication on superficial levels. To get stuck in dictionary meanings and wrong use of words is to quibble, so that all thread of the argument is lost.

Nations do the same by insisting on the legalities of actions while ignoring the actual facts. Genocide is mass murder and illegal but that does not help the victims. To stand by and say it is illegal is not telling a murderer anything new. The legality is lost on him. We do the same semantically when we quibble. It lowers the high energy level needed for direct perception and drains the electricity which comes from being-to-being communication. The way out is for someone to say, "I feel you are quibbling." Then someone can bring in another I-feel statement to bring the communication from the semantic level to a deeper level again. We all have to be alert and take full responsibility for the direction of the group. Even one person holding back, or one person feeling bored, or dwelling on the dishes to be done at home, is deflecting the energy and is not being integral. If you are that person, ask yourself, "Why am I separating? Am I bored? Why do I not feel involved and why am I not putting in my full energies to take responsibility?" If you cannot find the cause and release it, or simply let go of yourself when you recognize it and jump in, then ask for group help at the next appropriate time so that you can get in touch and be integral. Your *integrity* is important for group consciousness. The electricity flows in a group when all are integral.

Guideline #8

I WILL SEEK OUT THE CONFLICT IN THE HEART OF EACH PERSON AND THE CONTRADICTIONS IN THEIR MINDS, BUT NOT THE CONFLICT IN THEIR WORDS AND IDEAS. I WILL NOT ENGAGE IN THEIR INTERNAL CONTROVERSY. I WILL NOT CHALLENGE WHAT I DON'T UNDERSTAND. INSTEAD I WILL SIT BACK AND LISTEN.

When you are talking, communicating, or confronting a person, you look for the contradiction in *them,* not in their words and ideas.

To challenge what you do not understand is to quibble. It is not creative to put our ignorance out onto someone else and make them explain it all in detail for us, as though we are so stupid that we do not know anything. We will need to listen better and deeper. However, it could be that the person really is expressing himself poorly, leaving half of the story out. Then we will have to ask for specific points to be clarified. What we need to watch for is the kind of attitude which believes that the whole group must be held up while "I" wait to be enlightened. It is an egocentric attitude and not creative at all. It is like the beginner saying, "I don't understand what's going on, please explain," while the rest of the group mind is just about to share an important point, vital to the conflict. You can feel the group energy start to drain or be sapped off with this kind of comment and then you must ruthlessly remind the person of this guideline. To attempt to be "nice" at this point will siphon off all the group energy. You must be firm and not be sucked into another person's confusion. Remind them to read Guideline #8.

Guideline #9

MAKING A SPEECH

Under the guise of asking questions, some people will show how much knowledge they have or will display the contents of a book they have just read, ostensibly to share their insights with others. Whether those insights have been gained or books have already been read by others does not always occur to some egos. When asked to speak not from authorities or books, but from their own experience or to say what their real feelings are, they remain silent or back out of their position by saying, "I don't want to go into that now." Or they make statements about which they can offer no proof at all in their own life, only from hearsay. "Jesus said," "Marx said," "The authorities said," and they repeat all over the place for everyone's edification. But they are not prepared to test this philosophy out for themselves to prove it. They are continually coming out with suggestions which are not from their own experience. They want everyone else to test them. If they tested their own suggestions before they made them for others, then there would be value to their communication and their experience would contribute to the group energy. So before communicating, we must know that our own suggestions work and that they are not just theoretical. Theoretical knowledge and comment leads only to mental masturbation. Such people should be challenged for making a speech or asked if they are contributing theoretical information or whether they are speaking on behalf of everyone present, or from direct experience. We must as a group be prepared to fight for integrity. It is not Creative Conflict unless you say, "Hey, are you speaking for yourself? I'm not at the position you're speaking from!" or "I feel you are preaching and making an assumption that we are interested in your theories and you are not really experiencing the real issues we are dealing with!" So we must remind ourselves and each other: "I (THE BIG I) CAN ONLY SPEAK FOR MYSELF FROM MY OWN EXPERIENCE. I CAN'T SPEAK FOR EVERYONE."

This guideline also should be applied when someone begins speaking for other people about their problems. Married partners and parents often fall into the trap of speaking for others. "We just want him to find a nice hobby," says the well-intentioned wife or mother. The husband or child may not feel that way at all. So in Creative Conflict we must constantly ask each person to speak for himself or herself.

These nine guidelines to making conflict creative are deep studies of how human egos normally work. By looking for these patterns throughout our daily lives we can transform ourselves into incredibly perceptive and aware human beings. If these tools and techniques were taught in every classroom, in every home and in every business where people must cooperate, from the factory to big governments, we would have a tremendous understanding of human nature and of each other. The ancient advice, "Man know thyself!" would come true.

The following "Centering Meditation" is taken from the authors' book *Exploring Inner Space*, by Christopher Hills and Deborah Rozman, *University of the Trees Press*.

BEGINNING CENTERING MEDITATION

Start with a centering meditation in which each participant lets go of his personal self-sense to identify with and feel the oneness that links him with everyone else. The following centering meditation is one you can use to begin your Creative Conflict sessions. Perhaps other group members have centering meditations they would also like to share at different times. Whatever works best to bring the entire group to a feeling of the One in all is what you should use to begin your sessions. The centering meditation here is a step-by-step introduction into your inner space. In a group it will be a guided meditation, read or led by one person.

BACKGROUND

Real meditation is a wholistic experience that includes your entire being. The *first step* is to ask your body what it is trying to say to you. You get in touch with your body and relax it in this way. What is its message? In the East they use yoga postures as a means to relax the body and prepare it for meditation. The body is like a battery. It starts your consciousness going and gives it a storehouse of energy. To keep it running smoothly you have to keep the energy circuits free from tension. In "The Centering Meditation" we go through an exercise in tensing and relaxing to quickly put ourselves in touch with our whole body and at ease.

The *second step* is to get in touch with your feelings. Your breath is a very powerful tool you can use to change your emotional feelings at will. Conscious breathing puts you in touch with your feelings and charges your emotions and body with fresh life force. The *third step* is what we call concentration or centering. You draw all your life force into the center of your being. You draw your inner energies up to the point between your eyebrows, into your intuitive center of sensitivity connected with the pituitary gland. This is the magnetic part of your mind, beyond thoughts. You have tuned into your body and into your feelings, and now you want to tune into your center of direct perception. To do this successfully you have to have done steps one and two first, because only with a relaxed body and calm emotions can the energies be released to rise into this spiritual eye center between the brows, just in back of the forehead. Concentration is a focussing of attention so no distracting thoughts take you back into fidgeting, or into old memories and old dreams or feelings. We need all of our energies clear to meditate properly. Then, in this concentrated state, the intuition is given the chance to open. We stay there waiting, focussed, not demanding, just open. Let go of the mind, of any thoughts that come in. Just let them pass as they come. You wait in the stillness, centered, and you may experience intuitive flashes, an insight, a core feeling or thought where you just know it's real. You don't seize it with your mind and start to work on it, or try to remember it, because then you are back into the mind. Your intuition will remember what it needs to. Just let the thoughts go and higher consciousness can come in. If you stay centered and attuned throughout the Creative Conflict, intuition will come and work through you and work through all the levels as you explore.

The *fourth step* is expansion. Here you expand beyond your idea of being a separate self in a little body. The *fifth step* is the most important: You apply your newly expanded awareness into action. Like an electric current, you must ground this new energy into creative activity (whether it is work, play, writing, sharing or Creative Conflict) for it to become useful to your growth. Bring your whole self into your Creative Conflict relating.

When our activity serves our evolution, serves our expanded self, then it is the highest action we can be doing on earth. Not only do we go on an exciting adventure, but we serve the highest purpose in life: furthering evolution. The more you can bring these five steps into your everyday life, the more you gain the fulfillment of your own self-mastery.

THE CENTERING MEDITATION

The reader does as much of the same meditation as he can while slowly reading to the group. Whenever three dots appear (. . .) that means to pause. Whenever there is to be a long pause (over thirty seconds) it will be indicated. Anyone can read or lead a guided meditation. In the home and classroom we often have the children take turns guiding a meditation which they have made up or which they read from a book. The reader needs to be sensitive to the group while reading, in order to gauge the pace.

The leader reads the following:

Begin the centering by sitting with your spine straight, either cross-legged in a comfortable position on a pillow on the floor, or else sitting in a chair with your feet flat on the floor. It's important that you be comfortable. One way to help keep the spine straight is to place your hands at the junctures where the legs and pelvis meet. Keep the palms upturned unless you are used to meditating another way. Lean forward so that the pelvis is tilted forward, then sit up straight but keep the pelvis in the same tilted forward position. Now the pelvis will help you keep the spine in place by pushing the lower back forward while you relax. The hand position will help by keeping the shoulders back and the chest out. Keeping the back relaxed but straight is important so that the energy in the seven spinal centers can flow freely up and down the spine from your brain. You can even feel the energy moving in the spine after awhile if you tune your mind into it. Once your posture feels comfortable, you can begin to relax each part of the body in turn. It's best to close your eyes from here on and let yourself be guided by the leader until you know how to do it on your own.

Tense the toes, put your mind inside them and relax them. . . Then draw your awareness out of the toes into the feet. Tense them and let them go. Relax the feet. Draw your consciousness up into the ankles and legs. Tense the ankles and calves, don't tense too hard, then let them go, relaxed, released . . . Draw your awareness and your energy up your legs some more into the thighs. Tense the thighs, charge them with energy and then let them go, releasing all the muscle tensions, releasing all the pent-up energy. Relax. Tense the pelvis and buttocks and hip area, then let it all go relaxing it as you release the tension. As you practice this your body will feel so light that you will hardly know that it exists from the waist down . . . Now tense the stomach and let it go. Then the chest, tense and relax . . . Now the hands and lower arms. Tense and relax. Move your consciousness to the upper arms and shoulders and tense and relax them. Now put your awareness in your back and tense and relax your spine and back muscles in three parts. First the lower back, then the middle back, then the upper back and neck. . . Feel the consciousness move up the back as you withdraw your awareness up and up as you go. . . Now tense the face, squish it all up and tense all the facial muscles. Relax. Finally tense the head and scalp, let them go and focus your awareness into the center of the brain on top of the head. Your whole body should feel loose, free, relaxed, and your consciousness awake and ready. Ask it how it feels. If any part still feels tense, or fidgety, you tense it and then let it go, letting all its pent up energy relax. . .

Now begin to watch your breathing for one or two minutes. Watch it go up and down inside your nose and in your heart or lungs. . . Feel its rhythm slow you down and calm you inside-out as you let it flow up and down like a wave on the sea. . . Ask yourself, do I have any old feelings, old pains and hurts still in my heart? Or, when was the last time I got upset at someone, or someone got angry with me? Feel your old feelings and as the breath goes out let them go. Each time you breathe in, feel you are charging up with new life force and fresh feelings. . . Now inhale slowly and gently through your nostrils to a count of five, then hold the breath for the same count, then slowly exhale through the nostrils to the same count. . . Gradually you will be able to increase the count to twenty and feel deep effects in your feelings. As you breathe, you draw in fresh life and love which rides piggyback on the breath. As you hold your breath, circulate this love through your whole body, washing it with fresh life force and love, and as you breathe out you let go of any old worries, tensions, or painful feelings you may have. Get in touch with your deep feelings. Let go of your old emotions and inhale fresh, uplifting emotions. You are a child at heart. You are transforming your own inner space at will. Repeat this rhythmic breathing while imaging fresh love and life five times, the same count as you use in the breath. It's important to really put yourself into it, to bring yourself a new feeling, a new experience of energy. . . (long pause).

Now let yourself breathe naturally again. . . To relax your mind more deeply, get in touch with its thought-making. Let the thoughts go, don't hold onto any of them. . . Saying a sound in the mind as you watch your breath helps calm the thoughts. As the breath flows in naturally, say the word *sa* to yourself, mentally. As the breath flows out naturally, say the word *ha* to yourself. This will quiet your thoughts. Practice it a few moments. . . (long pause) . . . Now draw the mind and all the awareness into the center behind your forehead. You can do this by pretending all the energy is flowing up from all your nerves and collecting in one point at the place behind your forehead in between your two eyebrows. It may be like light rays focussing into the sun, or like all your energy flowing into a magnet at that point. Here, you feel centered inside yourself.

If you feel you are still having trouble keeping your mind steady, you can do the same centering, but this time bring the energy into your heart center which is near the center of your chest, and let your mind flow into a feeling of love. Send that love out like a sun shining from your heart into the room, and into every person present. Meditation on the heart opens up a feeling of love and sweetness. Meditation on the magnetic center between the brows opens up sensitive perception. Together they help each other to expand your whole being.

Now when you are centered, you are ready to expand into new awareness and to explore with a more refined and attuned consciousness.*

BEGINNING MIRRORING EXERCISE

Begin by dividing the group up so that pairs of two people sit knee to knee and one or more persons sit as observer at their side facing them. Alternatively you can choose just one pair to sit in the center of the group and the rest of the group can be the observer. If

---

* The instructions for five-step centering and beginning meditation are available on tape from the publishers.

there are only two of you, try to use a tape recorder as your observer, then play it back to hear what it has to say; otherwise do your best on your own.

#1   Begin with one of the pair sharing how he feels about himself right now in a few sentences.

The other person:
  (a) listens, saying back what was said, mirroring just the words.
  (b) then he mirrors again, this time bringing in the essence or meaning behind the words. To do this he has to use his own words.
  (c) next, he mirrors back the vibration of the person. This third mirror is reaching for the intuitive mind. The vibration may be different from the word message or it may be the same. He tries to mirror whatever nonverbal message he picks up.

The first person then confirms or corrects the mirror. If it is corrected then the other person tries to mirror again and keeps mirroring until the first person confirms the mirroring is accurate and complete.

The other person now can respond and say how he feels about what the first person said. The two switch roles and go through the same exercise. The observer comments and guides if he feels the mirroring is going astray and at the end shares whatever he felt was left out and how he experienced the sharing.

#2   Everyone chooses a partner (observer optional). Begin with the first person sharing with the partner how he feels about himself and how he feels about his partner right now. The partner mirrors until there is confirmation and then shares his feelings. The first person then mirrors these feelings. The two switch roles. People should pair off with those toward whom they have the strongest feelings. Remember to use the seven keys to real listening in their correct order. Review them or have them written down next to you if you don't know them by heart. The value of the observer is that he can point out gaps that you may not see while in the thick of the process. If you have the time and there are enough people, use an observer at least the first time you do this exercise and make it optional the second time if you feel it was too cumbersome. A good observer is a great help; a poor one will waste your time. Use your imagination to try different approaches to see what works the best for you.

THE LOVE SEAT

PREPARATION

You will need to make a chart of the group personality. If you have less than ten members in the group an 8½ x 11 piece of paper will do. More people will require a larger sheet or two. Write the first names of everyone down the side and again in the same order along the top. Draw lines both vertically and horizontally forming squares. Label the vertical lines "Reflectors" and the horizontal lines "Senders." Use the sample grid on page 278 as a model.

The Love Seat is a favorite awareness activity for many families and friends. It is an opportunity to share deep feelings about each other in a situation of trust, caring and openness. Both positive and negative qualities are used in this journey, and I have never failed to see a group emerge from this experience without a tremendous new awakening.

In addition to the benefits of the structured sharing for people who know each other, it is also an insightful experience for people who are seeing each other for the first time. Often our first impressions of people are deep insights into positive traits and personality flaws, which we later lose sight of because we get to know the person on other levels. In this exercise we draw from the intuition so we can see into people with penetrating insight.

Our goal is to overcome hostility and suspicion, and to demonstrate trust with each other by trusting and being open about our perceptions. Penetrating insight will come if you are willing to be honest in how you look at others and with yourself.

Still there may be those who hold back. You will not be contributing to the success of the journey by holding back. In fact, though you may feel you are preserving relationships, you may really be making them worse. Friendships are strongly cemented and people brought closer together through honesty and an atmosphere of respect for each other's views.

This is also an excellent exercise to do among those who work together. It allows business associates to give each other feedback creatively, constructively and in an atmosphere of trust. It is highly recommended for any group of people who relate closely together.

INSTRUCTIONS:

#1.   The group forms into a circle. If there are more than thirteen people, form two circles. Each circle will need its own chart. The first Sender sits in the love seat and the rest of the group are Reflectors. One person begins and then we move around the circle until everyone has had a turn. If people are shy about volunteering for center then go around the circle in order. One person from each circle is designated as the recorder for the entire time. Choose someone who can write well and write quickly. The Sender faces one person and looks him in the eyes. That person is now the first Reflector. If you are the Reflector try to tune into the Sender and share one thing (only one thing) that you feel is positive about the Sender or one thing you like most about him, and one thing (only one thing) that the Sender needs to work on to change or grow. The reason for the term Sender is because the person in the love seat is sending his vibrations from his being.

The Reflector mirrors or reflects them back in what he says about the Sender. After the Sender has heard the first person he nods a silent thank you and, *without answering,* moves to face the next person in the circle and sends his being out to the Reflector. The Reflector says one positive piece of feedback and one thing that he feels the Sender needs to work on. The recorder writes down both the positive and the item to work on in the square boxes next to the name of the Sender and under the name of the appropriate Reflector.

The Sender keeps moving around the circle one by one until everyone has had a chance to express their reflection. He does not talk until he has completed with everyone even though he may be bursting to say "yes, that's right" or "no" or "that's because . . . ", etc.

Before he leaves the love seat the Sender says one thing he likes best about himself and one thing he feels he needs to work on. This, too, is recorded. Then he may comment for a moment, if he wishes, on the feedback he has received from everyone. The next person takes the love seat and becomes the new Sender. When everyone has had a turn the chart will be filled.

Don't be afraid to share your feelings. The deepest thoughts, the ones you fear may not be right, are usually the ones that are most appreciated and the most right on. If you can't think of anything or your mind goes blank you can comment on simple and obvious things like dress, hairstyle, make-up, warmth, coldness, introvertedness, etc. But remember it is your responsibility to make the journey work by sharing something of yourself with each person. If you won't say anything then you are in fact telling the others they are perfect in your eyes. While you may admire someone greatly, it will not help him to grow or your friendship become closer unless you can share whatever you feel *that moment* on the positive and the negative.

#2. You may discuss reactions when everyone's been in the Love Seat, or go straight on to Part II.

End of Part I

PART II

Usually after finishing Part I the group is all energized and in a nice heartfelt vibration with each other. This next step is to analyze the chart for projections and direct perceptions.

#1. The charts are brought into the limelight. Each person reads what he or she has said as a Reflector about each of the other people in the group. *If the handwriting is difficult to read, the leader or the recorder can do all the reading.* As the Reflector's comments are read, both positive and negative, look for the following:

   (a) Has this Reflector said the same thing or very similar things to two or more people?
   (b) Is what the Reflector said about this Sender more true of himself than it is of the Sender?
   (c) Is what the Reflector said about this Sender right on in your eyes? Has he been very perceptive?

If the answer to (a) is yes, then it is likely that the feedback to the Sender was a "projection", meaning that the Reflector was seeing through his or her own personality. Sometimes the feedback may be true of both the Sender and the Reflector. This is called a "semi-projection". It is very easy to see our own good and not-so-good traits in another person because they are in ourself. If (b) is true it is also a "projection." But if it is, say, 50-50, just as true in both of them then it is a "semi-projection." If (c) is true and you feel "ah-ha, he's really right," or if it is mostly true about the Sender and doesn't apply much or at all to the Reflector's personality then it is a "right on", a "direct hit" or a "direct perception."

Decide as the comments are read whether they are P, S-P, or DP (Projection, Semi-Projection or Direct Perception). Call them off as the reader goes through the comments. Don't spend a long time discussing; your first feelings are usually correct. It may be that one person just cannot see what others see in someone. He may be correct ("50 million people *can* be wrong,") but a group usually is more accurate than any one individual. That person may be "identifying" with the Sender, feeling how he would feel if he were in the Sender's shoes (which may be totally off or may be true). Identification is not clear seeing either, because it is coloring the perceptions with your own personal fears and hopes. By reading the comments we gain further insight into our personalities.

#2.   This entire love seat experience is an exercise in seeing how the ego works in its relationships with others. Through the group mirror we get a many-faceted picture of ourself, which is how other people do see us, and we can get a wonderful idea of what parts of our egos we need to work on to enhance our evolution. Did you have thoughts you never before experienced? Did you enjoy the opportunity to give feedback and to have your own image reflected with mature clarity? Could you feel the human similarities despite the apparent differences between people? Discuss.

#3. Can you see any ongoing themes in the feedback a person has given to others? For instance, a person might say to three other people: "You need to develop confidence"—or something similar so we see a theme of self-confidence. Perhaps the speaker has a problem with self-confidence and therefore is seeing others through the filter of her own concern. See if you can spot any themes in the feedback and write the theme in the square provided on the right side of the grid, opposite the name of the person who gave the feedback.

Can you see any themes in the feedback given by the group to an individual? Maybe the group is all seeing the same thing in an individual that he or she needs to work on. Write the theme in the squares at the bottom of the grid, directly opposite and below the name of the person in the love seat.

By working at the themes we see if our own concerns or the issues that we're working on get projected onto others. We may discover that it's not that everybody else is working on the same thing as ourself, but that we're looking at others as if they need to, because we're looking through a filter of our own creation.

#4. Is the group learning how to dissolve bitter feelings or negativity with love, transcending the barrier of different inner worlds? Is the group getting beyond being offensive or defensive? Which people did you feel could have shared more? How accurate was the feedback overall? Discuss.

#5. Journal writing. The group may want to xerox the chart so that everyone can keep a copy of the feedback in their journals.

PSYCHODRAMA

The following is an exercise in Psychodrama that you can use to gain skills in tuning into people, in developing your intuition. Whenever the group Creative Conflict gets stuck on a verbal or head level and is out of touch with the deeper feelings of the heart, psychodrama is a useful technique. It can also be done as a structured exercise. If you bring psychodrama in as a technique when there is a need, then one person spontaneously gets up and stands behind the person they are identifying with to speak out as an alter ego. Others can do the same as they feel the need. Once you have taken the energy to a deeper level then the group can leave the psychodrama format and move naturally back into Creative Conflict. Psychodrama is a very useful exercise for learning how to identify with the inner world of another person positively which means feeling and becoming one with what that person is feeling but not letting it suck you into a negative space or get you down. At the same time as you feel one with the other, your intuition shows you a wider reality and you stay on center.

Psychodrama began as a form of therapy in the 1920's. It was developed by a psychiatrist named J.L. Moreno to enable people to release their feelings and to help each other see their internal blocks. Through acting out real scenes from our lives, role-playing other people's parts or replaying our own, we get a new perspective on what has happened.

In spiritual psychodrama, we use the action to help us expand our consciousness. We look at it as a form of growth, not necessarily as therapy. Healthy, normal people can benefit from this group experience as much, and often more, than people with serious problems. This type of psychodrama is a spiritual tool in that it gives you training and opportunity to enter into the inner worlds of others and experience them as they experience themselves. It also enables you to look back at yourself while looking through the eyes of others. Your angle of vision is widened from the purely personal tunnel-vision view, to a more inclusive picture from many centers.

Like Gestalt dream work, spiritual psychodrama sees every situation, every disagreement, every experience and every person as a projection of your inner self. You learn to make this truth part of your understanding through the action.

We normally use this dramatic method to break a deadlock in the Creative Conflict where a person has become moribund, out of touch with feelings or unable to relate to what the group is saying. The Creative Conflict process gives us a 360 degree wholistic view of our lives, but sometimes a person gets stuck in a tunnel. Then we try a radically different approach to get him out of his ego identification and into the worlds of other people. When the change of attitude occurs, we can then continue with Creative Conflict proper.

THE PSYCHODRAMA EXERCISE

#1. Everyone writes down in their journals a real life problem they are having, or recently have had with another person. It may be entirely an internal conflict about that person, or it may be a recent heated argument, or possibly an inability to communicate with someone. Pick a situation fairly fresh in your mind. Everyone has some difficulties in relationships with others, even if they are minor ones; otherwise their lives would be perfect. Pick out one such difficulty, and write it out. Then everyone shares their problem briefly with the group.

#2. The group now decides which situation has the greatest need for group help. The decision should be unanimous. That person's problem is chosen first. That person describes the scene of the problem, the last time it occurred, and what happened between the people involved.

#3. After the brief description, the group acts out the scene. Chairs are pushed out of the way so there is open space in the center of the room. The person whose problem it is will play himself. He is called the protagonist. He picks people from the group who he feels might best play the parts of the others in his scene. With just the brief facts described to go on, the others try to tune into how they might feel being in the shoes of the person they are to portray. Psychodrama is also called spontaneity theater. No roles are memorized, you don't try to figure out beforehand how you are going to act out in some situation. Rather you put yourself in the position of the person whose role you are going to play and respond spontaneously, incorporating the few facts you know into your actions and words. It is uncanny how often your spontaneous portrayal is exactly what has happened in the real situation. The protagonist is often astonished when you say something that was exactly what the person in real life had said. As the scene is being acted out, don't worry whether it changes direction from what was described. Often in the psychodrama we go deeper into issues that are more real than what has happened in real life. The rest of the group watches, not as observers, but as part of what is happening. When anyone has an insight or a flash, they jump up and stand behind the person who they want to speak for. They become a double or alter ego for the moment, and speak their piece, in the first person, using the word "I" just as if they were that person. They remain standing until the others have a chance to reply, and then the double sits down and lets the scene resume, only with new light. Don't be afraid to risk hopping up and down. The more input and insight, the more angles of vision are provided. Everyone will still have to be astute enough to see when someone's interjection is really way off base and distracting. If this happens, someone says how he feels and directs the scene onto the course he feels it needs to be going. Often deep emotions will come out and the action will get very intense. This action is real feeling and reaction, it is not play acting. Many people in the group will be able to recognize and identify with each other's scenes. When there is no more to say and the energy has faded, everyone goes back to their seats and the group discusses what occurred. The protagonist begins by sharing what feelings and insights came.

Choose another scene and do another psychodrama if there is time. Do as many as the group has time for. It is important for people in the circle to risk getting up and jumping in to act as double or alter ego. Encourage each other to participate. Don't be afraid to make a mistake, but always have the best intentions for the protagonist's world in mind.

Write any insights you have had into your journal.

PSYCHODRAMA TECHNIQUES:

1. *Alter Ego or Double*—One or more people stand with or behind the person to reinforce what he or she is trying to express, to tune into and speak for the person—what is going on inside but is unexpressed, to take on the same identity. This action spurs the person to get in touch more readily with what is really going on inside. You speak as though you are that person speaking.

2. *Psychodrama Mirror*—The person in the center is replaced by another group member in order to see himself as the other sees him. Through watching himself he is able to get more in touch.

#3. *Ideal Other*—The person in the center describes what his ideal type of image would be, either how he would like himself to be, or how he would like his spouse, parent, friend, business partner, etc., to be.

4. *Empty Chair*—When the person expresses that there are two parts of himself at war then he talks to one part in an empty chair and tells that part how he feels. Then he switches chairs and becomes that part and talks back to the other part, answering and saying how he feels from that point of view. He keeps switching places and identification back and forth until insight comes to him. Sometimes other members of the group need to guide the movement as intuitively as they can, and lead it in a new direction with a new technique if the person is still blocking.

In all these techniques, dare to make a mistake but always have the best intentions for the person. If you go on your own trip, projecting your own reality in the action, then it is the responsibility of other members to call you on it. Some people worry that these techniques will expose tender areas of a person's inner world that no one in the group would be capable of dealing with. But it is necessary to bring tender areas into daily communication if we are to improve our relationships and our communication. As long as there is care and concern and as long as you remember to use the Keys to Real Listening, all will go well. We have never seen anyone harmed in any way by this process. By putting integrity and honesty with one's feelings first as the core of the Creative Conflict we are dealing with life, with reality, not some psychological game. All these techniques are here and now intensifying of real thoughts and feelings.

AN ADVANCED MIRRORING EXERCISE

Purpose: Identification, Projection, and Basic Assumption, made clear to participants in Creative Conflict.

Note: It is important to tape record this exercise so any disagreement can be heard with more objective ears.

CENTERING USING CHANTING: (Someone read aloud. . . .)
As we chant let's see if we can listen to the ear of the ear and be aware

that the same One pure consciousness is doing the same listening inside the inner worlds of its other manifestations in the group. Get into that same ear of the ear, that same space which is in each of the others as well as in ourselves. Feel the unity of that One playing through you and the others. Listen to that One until you experience the group as One Self, One Body, One Instrument. Though capable of playing many different tunes through different people, the instrument is one . . . (pause) . . . Chant OOOOMMM fairly loudly in long resonant sounds together for a few minutes. Listen to the ringing of the microtones. Now in the silence, retaining that experience of the One, remaining in that deep center of being, know that when you open your eyes, that same consciousness will be looking through them at Itself in others just as It did through the ear of the ear. It is essential to stay in this space in order to perceive purely. To lose consciousness of this space is to revert to egocentric observer consciousness which is only listening to itself.

POSITIVE IDENTIFICATION: Pair off and we are going to practice what is called positive identification. First one pair will be the center of attention, then another pair and so on. The others observe what happens as openly as they can. One person of the pair tells, as nitty-gritty as he can be, how he feels about himself right now and how he feels about his relationship with the group. The other person of the pair listens with his mind empty, like a photographic plate receiving the impressions, the feelings and the thoughts. He finds out whether they are his own, like this: if you think they are just the other person's thoughts you are receiving and not your own, then they are not true because you haven't really become at one with the other, because if you are at one you will not be able to tell any difference. Only if you feel there is resonance, that the impressions are both yours and the other person's, consider them as true. Then you are truly consciously identified, being at one with the other for that time and there is no sense of separation. (After you finish then you can ask yourself whether or not you are *really* like that, but you'll never know the person as he is and as he experiences himself unless you are truly positively identified and not separate. You will probably be projecting your own world if you are not thus identified.) Now the test of your listening ability is the next step.

After the person has spoken and you feel you are identified, start to mirror back the person as you feel you know him to be, as you are *experiencing* him to be. If you don't feel identified yet, ask a few questions until you feel identified. It is important to be loose and free in order to really identify, so don't fear others' reactions; everyone is opening and exploring.

The others watch, make notes if needed. Perhaps make a video tape if you have access to one, to tell the listener what you feel is true positive identifying, and what is a *projection* of his own and what are *basic assumptions* he is making about the other. Discriminate between *direct perceptions* and *basic assumptions*. Then go around again and do the same thing on each other's evaluations of the pair, being aware of the same three factors of *positive identification, projection* or *basic assumptions* as you speak. As you hear each other speak, call the person on projection, or basic assumption when you hear it, or make a note of it on paper and bring it up at the next appropriate moment. The observers act like video cameras all taking their shots from different angles, different realities, and some will be true, while others may be projections too. The group will determine what is actually being communicated and what is real.

Then the pair switch roles.

Then another pair is chosen.

This advanced mirroring exercise is designed to enable you to experience in depth the inner world of another, the heart and soul of the other, and from that identification be able to look at the ego patterns.

19

COURSE SYLLABUS FOR CREATIVE CONFLICT

The following outlines are formats that you can use to guide your group through the beginning sessions of Creative Conflict practice. We have found a step-by-step introduction to the Creative Conflict process to be the most valuable way of learning how to integrate the methods into your consciousness. If your group is not ready for so complete an experience as the outlines provide, just begin simply with the seven keys to real listening and the two exercises in Chapter 18 called "Mirroring" and the "Love Seat". For each session, take one guideline, key, technique, block or principle and meditate on that one item. Study, discuss and apply each item one at a time. (See the listing on page 253.) Gradually you will make all of the Creative Conflict processes and methods your own. Apply the particular method you are studying each week not only in your group but in your daily relating. Look for illustrations in the environment around you, in the way people relate and speak to each other, and look for examples in your own inner thought life.

The ten-week course in beginning Creative Conflict requires a firm commitment to attend every class, to arrive on time and to take seriously the responsibility for phoning if you are too ill to attend.

Materials needed for the course:
★ Your own copy of *Creative Conflict* which you should read before you join the group.

★ A spiral notebook in which to keep an ongoing journal.

★ Cassette tapes and a tape recorder with microphone(s) that will pick up everyone's voice. The group as a whole will need to buy some blank cassette tapes to record the sessions. If each person contributes $1.00 you can purchase a stock of inexpensive tapes that can be used over again each week after the person has listened to his or her Creative Conflict on tape. If someone wants to keep a particular tape he must buy a new blank tape to replace the tape he keeps.

Each member of the class, including the facilitators, will keep a journal, week by week, in which insights into the Creative Conflict process and into oneself and insights into human nature are recorded. The journal supplies another dimension of experience to the class. Save fifteen minutes at the end of each session for people to write in their journals.

At the end of the course, your journal should reflect what you have learned about yourself, about human consciousness and about Creative Conflict. Your journal should reveal to you how much you have advanced in the expansion of your awareness and reflect your own strengths and weaknesses in such a way that anyone could benefit by reading what you have written (i.e., you have not just recorded your own self-obsessions but an ongoing process of discovery and bringing self-knowledge to light). Depending on how much consciousness you put into your journal, you will produce a creation whose shallowness or depth of expression will be an exact mirror for you. The journal will be a means by which you can learn not only the nature of the ego in general but the nature of your own ego structure, what it is made of and how it keeps you small. Once your ego structure is exposed and revealed for you to see, the very awareness itself begins to stretch your boundaries.

The beginning course is structured to focus intensively on one ego pattern per week so that you do not memorize these patterns with the head and then quickly forget them but rather you open your awareness to experience them so that you can never go back and be unaware of them again. The course will also focus on one of the guidelines of Creative Conflict each week. Although the course is divided into ten sessions to give you a broad introduction, you may find that spontaneously you will want to spend two or more weeks on each subject. It is quite good to stay with a topic until you feel your group has a workable grasp of its inner meaning. Always let people unanimously agree whether or not they feel it is in tune to spend an additional week on any issue.

BEGINNING CREATIVE CONFLICT OUTLINE

If the group has not been together before, take twenty minutes or more before you begin for each person to share a little about who they are and why they are here. You may want to do the "Getting to Know You" exercise in *Exploring Inner Space*, pages 60-63, to build trust and open the door to the deeper being before you begin the first exercise. For definitions and descriptions of the blocks to be discussed, refer to Chapter Four.

COURSE SYLLABUS: BEGINNING SESSION

First Week: Mirroring (guidelines #7 and #8, pages 284, and 285)
Refer to Chapter Thirteen for a proper understanding of mirroring. We will practice three levels of mirroring: mirroring back just the words: mirroring the essence of the words; mirroring the vibration of the being who is speaking the words. We will do the mirroring exercise on pages 291-293. Each person will share a feeling with another and the other will then mirror back what he or she has heard. This is an exercise in deep listening, in which we become aware what kinds of things block us from really listening and what this nonlistening does to the person with whom we are trying to communicate. It is also an exercise in tuning into vibrations, learning the difference between the head and the heart. We will become aware of the tapes we play in our consciousness. Real listening is to completely stop these thoughts and feelings and get them out of the way, and thus we go deep, beyond the ego, into the special vibration of the heart.

Second Week: Projections, semi-projections, and direct perceptions (guideline #4, pages 281-82)
We will do the love-seat exercise (pages 293-97) with a special focus on the accuracy of feedback. The purpose of this exercise is to learn the degree of our self-obsession and self-enclosure, or our ability to get into another's world.

Third Week: Basic assumptions and stereotyping (guideline #6, pages 283-84)

Basic assumptions and stereotyping are also ways of projecting our own realities onto others rather than tuning into their inner worlds. In this session, using the grid that we made the previous week, we will learn to see that our perceptions are not absolute and infallible, learning how to check with another person before judging. This takes us deeper down, to another level of the love-seat exercise.

Fourth Week: Negative identification, rationalizations, emotionalism, "yes, but" (guideline #1, page 280)

Negative identification is identifying with the emotions of another so that they pull you off center, or identifying with your own negatives. We will learn the difference between sympathy and empathy, the difference between compassionate ruthlessness and doing a power trip. We will practice various ways of saying the same thing to a person so that we develop skill in giving feedback. We will also look at the pattern of emotionalism—not only the genuine emotions that come from deep penetration but the ego feelings that we use to block the feedback from going any deeper. And we will explore two other major patterns for deflecting feedback—rationalizing and the "yes, but". What is the difference between being receptive and "buying" feedback that you should not buy because it is "off" or is coming from someone's ego trip? How do we do Creative Conflict safely.

Fifth Week: Motivations (guideline #5, page 282)

We will probe our motivations for coming to this class and probe motivations behind the things we say to each other. We will try to get from shallow levels of commitment to deeper parts of ourselves that we may not yet be aware of. We will look at motivation in our relationships and in all the various things we are doing with our lives and with our consciousness.

Sixth Week: Compliance and risk (guideline #2, pages 280-81)

Compliance is "going along" with what others say or decide to do and being unwilling to risk saying something different. We will examine private judgements that we are making in our minds. What is the difference between real openness and just plain folly? When do you risk? What kinds of things make a creative risk out of which good may come? What constitutes a negative risking in which your sharing becomes an energy drain instead of a venture into greater depth of communication? We will, either in this week's Creative Conflict or another, experience the "fog" that occurs when the ego's computer, backed into a corner, ceases to function. We will explore the different layers of integrity in order to discover that risk is what makes life deep.

Seventh & Eight Weeks: Self-image (guideline #9, pages 285-86)
Having probed motivation and our private judgements, we go deeper
still into the many self-images which shape and govern our relationships
and our life-styles. As these images stand between us and the
realization of our real self, superimposing "personality" upon our real
uniqueness, this is an adventure in self-discovery, bringing the
unconscious mind to light in each person.

Ninth Week: Banging Kilroy (Chapter 14, Identification)
Banging Kilroy is an exercise in self-mastery. Kilroy is the comic strip
character who sticks his nose over the fence. The idea is to knock him
down immediately, before he goes any further, because once he has a
foot into your mind, like the common cold, he will run his full cycle.
Having learned to risk, we now come out with our fears, doubts, ghosts
and negative mental patterns so that we learn mastery over these
powerful forces in our consciousness. We also learn to master our
habitual ways of interacting at the group level—how to change from a
retreating vibration to radiating; what constitutes a Kilroy not only at the
level of our daily thought life but also in actual challenging situations.

Tenth Week: Chakra* blocks (guideline #3, page 281)
Refer to Chapter Fifteen for an introduction to the chakras, the levels of
consciousness that determine our personality. Each person will share
his or her greatest block to fully expressing and entering into life, i.e.,
which chakra he feels is most closed and what steps can be taken to
open up that level of being. To avoid mere advice-giving, we will use
some techniques such as the psychodrama exercise, so that we get
deeper insight into these blocks and deeper motivations to change
them. Another way to tune into this is to ask, "What is our 'Achilles'
heel?" What is the one thing that keeps tripping us up? What most
blocks us from oneness with others, from feeling in tune, from finding
our hearts?"

Remember to use the Sequential Steps on page 270. Once you
understand the mechanics of Creative Conflict you will naturally
discover the ego blocks.

As you can see, a ten-week course will only touch the surface
of each of these areas mentioned. Don't worry, you can start over
again during your next ten-week commitment period or extend the
ten-week sessions into twenty weeks, allowing approximately two
weeks for each item. Spend the first fifteen minutes of each session

---

*Chakra—one of the seven psychic energy centers in the human consciousness that
determines our personality type.

discussing the topic, then go into the conflict needs at hand and apply all that you have learned. Re-read the applicable sections in this book before attending class. Remember to use this book, *Creative Conflict*, as a handbook to guide you and keep you in tune during your course. When you have learned and can apply the contents of these sessions to your normal life, you are ready for a step-up in commitment. You and your group need to decide what that will be. Set a new challenge for yourself. Draw up a new ten-week outline with additional principles and techniques from *Creative Conflict*, or if your group is ready, use the following syllabus for your intermediate class. Guidance is always available from University of the Trees facilitators.

INTERMEDIATE
CREATIVE CONFLICT OUTLINE

The focus of the next ten weeks is to understand more deeply the state of consciousness from which Creative Conflict originated and the attitude we must develop to practice the process purely. The following outline lists the themes for the next ten weeks. The themes are guideposts to take each session to a new dimension. During the discussion of the themes at the beginning of each class, deep issues in each person will appear and the group will then choose the priority needs to go into for the session. You may find that many needs will make themselves known and you will want to take an extra week or two to cover them. Decide unanimously as a group if you are going to postpone starting on a new theme until the following week and inform any absent members. Be careful not to get so embroiled in the conflict issues that you let discussion on the theme topics slide away from your weekly itinerary. The weekly theme should ever be in the forefront of the individual and group mind to help illumine and guide the specific issues brought up for Creative Conflict.

During the intermediate sessions of Creative Conflict the group will reach deeper levels of experiencing what was already begun in the beginning classes. The focus will be on developing teamwork, building the group consciousness and trust, working on clarity in the communication, as well as continuing to open the heart. To achieve greater depth and intensity, each person must be ready to commit himself to taking full responsibility for the whole, as if he were solely responsible for how the class is going, and commit himself to risking, even if he turns out to be misperceiving. Continue writing in your journals, expressing not only what you experience in the classes but what happens when you practice one of the keys, principles or guidelines during the week.

COURSE SYLLABUS:INTERMEDIATE SESSION

First Week: Commitment
Why are we still wanting to learn Creative Conflict? What end results of Creative Conflict have we personally discovered so far? What are we committing to when we commit ourselves to doing Creative Conflict? Has anyone any reservations about the process or any misgivings? We will go into these and try to find out why some of the process is set up the way it is and see how it mirrors life. Why does Creative Conflict get heavy sometimes? How far does our responsibility to others go? How did we feel toward those who left the class? How do we continue to build trust?

Second Week: Review of the Nine Guidelines (pages 280-86)
We will break into small groups and each group will go over the nine guidelines and think of concrete examples of them in their own lives and in previous Creative Conflict sessions that they can share with the group as a whole. When we come together again as one group, the task will be to re-express the guidelines in our own words so that everyone shares in their understanding of them. How has the knowledge of these guidelines and the practice of them affected our lives over the past ten weeks?

Third Week: Centering in the larger Self (Principle #1, page 224)
How does the principle of Creative Conflict, "Whatever is not mastered is the true quality of your manifested self," relate to the guideline, "You are whatever disturbs you"? How can we apply this principle in a Creative Conflict situation and what is its value? How does Creative Conflict nurture our spiritual realization? How have you experienced your spiritual insights expanding beyond the narrow confines of your little self in Creative Conflict?

Fourth Week: Confronting our fears and self-doubt (Principle #3, page 226)
Let each person share his or her deepest fear and greatest area of self-doubt. How can we renounce these Kilroys and ego knots without

repressing them and being out of touch? How can we learn to cease identifying with our egos in a way that will truly transform us? What enables us to create "opposite waves" that will truly counteract our negative thought vibrations of fear or self-doubt? How can we re-program these reactions in a deep way instead of the superficial levels of most positive-thinking programs?

Fifth Week: Self-image (Principle #2, page 225)

Let each person express his self-image, not facetiously, but how he really sees himself and how he would like others to see him. Then other group members, at random, give him a mirror of how they experience him so he can see whether he is actually manifesting what he thinks he is manifesting. What parts of ourselves have we not mentioned in our self-image that others strongly experience in us? How is our self-image apparent in our thinking and seeing? Why is self-image only an appearance created by thought? If only consciousness is real, how can we tune to its purity to transform our self-image and thereby transform our personality?

Sixth Week: Negative identification (Principle #4, page 229)

What is causing us to identify with what we feel we need and there-fore hang onto our egos defensively? Why are we defensive at times in the group, instead of identifying with the perceptions of those who are trying to give feedback for the purpose of making us or someone else whole? Why is truth frightening? What is the one thing that we each feel we most need and would not want to give up? Does this need block us from change? How attached are we to it? Each member shares a personal experience of when they have found truth difficult to accept. What are each of our worst areas of negative identification and how are they blocking us from changing?

Seventh Week: Judgements (Principle #5, page 230)

What arises in our consciousness that allows us to judge another? Let each person share whatever judgements of the class or of any individual member are going on in their minds. Let us share not just the shallow judgements but the real, gut-level feelings that we have pushed down inside us. How can we discriminate between true nonattachment to other people's judgements or actions and the kind of detachment that masks feelings? How can the group function more as an organism, a precision force, skilled in combat with the elusive ego and yet still be in the heart? When is love not visible to the ego? Can we list examples of when love has been present but it has been blocked by personal reactions?

Eighth Week: Motivations

How do we feel about the motivations of everyone in the class now? Is there anyone who we feel has not experienced in themselves the dynamic of the Creative Conflict process taking them past their projections or other ego blocks into their real underlying motivations? Has everyone experienced some penetration of their self-image? Has anyone not touched the vulnerable space in a Creative Conflict at some point in the class? The purpose of this session is to get a general idea of what level each person is at and what direction the group needs to go in order to bring each member to his or her next step in self-confrontation.

Ninth Week: Levels of consciousness (See Chapter Fifteen)

Each group member should read Chapter Fifteen before coming to the class and meditate on which level of consciousness he or she resonates with most. Which block is the most common block to real listening that each person keeps coming up against? What most blocks us from oneness with others or from feeling in tune and being in our hearts? How is this pattern reflective of the level of consciousness on which we most often function? What can we specifically do to overcome the negative pattern we have seen in our level of consciousness? The entire group explores these questions together in the session and gives each other feedback. During the week between this session and the next, each member practices overcoming the particular block they have isolated in their own predominant level of consciousness.

Tenth Week: How do we feel about God?

What is God to each one of us? How can we feel more connected to the source of our consciousness? How selfless do we feel both in relation to our commitment to be responsible for the evolution of the group and in relation to our daily lives? How does selflessness affect our attunement with the greater Self? What do we want to commit ourselves to both individually and as a group in the next ten-week session?

As you can see, the outline for the intermediate session progressively leads the group into very nitty-gritty areas of self-confrontation. Advanced Creative Conflict continues to go more deeply into the areas explored in the beginning and intermediate sessions. In advanced Creative Conflict we look more deeply for the different levels of consciousness that people function on and see specifically how our basic personality type colors the way we relate to others and conditions our reality. We deal almost exclusively with subtle self-images and identification patterns since, by this time, participants have done a great deal of work on their motives. At University of the Trees we also use an electronic soul mirror in advanced Creative Conflict, a video recording of Creative Conflict sessions so people can watch themselves and learn to see their own egos in action as others see them. One person then videotapes individuals' candid reactions *while* they are watching themselves on TV. The facial expressions that come from watching ourselves watching ourselves are incredibly revealing of our self-consciousness and self-image. They make excellent material for further Creative Conflicts. The more we can see ourselves from the most universal perspective possible, then the more we approach total awareness, a 360 degree view of life that includes all lesser perceptions and brings us to the apex of human evolution.

The goal is to learn to use the process increasingly in daily relating so that it becomes an integral part of us. When we can live our lives seeing everyone and everything as ourself, as the mirror of our own consciousness, and can stand in the still center of our own souls as we work and play and serve, we will find ourselves in tune with the laws of the cosmos. This expansion is the outcome of living with total self-realization. A life rich and full in communion with nature, with other humans and with the cosmic being increasingly unfolds with this deep practice.

20

GROUP CONSCIOUSNESS–
THE CALL OF THE HEART

The ultimate evolution of Creative Conflict is to imitate nature's intelligence in bringing all organisms into harmony with the total environment in which they live. At the nuclear center of all organisms, whether physical or mental, inorganic or organic, there is a drive which we can call emotional because all emotions are basically chemical, whether they are physically or mentally induced. Such drives exist as emotional reactions in the leaves of the sensitive plant, or the reaction of an animal or plant to a scent, or an insect to a color. Humans are no different in their emotional responses to thoughts, people or situations. There are emotional responses to groups just as there are sexual responses to individuals. Learning to discriminate the validity of these responses, our emotions and feelings, is what we mean by the examined life. The human life which is not examined is no more free of nature's primal drives and instincts than the life of a plant or an insect. Conflict is nature's way of purifying all separate organisms, individuals, or parts of larger wholes, which are guided by an invisible hand towards their destiny. How can we quickly discover this hand and look in the direction in which it is pointing? Creative Conflict enables us to see the difference between the emotional state of our inner being and the true reality that we can perceive in our mind only when we have a purified heart.

Discriminating the true and false promptings of the mind and heart is the task of life. Often it seems as if humans are made up of two opposing forces—the heart, which is wholistic, not separate from either its own experience or from the whole, and the mind, which gives us a binding image of ourself and wants to dictate a separate egocentric reality. The heart controls by surrender, but surrender is unthinkable to the mind which fears loss of clear-seeing and rationality. But mind's logic, when divorced from heart's love, actually narrows the seeing of the mind's own presumptions and cuts us off from the whole vision. The promptings of the heart will get us into problems only if we allow them to get garbled by ego-mind motivations. When the heart can follow selflessness it is gradually refined until it becomes pure love and clear seeing into the worlds of others. The heart radiates well being to others as well as into its own world. A group of people who have plumbed the depths of the heart are one in being and can become a powerful force for change. Their vision and purpose are one, and their minds serve their hearts.

Group consciousness is a new spirit in the world, not like any we have experienced before. Its power is not only worldly power, although the efficiency and clear-seeing of groups of individuals who live and work wholistically does bring practical power, as we see in scientific endeavors like putting a man on the moon. Group consciousness is a spiritual power that arises out of individuals who have quelled the conflict of head and heart. Group consciousness is not to be confused with the power of the State collectively forcing compliance upon all its subjects in the name of the good of the whole, but rather it is the power of those individuals who think for themselves and are one because they are in tune with natural laws. Only individuals can recognize this power when they hear about it, read about it or see it in action. Evolutionary groups are made of such individuals. The evolution of group consciousness and its implementation on our planet lies in the evolving awareness of each individual and not with the identity of any specific group. But groups of individuals who themselves transcend the separative functions of the ego and who live and think wholistically as one integrated being, become spiritually very powerful.

At certain points in the life of each individual, the heart adopts a strategy to dig a pit for the ego to fall into. This is heart's way of teaching mind the consequences of being separate, to help us evolve and refine our egos to be more in tune with the whole. Whether or not we achieve a leap into higher consciousness depends on how we respond to heart's tests. Most people need to experience the same tests over and over in different disguises before they are ready to choose a new direction. Heart is nature's channel for waking us to our next step in evolution—if we can learn to listen to its guidance. But if in following our heart we seek confirmation, the vanity of fame or recognition, or we expect something in return when we give to another, then our love contains that quality of ego, that impurity. Ego riding piggy-back on the heart leads us into one pit after another, all for the purpose of refining us. Heart seduces head very cleverly by going along for awhile with head's rationalizations and assumptions, but these are just ruses of the heart to create the situation where head can confront itself.

The mind and intellect that are married to the heart produce wisdom. The heart that, through Creative Conflict, has been sifted and penetrated by the intellect, has been refined, and that heart's wisdom and love shines like the sun on all people the same. Minds that love the light, that want to be purified at any cost, run towards the light and truth however vulnerable they feel in the heart. The heart sifts them more rapidly and they embrace the changes as they are brought to more love. The challenge for each human being who has the will to evolve is to fall in love with love itself. Refined love is self-validating, self-illuminating, self-recognizing, self-realizing, feeding off its own love which is generated within, everywhere, like the sun. The sun shines of itself and does not need another light to see its own light. You might say, "Well, I *want* someone else to confirm me." But such a need stems from an unfulfilled separate state of being. The heart that is in resonance with the head sees its own love reflected in itself like a mirror without any need for recognition from "the other". Recognition and love come in abundance anyway, because the universal mirror is not separate from your own. People blind in the ego may not be able to recognize your love, but you understand their blindness. If your love is recognized by people, that is just the cream. When you become unitive love, there is no separate head or heart left, just your Self— the One.

Everything we do is ultimately for ourself. We fool ourselves thinking our love is for the other, or thinking we get married for the other, or that we have children for the children's sake. In truth you get married for yourself, you have children for yourself. Everything you do is ultimately totally selfish, because it is the self that does everything and wants everything. You do Creative Conflict and open the heart for yourself. You even become selfless for your self. If we have to become unselfish in order to get something like harmony, or greater love, bliss or fulfillment then we have a drive or motivation for becoming more and more selfless. Your self is the one that must confirm everything. Nature teaches us that selflessness pays greater dividends in terms of joy and fulfillment, and the more we taste of joy the more we acknowledge selflessness as its own reward. Ultimately you *have* to be selfless because nothing else will satisfy. There is no other work you would rather do, no one else you would rather serve. Selflessness is a choiceless choice. And who is driving you? Self! Who do you surrender to? Self!

Ask yourself who you are working for and whether or not you are getting fulfillment? If not, you had better find out why not. What motives are screwing you up? Because if you are not getting fulfillment, whatever your circumstances are, you are not in tune with nature in some way and are not doing the will of God. When you deeply believe in what you do, you can take on tasks and enormous problems that no one else is prepared to tackle. You have indefatigable energy and consciousness. You go to *meet* problems, instead of retreating from them. The more Self-realized you are, the more hands and feet you wish you had to do all the things you know need to be done for the good of the whole. Great lovers constantly beautify the world they live in to make the earth planet a better environment. Your attitude to doing work on yourself or your attitude to any work determines how much you love yourself. In turn, this will determine your happiness, because work done with love is love made visible and that work is made totally fulfilling because *love* is our own reward to ourself.

When a group of Self-realized people work together in love for this same purpose, a powerful force is unleashed in the world. That fusion at the nucleus of being, like the nuclear fusion in the heart of the sun is the spirit and vision of group consciousness, and Creative Conflict is its vehicle. All those who work in this spirit and in love, work now for eternity. They are the torchbearers of now, who will pass the flame to those who will carry it on. You who do this work on yourself will carry that flame in your heart and you will pass it to those who come later who, together in true group consciousness, will build a new world, a new vision, a new humanity. This is spiritual genius. It is your legacy to the future.

If you hear the Call of the Heart and want more, write or visit the University of the Trees community. One of the greatest ways you can give of yourself is to live in a loving, supportive community. We invite you to come for a visit to see if this is where you want to live. Please do not come without first writing or calling.

Our address is University of the Trees, P.O. Box 347, Boulder Creek, CA 95006. If you have obligations that prevent you from visiting, perhaps you would like us to come to you. If you wish to help sponsor or attend a Creative Conflict workshop in your area please write and let us know. Send us your phone number. Someone will be in touch with you.

INDEX

H

happiness 33
head, the 26, 47, 54, 56, 57, 61, 73, 112, 113,
115, 201, 240, 260, 269, 281, 316
heart, the 26, 29, 32, 39, 41, 43, 47, 54, 56,
57, 60, 61, 63, 64, 73, 91, 112, 113, 114,
115, 116, 126, 158, 200, 202, 260, 268,
275, 276, 277, 314, 315, 316, 317
honesty 13, 39, 82-3, 85, 162, 203
humility 16, 39, 40, 44, 61, 62, 106, 122, 123,
157, 269
hypocrisy 63, 118

I

identification 28, 29, 33, 69, 214-34, 280,
302-3
    negative 43, 45-7, 126, 227
imagination 5
I-message 206-8
indigo level 241
individuality 99, 100, 108, 116
inner worlds 23, 25, 39, 44, 60, 152, 153,
191, 243
insecurity 45, 66, 67, 70, 71, 77, 240
integrity 13, 19, 24, 38, 57, 82, 135, 136,
162, 166, 171, 181, 187, 188, 199, 208,
285
internalization 43, 51, 52
in touch 35, 59, 73, 76, 153, 200, 205, 207,
266, 269, 271
in tune 29, 273

J

judgements 16, 43, 45, 50, 60, 116

K

Kilroy 33
    banging 33
Kundalini 244-46

L

letting go 35, 62, 77, 202
listening 23, 24, 36, 38, 41, 43-64, 65, 84,

117, 148, 206, 252
    real 23
    active 30, 180, 199, 200
light 30, 124, 198, 235
love 25, 26, 31, 38, 50, 56, 59, 61, 63, 65,
69, 70, 74, 77, 79, 85, 87, 91, 112, 113,
115, 121, 133, 162, 175, 220, 265, 277,
317

M

meditation 14, 23, 24, 35, 36, 41, 250, 274,
287, 289-91
mirror 9, 14, 25, 26, 30, 31, 35, 37, 45, 49, 50,
58, 61, 83, 123, 138, 226, 273
mirroring 38, 53, 72, 83, 107, 134, 138, 139,
161, 178, 200-5, 209-12, 259, 292, 301-3
motivation 20, 25, 32, 37, 47, 55, 56, 57, 63,
131, 142, 181, 191, 282-3

N

nature 17, 41, 50, 58, 98, 99, 119, 127, 149,
227, 314
    natural 317
negative identification 43, 45, 46, 47, 126,
227
negativity 16, 34, 56, 69, 104, 139, 227, 268
nothing 40, 62, 204

O

oneness 20, 22, 33, 38, 41, 56, 58, 116, 221,
268
openness 37, 39, 62, 64, 79, 81, 82, 85, 160,
163, 168, 174, 198, 204, 205
orange level 239
owning 35, 69, 85, 87

P

pain 17, 26, 29, 30, 33, 35, 37, 44, 49, 50, 56,
88, 92, 97, 103, 113, 127, 232, 267, 272
patterns 29, 36, 93, 135, 148, 305
penetration 26, 30, 35-6, 37, 40, 43, 57, 59,
62, 267
perception 34, 39, 40, 41, 43, 44, 136, 138

WHAT IS UNIVERSITY OF THE TREES?

Common Ownership Press/Meditation Community/
Ion Research Center/Light Force Spirulina Co.
Degree Granting University/Children's School/Researchers
into Supersensonics & Supersensonic Healing Energies

The University of the Trees is an experimental school for world change. We exist for the purpose of synthesizing the efforts of those who believe man is about to make a spiritual breakthrough and take a million year leap in evolution. In preparation for the next step, real change must begin within the individual. Individuals at the University of the Trees find their hearts opening to express their potential through an open learning situation in which the subject and object of study is consciousness. Through meditation and "Creative Conflict", the probing of the ego's blind spots in real life situations, the person comes to the real awareness of his inner being—thus building a dynamic individual in the true meaning of that word—"not to be divided".

Every individual in the community is unique and there is no set mold, for we encourage each other to develop our own potential. With a group of individuals dedicated in the heart to the betterment of each other "as ourself", a new quality of consciousness is experienced; we have called it "group consciousness". A group consciousness experience happens when everyone in the group/family is caring for the evolution and vision of the whole more than for their personal self. There's never a dull moment when you live with thirty or forty people building openness and trust with each other based on Truth. Facing our blindspots and going towards the problems in our consciousness is not easy but it is challenging!

Daily we explore together the deeper meanings of Nuclear Evolution as it relates to actual day to day living, practice Creative Conflict and work on our latest project of common ownership in business. We meditate together and use meditation in our decision-making and in our children's school. We chant together and discover ever new dimensions in the realm of sound and the profound effects of resonance on human consciousness. Wholeness and health are vitally important here, so we are constantly researching methods both to discover nutritional imbalance and to restore balance on the seven levels of being and to nourish the useful vehicle of the body with light and pure survival foods. In conjunction with our tape department we are also now working on a vast expansion into home computer programs for meditation and development of consciousness. We have purchased a sophisticated microcomputer system and eight Apple computers and together this gives us a computer capacity equal to any university in the country.

We welcome you to explore more of "The Trees"—our community, our publications, cassette taped lectures and meditations, university courses by correspondence and our products. Please write for more information in the area of your interest.

MEDITATING WITH CHILDREN . . . MEDITATION FOR CHILDREN

MEDITATING WITH CHILDREN and *MEDITATION FOR CHILDREN* by Deborah Rozman are two unique books for enhancing peace and awareness in children. *MEDITATING WITH CHILDREN* is written for the teacher or group leader while *MEDITATION FOR CHILDREN* is written for the parent, family or individual and applies meditation to interpersonal relating in the home. Both books are excellent complements to *CREATIVE CONFLICT, Learning to Love with Total Honesty.*